THE COMPLETE IDIOT'S GUIDE® TO

SQL

Wauconda Area Library
801 N. Main Street
Wauconda, IL 60084

by Steven Holzner, Ph.D.

ALPHA

A member of Penguin Group (USA) Inc.

ALPHA BOOKS

Published by the Penguin Group

Penguin Group (USA) Inc., 375 Hudson Street, New York, New York 10014, USA

Penguin Group (Canada), 90 Eglinton Avenue East, Suite 700, Toronto, Ontario M4P 2Y3, Canada (a division of Pearson Penguin Canada Inc.)

Penguin Books Ltd., 80 Strand, London WC2R 0RL, England

Penguin Ireland, 25 St. Stephen's Green, Dublin 2, Ireland (a division of Penguin Books Ltd.)

Penguin Group (Australia), 250 Camberwell Road, Camberwell, Victoria 3124, Australia (a division of Pearson Australia Group Pty. Ltd.)

Penguin Books India Pvt. Ltd., 11 Community Centre, Panchsheel Park, New Delhi—110 017, India

Penguin Group (NZ), 67 Apollo Drive, Rosedale, North Shore, Auckland 1311, New Zealand (a division of Pearson New Zealand Ltd.)

Penguin Books (South Africa) (Pty.) Ltd., 24 Sturdee Avenue, Rosebank, Johannesburg 2196, South Africa

Penguin Books Ltd., Registered Offices: 80 Strand, London WC2R 0RL, England

Copyright © 2011 by Steven Holzner

International Standard Book Number: 978-1-61564-109-3
Library of Congress Catalog Card Number: 2011902717

13 12 11   8 7 6 5 4 3 2 1

Interpretation of the printing code: The rightmost number of the first series of numbers is the year of the book's printing; the rightmost number of the second series of numbers is the number of the book's printing. For example, a printing code of 11-1 shows that the first printing occurred in 2011.

Printed in the United States of America

Publisher: *Marie Butler-Knight*

Associate Publisher/Acquiring Editor: *Mike Sanders*

Executive Managing Editor: *Billy Fields*

Development Editor: *Ginny Bess Munroe*

Senior Production Editor: *Kayla Dugger*

Copy Editor: *Amy Borrelli*

Cover Designer: *William Thomas*

Book Designers: *William Thomas, Rebecca Batchelor*

Indexer: *Tonya Heard*

Layout: *Brian Massey*

Proofreader: *John Etchison*

To Nancy, of course.

Contents

Introduction

Welcome to *The Complete Idiot's Guide to SQL*. The goal of this book is to give you a real, working knowledge of SQL, the language you use to communicate with databases.

Here, you're going to get a guided tour of SQL. But that's not all. You're also going to get a guided tour of SQL as it's used by your Database Management System (DBMS).

SQL is defined according to a strict standard. However, all modern DBMSes stray from that standard considerably. Most books on SQL ignore that fact and just give you the standard SQL story. But that story doesn't work a lot of the time in today's DBMSes.

That's why we give you both the standard story and the story for the DBMS you're using. If any of the four major DBMSes—MySQL, Oracle, Microsoft SQL Server, or PostgreSQL—use different syntax for a particular task, we'll let you know what that syntax is.

This book also differs from other books in that every point is illustrated with at least one example. You won't see just theoretical discussions of SQL tasks here—you'll see the actual tasks run in real DBMSes so you can get up to speed simply by taking a look at the examples.

What's in This Book

This book consists of four parts, all of which give you the full SQL story with syntax relating to specific DBMSes. The following paragraphs discuss what's in those parts.

In **Part 1, Mastering the SQL Basics,** you'll lay the foundation of your SQL journey. Here, we'll start with the SQL basics like understanding databases, tables, rows, and columns.

Then we'll see how to create database tables, store data in them, and retrieve that data. When you're done with this part, you'll be able to take your data, put it into a database, and retrieve it from the database, all with the help of SQL.

In **Part 2, Crunching Your Data,** you get deeper into SQL, seeing what it can do for you and your data. Here, you investigate different options for sorting your data, such as simple sorts, group sorts, reverse sorts, custom sorts, and more.

Then you learn about filtering your data to extract just the information you want. This is where you see how to get all the data that matches the criteria you want.

Finally, in this part, you take a look at how to make changes to your stored data by updating it. You see how to update individual data items in a table, an entire row in a table, or even in a whole table.

In **Part 3, In-Depth Data Handling,** you'll plunge a little deeper into manipulating data. You start by connecting tables so that the data items you read can come from one table or from a connected table. (Connecting tables like this means you don't have to store all your data in the same table.)

Next, you examine how SQL lets you group data inside the same table. Say, for example, that you have a table that keeps track of a set of employees, some of whom are in Sales and some of whom are in Accounting. By grouping the records in the table, you can collect those in Sales together and those in Accounting together, effectively forming two subtables in the same table. Then you can sort or examine each group of employees independently.

You also look at SQL views in this part. Views are temporary tables that you can use when you don't want to interfere with the data in a real table. You can assemble a view from some or all of the data in a real table, or combine data from two or more tables.

In **Part 4, Power Techniques,** you see the muscle of SQL. Here, you see how to store SQL code in procedures that you can call at any time. That's great if you have long scripts of SQL that you need to execute over and over.

You also learn how to make your SQL operations secure with transactions. When you execute SQL as part of a transaction, you can undo or roll it back if you want to—if something goes wrong at some point in a transaction, you can roll it back, leaving things as if the transaction never happened.

Finally, you look at SQL constraints and triggers. Constraints are rules you can set up for tables that limit the values you can enter into the table. For example, if you have a set of employees, you can constrain their ID values in the table to be in a certain range that you specify. Triggers are like more complex, more powerful constraints. They let you check what's going on every time someone inserts, updates, or deletes data in a table, and cause the action to fail if you don't approve. Using triggers, you can guard your data down to the last detail.

At the back of the book, there are two appendixes. Appendix A is a glossary of SQL terms. If you need fast access to a definition, this is the place to look. Appendix B is all about how to type in and run the examples in this book. Just how you do that depends on your DBMS, so take a look at how to enter SQL and execute it in Appendix B in order to follow along with the examples in this book.

Extras

You will also see sidebars throughout the book. These have the following meanings:

DEFINITION

These sidebars define unfamiliar terms scattered throughout the text.

SQL CAUTION

These sidebars warn you about potential problems you might encounter while using SQL.

SQL TIP

These sidebars give you inside information on SQL and what you will encounter as you work through the examples in the book.

Special Thanks to the Technical Reviewer

The Complete Idiot's Guide to SQL was reviewed by an expert who double-checked the accuracy of what you'll learn here, to help us ensure that this book gives you everything you need to know about SQL. Special thanks to Ken Bluttman.

Trademarks

All terms mentioned in this book that are known to be or are suspected of being trademarks or service marks have been appropriately capitalized. Alpha Books and Penguin Group (USA) Inc. cannot attest to the accuracy of this information. Use of a term in this book should not be regarded as affecting the validity of any trademark or service mark.

Mastering the SQL Basics

We're going to get our feet wet with SQL, first learning about crucial database concepts like tables, rows, columns, and even databases themselves.

Then we'll jump right in to see what SQL can do. We'll create a table of data and see how to extract data from that table, and how to sort and filter that data to get just what you want.

When you've finished this part, you'll be able to create database tables, insert data into them, and get that data back out again when you want it.

Getting into SQL

In This Chapter

- An introduction to SQL
- An overview of databases
- Understanding tables
- Working with table columns
- Storing records in rows
- Putting some SQL to work

Databases. You can't live without them—even if you don't know it. Every day, your name is retrieved from more than a dozen databases. If you use an ATM, for example, the bank's software looks you up in a database and finds your account. Someone might send you an e-mail and get your e-mail address from an address book, another form of a database. Even things we'd rather do without come from databases, such as bills and junk mail. Just think of all the electricity, gas, phone, cable, and other bills that are prepared from a database (or perhaps you'd rather not).

Databases are a huge part of modern life, and because you're reading this book, you most likely have some need to learn how to interact with them. You've come to the right place—in this book, we're going to cover SQL (that is, Structured Query Language) in depth, and SQL is the language of databases.

We're going to take things step-by-step to ensure you get the whole story in an easily accessible way. In this chapter, we start with an introduction to the concepts you'll need throughout the book, such as what a database is, what a table in a database is, and what SQL is. Then we put SQL to work immediately, creating a database table and working with the data in it to show how easy SQL is.

That's what's coming up in this chapter, as well as your guided tour to an overview of databases so that you have a good foundation for the rest of the book. We're also going to see some SQL at work here to demystify it and show how simple it is to make it work for you.

Let's get started by understanding some fundamental database concepts.

Understanding Databases

So just what is a *database?* As you can tell from the name, a database is where you store data—typically, individual items like numbers or text strings. How do you get from those data items to a database?

 DEFINITION

A **database** is a container for tables.

Those items are stored in tables—two-dimensional grids of data items, organized into rows and columns. A database is made up of one or more of those tables.

To understand how databases work, let's take a look at an example.

Creating Tables

Say that you're a famous professor, teaching a class all about SQL. You want to keep track of your students. You might set up a table on a piece of paper to record their grades. You'd have two columns: one for their name, and one for their grade:

```
---------------------
| name    | grade  |
|---------|--------|
|         |        |
|---------|--------|
|         |        |
|---------|--------|
|         |        |
|---------|--------|
|         |        |
|---------|--------|
|         |        |
|---------|--------|
|         |        |
---------------------
```

So far, so good. Now you can record the names of each student and their grades in your table like this:

```
---------------------
| name    | grade  |
|---------|--------|
| Ann     |   C    |
|---------|--------|
| Mark    |   B    |
|---------|--------|
| Ed      |   A    |
|---------|--------|
| Frank   |   C    |
|---------|--------|
| Ted     |   A    |
|---------|--------|
| Mabel   |   B    |
---------------------
```

Great—you've created your table of student grades on paper. And you've also created one of the fundamental structures used in databases: a *table*. That's how you store data, in gridlike tables.

DEFINITION

A **table** is a grid that has rows and columns that hold data. Note that an individual cell in the table is called a *field,* and rows are also called *records.*

Modern databases are set up to contain tables of data just like the one you've just created. The tables are divided into *rows* and *columns.* It's that easy.

DEFINITION

A **column** in a table has both a name (such as "grade" to hold student grades) and a data type (such as VARCHAR or INT).

A **row** holds a record in a table, such as a record for each student in your class. Each row is divided into columns, such as the name column and grade column in our example. Thus, rows are collections of data items (held in columns) to make a record.

Creating Rows and Columns in Tables

The rows and columns in a database table have just the same meaning as in your paper table. Each column is designed to hold a different data item—in this example, the student's name and grade:

```
-------------------
| name    | grade  |
|---------|--------|
|         |        |
|---------|--------|
|         |        |
|---------|--------|
|         |        |
|---------|--------|
|         |        |
|---------|--------|
|         |        |
|---------|--------|
|         |        |
-------------------
```

That's the way it works with database tables, too. Each column in a table holds a different data item(s); for example, if the table you've created were in a database, the first column would be named "name" and the second column "grade." In databases, each column has its own data type so you know what kind of data can be stored in that column. For example, if the data type of a column is a numeric data type like an integer, you wouldn't expect to see text data stored in that column. Columns are given their own data types so the database knows what kind of data is going to go into that column and can prepare to store it the most efficiently.

Data types include INT for integer, DECIMAL for decimal, VARCHAR for variable-length text string data (the most common way to store text—you can add or remove text to a variable-length string at any time), and so on. (You learn about all the data types in Chapter 2.)

In this table, the name column might be set up to hold text data (data of type VARCHAR, for variable-length text data), the grade column might be set up to also hold text data if you want (data of type VARCHAR again) or, if you want to record students' grades as numbers, as a number (such as the INT data type).

So in a database table, each column gets its own name (such as "grade") and data type. It works just like the paper table we've created.

Each row in the paper table holds the record of a single student, such as Ted's record here:

```
 --------------------
| name     | grade  |
|----------|--------|
|          |        |
|----------|--------|
|          |        |
|----------|--------|
|          |        |
|----------|--------|
|          |        |
|----------|--------|
| Ted      | A      |
|----------|--------|
|          |        |
 --------------------
```

It's the same in database tables. Each row contains a separate record. Each record may be as simple as the record we have for Ted here, or may be as complex as your record in a bank's internal accounting system.

SQL CAUTION

A record is a row, and a row is a record. What's the correct term, row or record? While both refer to the same thing—a single entry in a database table—row is the correct term in SQL.

Each row is made up of the various columns in that row, of course, and in database terminology, each column's location in a row is called a *field*. A field corresponds to a single cell in a database table. Thus, in our example, each row has a name field and a grade field. The values in those fields for Ted's row are: "Ted" in the name field and "A" in the grade field.

DEFINITION

A **field** is a single cell in a table.

To sum up, then, database tables are made up of columns and rows. A column holds data items with a specific data type (such as bank account numbers of the DECIMAL type or temperatures of the INT type). Each row represents a record in the table (such as Ted's record, which records that he got an A, or your record in the bank's database tables, which record your name, balance, and so on). And each cell in a table is called a field.

That's all great, but what is a database? We haven't answered that question clearly. To see what a database is, imagine that your SQL class is so popular, you've been asked to teach a second class. So you end up with two tables, which you name class1 and class2:

```
        class1                      class2
-----------------------     -----------------------
| name     | grade  |       | name     | grade  |
|----------|--------|       |----------|--------|
| Ann      | C      |       | Tamsen   | A      |
|----------|--------|       |----------|--------|
| Mark     | B      |       | Vickie   | B      |
|----------|--------|       |----------|--------|
| Ed       | A      |       | Tina     | C      |
```

```
|----------|--------|          |----------|--------|
|  Frank   |   C    |          |   Cary   |   A    |
|----------|--------|          |----------|--------|
|  Ted     |   A    |          |   Jim    |   B    |
|----------|--------|          |----------|--------|
|  Mabel   |   B    |          |   Mike   |   D    |
 --------------------            --------------------
```

Now you have two tables, class1 and class2, and you also have a database, because a database is just a collection of tables. That's it—a database is a collection of one or more tables.

Adding Primary Keys

We're just about done with our guided tour of the concepts behind a database, but there's one more concept to get down before we jump in and start creating tables and stocking them with data in the rest of this chapter: *primary keys.*

DEFINITION

A **primary key** represents a guaranteed unique identifier for each record.

Think about the grades table for a moment. The table records students by first name, and it's easy to imagine two students having the first name, giving you two records with the same name field. You can avoid that by adding a field to each record that holds a unique value, and such a field is called a primary key in database language.

It's not a concept that's unique to databases. Students in universities get IDs for the same reason—to avoid problems if two students have the same name. So you might add each student's ID to your table like this:

```
 ----------------------------
| name     | grade  |   id   |
|----------|--------|--------|
| Ann      |   C    |   01   |
|----------|--------|--------|
| Mark     |   B    |   02   |
|----------|--------|--------|
| Ed       |   A    |   03   |
```

```
|---------|---------|---------|
| Frank   |    C    |   04    |
|---------|---------|---------|
| Ted     |    A    |   05    |
|---------|---------|---------|
| Mabel   |    B    |   06    |
---------------------------------
```

Now you've added a primary key field to each record. Primary keys are no more than unique identifiers for records, and database tables usually include a primary key field (which is marked as the primary key for the table). Using primary keys is not mandatory, but most database tables do use them to have a guaranteed unique identifier for each record. Primary key values must be unique; no two records can have the same primary key. In fact, they're so unique that you are not supposed to reuse them. So if you delete a record, you aren't supposed to use its primary key value anywhere else in your table as a primary key.

And now that we've got the basic concepts down—tables, rows, columns, fields, databases, and primary keys—let's actually create them in real life to demystify them. The language we'll use to create them with is SQL.

Getting Your Database Ready

The actual software you use to keep track of databases and the tables in them is called a Database Management System, or DBMS. There are plenty of DBMSes out there, and you may already have access to one.

If You Don't Already Have a DBMS

If you don't already have a DBMS to run the examples in this book, consider MySQL. It's free, and it's the most widely installed SQL DBMS. Using MySQL to enter the examples in this book is easy; just follow the directions in Appendix B.

If you're interested in getting MySQL to follow along as we build the examples, go to www.mysql.com, click the **Downloads** tab, and download and install the MySQL Community Server package. It's free, and it will let you run SQL immediately.

If You Already Have a DBMS

You aren't restricted if you already have access to a DBMS and want to use it. You'll find directions on how to enter SQL and run SQL examples like the ones developed in this book for Aqua Data Studio, DB2, MacroMedia ColdFusion, Microsoft Access, Microsoft ASP, Microsoft ASP.NET, Microsoft Query, Microsoft SQL Server, MySQL, Oracle, PHP, PostgreSQL, Query Tool, Sybase, and ODBC data sources in Appendix B.

No matter what DBMS system you have, it will run SQL, and that means it runs the type of SQL we're going to be talking about in this book—ANSI (American National Standards Institute) SQL—using the most current version, SQLL2008. Many DBMS manufacturers add their own extensions to SQL, and if we use such an extension from time to time, we'll clearly label it as DBMS-specific. But what we're really covering is the latest standard ANSI SQL, which all current DBMSes run, so you're ready to go if you have access to any DBMS; you can enter the SQL for the examples in this book into your own DBMS by following the directions in Appendix B.

Introducing SQL

Now we'll introduce *SQL* itself. SQL stands for Structured Query Language (pronounced S-Q-L or "sequel," your choice), and it's the language you talk to databases in.

DEFINITION

SQL is Structured Query Language, the language you talk to databases in. It lets you store, manipulate, and extract your data and modify the structure of the database.

Everything you can do with a database, you can do with SQL. And that's good, because SQL doesn't need many keywords (the words that make up SQL) to do what it does, so it's easy to learn.

Creating a Database

We're going to jump into SQL right now by creating a database—that is, a place to store our tables. If you already have a database you'd like to work with, you can use it and skip ahead to the section "Creating a Table."

If you want to follow along, start your DBMS according to the directions in Appendix B so that you get a prompt that will accept SQL statements, called *queries*. We represent that prompt like this:

> >

> **DEFINITION**
>
> SQL is made up of individual statements, each of which performs some action. A statement is also called a **query** (which is why SQL is called the Structured Query Language).

Let's create an example grocery store with a table for fruit items. The database will be called groceries and the table in it will be called fruit.

To create a database that can hold tables in SQL, you use the SQL CREATE statement. To create a database named groceries, you use the SQL statement CREATE DATABASE groceries. Note that you need to end the SQL statements with a semicolon (;) because almost all database systems require it:

```
> CREATE DATABASE groceries;
```

> **SQL TIP**
>
> You might notice the use of capital letters for SQL keywords, like CREATE. Why is that? Is that mandatory? Actually, SQL is case-insensitive, so CREATE is the same as create, which is the same as CrEaTe. However, it's become standard in the SQL community to use all capital letters for the SQL keywords because for many people, it makes SQL statements easier to read because you can tell the difference between the SQL keywords and items like table or column names at a glance. So for the most part, when you see SQL statements anywhere in the world, the SQL keywords are capitalized.

The DBMS answers that the SQL query has executed successfully with a statement like this (your actual response will vary with what DBMS you use):

```
> CREATE DATABASE groceries;
Query OK, 1 row affected (0.03 sec)
```

That's it—we've just used SQL to create our first database. Not so bad. The next step is to add a database table, the fruit table, to it.

Creating a Table

Now that you've got a database to work with, you can create the fruit table. In this table, you might want to keep track of various fruits and the number of each you have in our grocery store, so the table columns would be named as follows:

```
--------------------
| name    | number |
|------------------|
|         |        |
|------------------|
|         |        |
|------------------|
|         |        |
|------------------|
|         |        |
--------------------
```

You can store the various fruit items in the database table this way:

```
--------------------
| name    | number |
|------------------|
| apples  | 1020   |
|------------------|
| oranges | 3329   |
|------------------|
| bananas | 8582   |
|------------------|
| pears   | 234    |
--------------------
```

Actually, there's one item missing: the primary key column, which holds a unique identifier for each fruit. You're free to name the primary key field what you want, so we'll call it id:

```
-------------------------------
| name    | number |  id     |
-------------------------------
| apples  | 1020   | 109     |
-------------------------------
| oranges | 3329   | 103     |
-------------------------------
| bananas | 8582   | 107     |
-------------------------------
| pears   | 234    | 101     |
-------------------------------
```

So that's the new table we want to create, the fruit table. Now let's create it in SQL.

Each column in a table has its own data type as well as name, so we'll use the VARCHAR type (variable-length text string data type) for the name field and the INT (integer) type for the number and id fields. To create a table with those fields, you'd use the CREATE TABLE SQL statement like this:

```
CREATE TABLE fruit (name VARCHAR(20), number INT, id INT);
```

Note how this works. You create the table fruit with the statement CREATE TABLE fruit, and then specify the columns in parentheses. For each column, you give the column's name and its data type. For the VARCHAR data type, which is what you use for variable-length text strings, you can indicate the maximum size of the text in characters by adding that in parentheses after the word VARCHAR, so here, we're allowing fruit names of up to 20 characters.

In fact, you can do more here by marking the id field as the primary key. That way, your DBMS will use it to sort on if you sort the table by default. To indicate that a field is a table's primary key, you just add the words PRIMARY KEY when you're creating the table like this:

```
CREATE TABLE fruit (name VARCHAR(20), number INT, id INT PRIMARY KEY);
```

SQL CAUTION

Now that you've marked the id field as the table's primary key, your DBMS won't let you enter the same ID for any two records. You could have chosen the name field as the primary key, but that would mean you can't enter two students with the same first name in your table.

Okay, we're ready to create our first table. We have to indicate to the DBMS which database to create the table in, and you can always refer to a table in a database with the syntax *database_name.table_name*, so you can create the fruit table in the groceries database like this:

```
CREATE TABLE groceries.fruit (name VARCHAR(20), number INT, id INT
    ➥ PRIMARY KEY);
```

However, most DBMSes have a shortcut here that you can use at the command-prompt line. You can use the USE statement to make a specific database the default like this:

```
> USE groceries;
Database changed
```

Now for all future operations, the DBMS will assume you are working with the groceries database, which means you don't have to qualify table names as *database_name.table_name*. You can use only the table name to refer to that table.

The USE statement is not a part of ANSI SQL—it's just a convenience statement supported by many DBMSes we can use to set the default database. If your DBMS command-line prompt doesn't support it, use the *database_name.table_name* syntax.

Now it's time to create that table. It looks like this:

```
> CREATE TABLE fruit (name VARCHAR(20), number INT, id INT PRIMARY KEY);
Query OK, 0 rows affected (0.06 sec)
```

As you can see, the fruit table was created successfully. Congratulations! You've created your first database table, and all with only a few SQL statements.

Now let's add some data to the new table.

Adding Data to a New Table

Here's the data we want to put into the fruit table:

```
------------------------------
| name    | number |  id    |
------------------------------
| apples  | 1020   |  109   |
------------------------------
| oranges | 3329   |  103   |
------------------------------
| bananas | 8582   |  107   |
------------------------------
| pears   | 234    |  101   |
------------------------------
```

So far, we've used SQL to create a database and to create the fruit table in it. Now you can insert data into the table using SQL.

You insert data into tables with the, you guessed it, INSERT statement. To insert data into the fruit table, you'd use an INSERT INTO fruit statement. When using this statement, you give the values you want to insert in parentheses following the word VALUES like this:

```
INSERT INTO fruit VALUES ('apples', 1020, 109);
```

And here's what it looks like:

```
> INSERT INTO fruit VALUES ('apples', 1020, 109);
Query OK, 1 row affected (0.03 sec)
```

And that's it! We've just stocked the first row of the first table with data. Now you can add the other rows like this:

```
> INSERT INTO fruit VALUES ('apples', 1020, 109);
Query OK, 1 row affected (0.03 sec)

> INSERT INTO fruit VALUES ('oranges', 3329, 103);
Query OK, 1 row affected (0.00 sec)

> INSERT INTO fruit VALUES ('bananas', 8582, 107);
Query OK, 1 row affected (0.00 sec)

> INSERT INTO fruit VALUES ('pears', 235, 101);
Query OK, 1 row affected (0.03 sec)
```

Great, you have successfully inserted data into the table. Now what? It's time to get that data out again and actually access it using SQL.

Accessing Data from a Table

Now that we've loaded up our database table, we're going to introduce the SQL statement we'll use most often in this book, the SELECT statement.

The SELECT statement lets you retrieve data from tables. We'll put it to use right away to check on the data we've entered into the fruit table.

We can select all data in the fruit table with the SELECT * FROM fruit SQL statement. In SQL, the asterisk (*) is a wildcard, standing in for any matching item. So SELECT * FROM fruit is a typical SQL statement—you specify what you want to select (everything in this case, which means using the * wildcard) and then indicate from which table you want to fetch the data.

Here's what using that SELECT statement looks like, now that we've set up our fruit table:

```
> SELECT * FROM fruit;
+---------+--------+-----+
| name    | number | id  |
+---------+--------+-----+
| pears   | 235    | 101 |
| oranges | 3329   | 103 |
| bananas | 8582   | 107 |
| apples  | 1020   | 109 |
+---------+--------+-----+
4 rows in set (0.02 sec)
```

Bingo. The entire table is returned and displayed, just as we wanted it. And as you can see, everything in the new table is just as we put it there.

SQL TIP

Note that our DBMS has returned the table automatically sorted on the primary key value. That's usually the case, but you can't rely on that sort order.

The usual return value from a SELECT statement is an array. In this case, that array (that is, an indexed set of values) contained the whole table because we asked for all data, but you can get more selective.

For example, you might just want to extract all names from the fruit table. You could do this easily. Just use the SQL query SELECT name from fruit, indicating that the name column is all you need.

That looks like this:

```
> SELECT name from fruit;
+---------+
| name    |
+---------+
| pears   |
| oranges |
| bananas |
| apples  |
+---------+
4 rows in set (0.00 sec)
```

Now you can determine what fruit items you're selling with a single statement.

Or you might find you're interested in both the name and number of the various fruits to check inventory on hand. Simple enough; just execute this statement: SELECT name, number from fruit. Here's what it looks like in our DBMS, which, as you can see, returns a two-column array.

```
> SELECT name, number from fruit;
+---------+--------+
| name    | number |
+---------+--------+
| pears   | 235    |
| oranges | 3329   |
| bananas | 8582   |
| apples  | 1020   |
+---------+--------+
4 rows in set (0.06 sec)
```

That was easy. You haven't even begun to scratch the surface. Let's take a look at drilling down even more precisely when we extract data.

Adding a WHERE clause

The WHERE clause lets you add further conditions on your query. For example, what if you want to zero in on just apples? SELECT apples FROM fruit wouldn't work, because the SELECT statement expects the name of a column or columns, not a name of a data item like apples.

Fortunately, we have the WHERE clause. The WHERE clause lets you get a little more picky when you're extracting data. For example, if you want to extract just data on apples, you can use the SQL SELECT * FROM fruit WHERE name= "apples". See? Very simple.

Here's what it looks like:

```
> SELECT * FROM fruit WHERE name= "apples";
+--------+--------+-----+
| name   | number | id  |
+--------+--------+-----+
| apples | 1020   | 109 |
+--------+--------+-----+
1 row in set (0.01 sec)
```

SQL TIP

Note that what you pass to SELECT (* or column names) retrieves columns, but when you start using the WHERE clause, you can retrieve rows instead. So as you can start to see, SQL serves up your data any way you want it.

Adding an IN clause

Too bad you can't retrieve both the apples and oranges rows at the same time with the same SQL statement. Or can you? Of course you can; you just have to specify a set of acceptable names to search for by adding an IN clause to the WHERE clause like this: SELECT * FROM fruit WHERE name IN ("apples", "oranges"). Note that even though this is a long SQL statement, it reads more or less like simple English. Here's how it looks when you execute it:

```
> SELECT * FROM fruit WHERE name IN ("apples", "oranges");
+---------+--------+-----+
| name    | number | id  |
+---------+--------+-----+
| oranges | 3329   | 103 |
| apples  | 1020   | 109 |
+---------+--------+-----+
2 rows in set (0.02 sec)
```

What if you just want to find the number of apples and oranges on hand? No problem at all. Try SELECT name, number FROM fruit WHERE name IN ("apples", "oranges"). Here's what it looks like:

```
> SELECT name, number FROM fruit WHERE name IN ("apples", "oranges");
+---------+--------+
| name    | number |
+---------+--------+
| oranges | 3329   |
| apples  | 1020   |
+---------+--------+
2 rows in set (0.00 sec)
```

There's just no end to it. What if you wanted the inventory of all fruit *except* apples and oranges? Why for that, you'd add a NOT keyword like this: SELECT name, number FROM fruit WHERE name NOT IN ("apples", "oranges"). Here's what you get:

```
> SELECT name, number FROM fruit WHERE name NOT IN ("apples", "oranges");
+---------+--------+
| name    | number |
+---------+--------+
| pears   | 235    |
| bananas | 8582   |
+---------+--------+
2 rows in set (0.00 sec)
```

Wow. And that's just for simple data retrieval. What if you wanted to check on fruit items where inventory is less than 1,000? You could do that like this: SELECT * FROM fruit WHERE (number < 1000). Here's what it looks like:

```
> SELECT * FROM fruit WHERE (number < 1000);
+-------+--------+-----+
| name  | number | id  |
+-------+--------+-----+
| pears | 235    | 101 |
+-------+--------+-----+
1 row in set (0.00 sec)
```

So as we can see, there are less than 1,000 pears—and that's the only fruit with less than 1,000 on hand. What if we wanted to know the total number of fruit? Nothing could be easier. Just use the built-in SQL SUM function this way:

```
> SELECT SUM(number) FROM fruit;
--------------+
  SUM(number)  |
--------------+
  13166        |
--------------+
  row in set (0.03 sec)
```

There are many built-in functions in SQL, so besides finding the total number of fruit, you can also find the average number of each fruit, the square root of each fruit, or just about anything numerical you want.

SQL TIP

The SQL built-in functions come with SQL, and they're one of the most powerful parts of SQL. Unfortunately, most of these are not standardized, so they vary by DBMS. Nevertheless, there are dozens of common built-in functions, and we'll get an overview of what's available in this book.

In fact, the real fun starts when you have multiple tables. Say, for example, that in addition to the fruit table, there was a suppliers table listing the wholesalers you get your groceries from. With a single SQL statement, you can look up which fruits are getting low in inventory, find their IDs, look up those IDs in the suppliers table, and display not only the number of fruit you need to order of each kind, but also the phone numbers of the associated wholesalers from the suppliers table. You can get really crazy with SQL.

SQL TIP

Connecting two tables together by relating them with a key (the ID value, in this case) gives you what is called a relational database. We'll connect tables together often in this book.

Now I hope you're getting an idea of how SQL lets you grab and work with data. SQL is a tool for retrieving your data from database tables and filtering it, sorting it, or otherwise massaging it. SQL gives you a window into your data and lets you manipulate it. Handling your data becomes a breeze.

Now that we've gotten an overview of databases, tables, rows, columns, fields, and SQL and have seen SQL at work, we're in good shape to dig into SQL in depth. Now that we've demystified SQL and built our foundation with the concepts we'll need, we're good to go.

We'll start in the next chapter with a detailed look at the most popular (and powerful) SQL statement—the SELECT statement.

The Least You Need to Know

- Databases are containers for tables.

- Tables are grids that hold data in rows and columns. Each column in a table has a name and a data type. Each row in a table is a record, a separate entry in a database table.

- It's a good idea to give your tables primary keys so that each record has a guaranteed unique identifier.

- You use the CREATE TABLE statement to create SQL tables. You use INSERT statements to add data to tables. You use SELECT statements to access data from tables.

- You can filter your data, selecting just the data you want, with a WHERE clause.

- Your DBMS will often come with many built-in functions.

Storing Data in Tables

In This Chapter

- Creating tables from scratch
- Working with the types of data you can put in tables
- Storing your data in tables
- Reading data from your tables
- Deleting a table when you don't need it anymore
- Adding and deleting columns in tables

Tables are at the very heart of SQL. Most SQL operations have to do with tables: storing data in tables, getting data out of tables, modifying the data in tables, and so on. You need to create tables before you can do anything with your data.

We're going to master tables here—creating them, inserting data into them, adding columns, deleting columns, renaming columns, modifying a table's data type—even renaming whole tables and deleting whole tables.

In this chapter, we're also going to create the sample table that we'll use throughout much of this book. We'll create that table here and fill it with data, and then use it as the basis for retrieving data from tables, filtering data, sorting data, and so on.

As you can see, there's plenty coming up in this chapter. Let's start with an overview of tables.

All About Tables

Database tables are just grids of data like this:

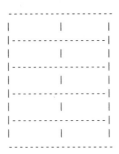

As you know from Chapter 1, each column in a table has a name and a data type. In that chapter, we created a table to hold fruit inventory with two columns—*name* to hold the names of the fruit, and *number* to hold the numbers of fruit on hand. The name column was of type VARCHAR, and the number column was of type INT:

```
-------------------
| name    | number |
|------------------|
|         |        |
|------------------|
|         |        |
|------------------|
|         |        |
|------------------|
|         |        |
-------------------
```

Then we slapped some data into the table. Each data set (the name of a fruit and the number available) made up a record, which was stored in a row in the table:

```
-------------------
| name    | number |
|------------------|
| apples  | 1020   |
|------------------|
| oranges | 3329   |
|------------------|
| bananas | 8582   |
|------------------|
| pears   | 234    |
-------------------
```

That wasn't the end of it—most tables also contain a primary key column, which stores a unique identifier for each record. That way, two records might have the same name, but their primary keys will always be different. We named our primary key column id and place values in it like this:

```
-----------------------------
| name    | number |  id    |
-----------------------------
| apples  | 1020   |  109   |
-----------------------------
| oranges | 3329   |  103   |
-----------------------------
| bananas | 8582   |  107   |
-----------------------------
| pears   | 234    |  101   |
-----------------------------
```

And that's it—that's a complete database table, good to go. Now let's see about creating a new table and understanding all the options you have when creating one.

Creating a Table

You create a table with the SQL CREATE TABLE statement, and in that statement, you specify all the columns in the table, which includes each column's name and data type. Here are the steps:

1. Start with the CREATE TABLE keywords.

2. Specify the table name.

3. Add an open parentheses—that is, (.

4. Enter the column name.

5. Add the column's data type.

6. Add a comma.

7. Repeat Steps 4 through 5 for the other columns.

8. End the CREATE TABLE statement with a closing parenthesis.

Here's how it looks formally:

```
CREATE TABLE table_name
(column_1 data_type,
 column_2 data_type,
...
 column_n data_type);
```

SQL CAUTION

The *table_name* item takes a little looking at as well. When you create a table, you have to specify what database you want that table to be in. In this book, we use the USE statement, which sets the default database for all subsequent SQL statements. However, USE is not standard ANSI SQL, so if your DBMS doesn't support USE, you can always refer to the table you're creating by its full name as *database_name.table_name*. In Chapter 1, we created the fruit table in the groceries database, so we could have referred to that table as groceries.fruit.

In fact, there's more here, because you can also add *constraints* for every column. A constraint limits the values you can put in a column, and you specify column constraints when creating the table (note that items in brackets are optional, so you need not specify any constraints at all if you don't want to):

```
CREATE TABLE table_name
(column_1 data_type [constraint],
 column_2 data_type [constraint],
...
 column_n data_type [constraint]);
```

DEFINITION

A **constraint** is a limitation on the values a column can hold.

We created the fruit table in Chapter 1 by constraining the id column to be the primary key:

```
CREATE TABLE fruit (name VARCHAR(20), number INT, id INT PRIMARY KEY)
```

You will see the more common constraints in this chapter, such as a popular constraint called UNIQUE, which constrains the column to contain only unique values (that is, no two rows can contain the same value in that column). For example, we might make the name field unique like this:

```
CREATE TABLE fruit (name VARCHAR(20) UNIQUE, number INT, id INT PRIMARY KEY)
```

As your table creation statements become longer, you'll need to break them up on to separate lines, but that's no problem for SQL:

```
CREATE TABLE fruit
(name VARCHAR(20) UNIQUE,
number INT,
id INT PRIMARY KEY);
```

SQL TIP

In SQL, extra white space like spaces, tabs, and carriage returns are stripped out before the SQL statement is processed, so feel free to use as much extra white space as you like to make your SQL clearer to read.

So that's how you create a table—you specify a name, data type, and optional constraints for every column. So what data types are possible? And what constraints? Those are coming up next.

Working with Data Types

We've already seen the VARCHAR and INT data types, but what other types are there? You can see the standard ANSI SQL data types in Table 2.1. Note that the range of a data type shows the allowed range of values, from minimum to maximum.

Table 2.1 SQL Data Types

Data Type	Meaning	Range
ARRAY	Using this data type, a field can hold an entire collection of data items; arrays have a defined element order	Varies
BIGINT	A big integer	Larger than the INT type, but varies depending on implementation
BINARY LARGE OBJECT or BLOB	Huge binary data objects, such as images or videos	Varies
BIT VARYING(n)	An array of up to n bits	$1 < n < 15000$
BIT(n)	An array of n bits	$1 < n < 15000$
CHARACTER LARGE OBJECT or CLOB	Used for huge text strings, like whole books	Varies by implementation
CHARACTER VARYING(n) or VARCHAR(n)	Variable-length character string, maximum length n	$1 < n < 15000$
CHARACTER(n) or CHAR(n)	Character string, fixed length n	$1 < n < 15000$
DATE TIME TIMESTAMP TIMESTAMPTZ	Composed of a number of integer fields; represents an absolute point in time	DATE, TIME, TIMESTAMP or TIMESTAMPZ (TIMESTAMP with time zone) data
DECIMAL(p, s) or NUMERIC(p, s)	Exact numerical, number of digits p, number of decimal places s	$1 < p < 45$ $0 < s < p$
DOUBLE PRECISION	Approximate numerical, mantissa number of digits 16	Zero or absolute value 10^{-308} to 10^{+308}

Data Type	Meaning	Range
FLOAT	Approximate numerical, mantissa number of digits 16	Zero or absolute value 10^{-308} to 10^{+308}
FLOAT(p)	Approximate numerical, mantissa number of digits p	$1 < p < 45$ Zero or absolute value 10^{-999} to 10^{+999}
INTEGER or INT	Integer numerical, number of digits 10	-2,147,483,648 through 2,147,483,647
INTEGER(p) or INT(p)	Integer numerical, number of digits p	$1 < p < 45$
INTERVAL	Composed of a number of integer fields; represents a period of time, depending on the type of interval	N/A
MULTISET	Using this data type, a field can hold an entire collection of data items; multisets have no defined element order	Varies
NATIONAL CHARACTER LARGE OBJECT	Used for huge text national character strings, like whole books	Varies by implementation
NATIONAL CHARACTER VARYING(n) or NVARCHAR(n)	Variable-width string supporting an international character set	$1 < n < 15000$
NATIONAL CHARACTER(n) or NCHAR(n)	Fixed-width string supporting an international character set	$1 < n < 15000$
REAL	Approximate numerical, mantissa number of digits 7	Zero or absolute value 10^{-38} to 10^{+38}

continues

Table 2.1 SQL Data Types (continued)

Data Type	Meaning	Range
REF	A pointer to another data field	Varies
ROW	Creates a data type of an abstract row (including all its fields) that you can use in table definitions	Varies
SMALLINT	Integer numerical stored as 16 bits	-32768 through 32767
USER-DEFINED DATA	You can declare your own data types from existing data types	Varies
XML	The XML data type takes XML data in a tree structure	Varies

SQL TIP

Most DBMSes add their own data types to those listed in Table 2.1. For example, Microsoft's SQL Server adds such types as TINYINT, MONEY, SMALLDATETIME, and more. Check your DBMS's documentation for the data types it might add.

Table 2.1 is pretty big, so what are the most common data types? They are:

- INT
- VARCHAR (or TEXT)
- FLOAT
- DATE
- TIME

We've seen the INT and VARCHAR types at work. The FLOAT type holds floating point numbers, and it's easy to use. You insert values like "3.23453" into FLOAT fields. If you want to use an exponent, you can use E such as this: "3.2E-6." which gives you a value of 3.2×10^{-6}.

The DATE and TIME types require a little more discussion. The DATE type holds, as you might expect, dates. The format you pass dates to SQL is as "YYYYMMDD," so if you wanted to store September 2, 2012 (that is, 09/02/2012) in a table, you'd tell SQL to store the date "20120902."

The TIME data type is easier to use; you just record a time. For example, to record 01:02:03, you'd tell SQL to store the time string "010203." We'll see how to work with dates in this chapter.

That gives us a good picture of the available data types. Now what about the constraints you can put on columns?

SQL TIP

You might be interested in the user-defined data types you see in Table 2.1. Can you define your own data types? User-defined types are based on predefined SQL types. So, for example, you can rename one existing data type as another like this: CREATE DISTINCT TYPE Euro AS DECIMAL (10, 2);. Now you can refer to a new data type when creating tables— the Euro type. The second type of user-defined types is more complex, because it involves data structures.

Working with Constraints

For each column in a SQL table, you specify the name of the column and its data type. But you can, optionally, add a constraint (items in brackets are optional):

```
CREATE TABLE table_name
(column_1 data_type [constraint],
 column_2 data_type [constraint],
...
 column_n data_type [constraint]);
```

Constraints are ideal because they let you put bounds on your data so your DBMS can check that data for you, saving you the trouble. A full discussion of constraints is included in Chapter 14, but you can take a look at what makes them valuable here.

We've already seen that one constraint is UNIQUE, which means that all values in that column must be unique, and another is PRIMARY KEY, the field that holds a guaranteed unique identifier for a row:

```
CREATE TABLE fruit
(name VARCHAR(20) UNIQUE,
number INT,
id INT PRIMARY KEY);
```

Another constraint is NOT NULL, which means you cannot insert a *NULL* value into a column.

> **DEFINITION**
>
> When a cell contains **NULL**, it is understood as containing no value at all. Typically, that means the data in the cell hasn't been initialized (that is, no data has been entered into the cell).

In SQL, a NULL value stands for no value at all, not even zero. When a cell contains a NULL, it's understood that it doesn't contain a value. Usually, cells in a table are all initialized to NULL. When you use a constraint of NOT NULL, you indicate that you cannot insert a NULL value into the fields of a particular column. In other words, you demand a value of some kind in a particular cell, not just NULL.

Here's another cool constraint: CHECK. The CHECK constraint lets you constrain values stored in your table. For example, say you have a table with a column named length for particular items. You can make sure the values stored in the length field are positive this way:

```
CREATE TABLE Items
(Length INTEGER CHECK (length > 0),
name VARCHAR(30));
```

That's very handy. Now you don't have to check that data yourself.

Another constraint if the DEFAULT constraint, which gives all fields in a column a default value. Nice.

As mentioned, a full treatment on constraints is included in Chapter 14. In the meantime, let's create the example table we'll use in the coming chapters.

Creating Our Example Table

We created a simple table in Chapter 1, the fruit table, but we're going to need more than that to explore what's possible in SQL. So imagine that you're the fabulously wealthy CEO of a corporation and you want to keep track of your employees.

To do that, you start by creating a database named Corporation to hold data about your corporation:

```
CREATE DATABASE Corporation;
```

SQL TIP

As we create our sample table and fill it with data, we're going to be using a lot of SQL. Do you really have to type all that to create the sample table we'll use in this book? No. Just take a look at createtable.txt in the sample code for this book at www.completeidiotsguides.com. In that file, you'll find all the SQL statements used to create the table and insert data into it, ready to copy and paste into your DBMS. Whew.

Next, you create a table named Employees with the following columns:

- **firstname**   The employee's first name.

- **lastname**   The employee's last name.

- **department**   The employee's department, such as Sales or Accounting.

- **hiredate**   The date the employee was hired.

- **supervisor**   The ID of the employee's supervisor.

- **id**   The employee's ID.

So our Employees table will look like this (this is the table we'll be using in the coming chapters):

```
------------------------------------------------------------------
| firstname   | lastname  | department | hiredate   | supervisor | id     |
------------------------------------------------------------------
|             |           |            |            |            |        |
------------------------------------------------------------------
|             |           |            |            |            |        |
------------------------------------------------------------------
|             |           |            |            |            |        |
------------------------------------------------------------------
|             |           |            |            |            |        |
------------------------------------------------------------------
|             |           |            |            |            |        |
------------------------------------------------------------------
|             |           |            |            |            |        |
------------------------------------------------------------------
```

Do we have any constraints? Yes, we want to make the id field the table's primary key, which automatically makes the value in the id field unique. Let's also have the ID values run between 1000 and 2999 with a CHECK constraint, and the supervisor ID values run between 1000 and 1999. That makes our CREATE TABLE statement look like this:

```
CREATE TABLE Employees
(firstname VARCHAR(20),
lastname VARCHAR(20),
department VARCHAR(20),
hiredate DATE,
supervisor INT CHECK (supervisor > 1000 AND supervisor < 2000),
id INT PRIMARY KEY CHECK (id > 1000 AND id < 3000));
```

Note that you can specify multiple CHECK constraints if you use the handy AND keyword, as we're going to see in Chapter 14.

And that's it. Now you've created the example database Corporation with the Employees table in it. The next step is to put some data into that table.

Adding Data to a Table

You use the INSERT SQL statement to insert data into tables. In particular, you can use the INSERT INTO *tablename* VALUES (...) statement, and we'll do that here.

Say you have an employee named John Wood in Sales, hired on 1/15/2012, whose ID is 1501 and who has a supervisor with the ID 1001. You can insert John into the Employees table like this in your own DBMS:

```
>INSERT INTO Employees VALUES ("John", "Wood", "Sales",
  ➥ "20120115", 1001, 1501);
Query OK, 1 row affected (0.01 sec)
```

You can also check if John is now in the table with a SELECT statement:

```
> SELECT * FROM Employees;
+-----------+----------+------------+------------+------------+------+
| firstname | lastname | department | hiredate   | supervisor | id   |
+-----------+----------+------------+------------+------------+------+
| John      | Wood     | Sales      | 2012-01-15 | 1001       | 1501 |
+-----------+----------+------------+------------+------------+------+
1 row in set (0.00 sec)
```

So far, so good. Now let's add a few more employees. Remember, you don't have to enter the INSERT statements for these employees from scratch; all the SQL needs to create the Employees table is for you to copy and paste from the createtable.txt file in the book's code:

- Mary Green in Sales, hired 1/15/2012, ID 1601, supervisor ID 1501.

- Daniel Grant in Sales, hired 1/15/2012, ID 1602, supervisor ID 1501.

- Nancy Jackson in Accounting, hired 2/20/2012, ID 1701, supervisor ID 1501.

- Tom Smith in Accounting, hired 3/15/2012, ID 1801, supervisor ID 1701.

- Jessica Smith in Accounting, hired 3/15/2012, ID 1901, supervisor ID 1701.

Inserting these additional employees into the table looks like the following:

```
> INSERT INTO Employees VALUES ("Mary", "Green",
   ➥ "Sales", "20120115", 1501,  1601);
Query OK, 1 row affected (0.00 sec)

> INSERT INTO Employees VALUES ("Daniel", "Grant",
   ➥ "Sales", "20120115", 1501, 1602);
Query OK, 1 row affected (0.00 sec)

> INSERT INTO Employees VALUES ("Nancy", "Jackson",
   ➥ "Accounting", "20120220", 1501, 1701);
Query OK, 1 row affected (0.02 sec)

> INSERT INTO Employees VALUES ("Tom", "Smith",
   ➥ "Accounting", "20120315", 1701, 1801);
Query OK, 1 row affected (0.00 sec)

> INSERT INTO Employees VALUES ("Jessica", "Smith",
   ➥ "Accounting", "20120315", 1701, 1901);
Query OK, 1 row affected (0.00 sec)
```

And now we can check on the table with a SELECT statement:

```
> SELECT * FROM Employees;
+-----------+----------+------------+------------+------------+------+
| firstname | lastname | department | hiredate   | supervisor | id   |
+-----------+----------+------------+------------+------------+------+
| John      | Wood     | Sales      | 2012-01-15 | 1001       | 1501 |
| Mary      | Green    | Sales      | 2012-01-15 | 1501       | 1601 |
| Daniel    | Grant    | Sales      | 2012-01-15 | 1501       | 1602 |
| Nancy     | Jackson  | Accounting | 2012-02-20 | 1501       | 1701 |
| Tom       | Smith    | Accounting | 2012-03-15 | 1701       | 1801 |
| Jessica   | Smith    | Accounting | 2012-03-15 | 1701       | 1901 |
+-----------+----------+------------+------------+------------+------+
6 rows in set (0.00 sec)
```

Excellent. That's our sample table you use throughout the book. Now we're all ready to face the coming chapters.

If you need to add more rows to the table—as you hire more employees, for example—you can use additional INSERT statements.

> **SQL TIP**
>
> What about modifying your data when you have to? Say that an employee quit. How could you remove their record? Or say that someone changed departments—how could you update their record? All that is coming up in Chapter 7, which covers working with rows and individual cells after such tables have been filled with data.

Modifying a Column's Data Type

What if, after you created a table, you decided you wanted to modify a column? Say that, for example, you wanted to modify the hiredate column from the DATE type to the VARCHAR type.

Could you modify the table to do that? Yes, you could, using the ALTER TABLE statement. Just give the new data type of the column and any constraints:

```
ALTER TABLE table_name
MODIFY column_name data_type [constraints]
```

For example, to change the type of the hiredate column to VARCHAR, you could do this:

```
ALTER TABLE Employees
MODIFY hiredate VARCHAR(20) NOT NULL;
```

You can modify a number of columns at once like this:

```
ALTER TABLE table_name
MODIFY (column_1 data_type [constraints],
column_2 data_type [constraints],
...
column_n data_type [constraints]);
```

For example:

```
ALTER TABLE Employees
MODIFY hiredate VARCHAR(20) NOT NULL,
lastname CHAR(50);
```

Renaming a Column

Can you rename a column? You can change names of columns in some DBMSes, but not in most (for example, this functionality was added to Oracle as late as version 9i, release 2).

Renaming a column works like this in SQL:

```
ALTER TABLE table_name
RENAME COLUMN old_name TO new_name
```

Because many DBMSes won't let you rename columns at this time, your only recourse is to delete the column and add a new one with the name you want. This is discussed more in a following section.

Adding Columns to a Table

What if you wanted to add a new column to the Employees table—for example, a title column, which recorded each employee's title? You can add new columns to tables like this:

```
ALTER TABLE table_name
ADD column_name data_type [constraints];
```

For example:

```
ALTER TABLE Employees
ADD title VARCHAR(50);
```

This will add a column named title to the Employees table, as we can verify with a SELECT * FROM Employees statement (note the empty title column at the end):

```
> SELECT * FROM Employees;
+-----------+----------+------------+------------+------------+------+-------+
| firstname | lastname | department | hiredate   | supervisor | id   | title |
+-----------+----------+------------+------------+------------+------+-------+
| John      | Wood     | Sales      | 2012-01-15 | 1001       | 1501 |       |
| Mary      | Green    | Sales      | 2012-01-15 | 1501       | 1601 |       |
| Daniel    | Grant    | Sales      | 2012-01-15 | 1501       | 1602 |       |
| Nancy     | Jackson  | Accounting | 2012-02-20 | 1501       | 1701 |       |
| Tom       | Smith    | Accounting | 2012-03-15 | 1701       | 1801 |       |
| Jessica   | Smith    | Accounting | 2012-03-15 | 1701       | 1901 |       |
+-----------+----------+------------+------------+------------+------+-------+
6 rows in set (0.00 sec)
```

To add multiple columns to an existing table, you can use ALTER TABLE like this:

```
ALTER TABLE table_name
ADD (column_1 data_type [constraints],
column_2 data_type [constraints],
...
column_n data_type [constraints]);
```

SQL TIP

Now that we've added a new column to our Employees table, how would you put some data into that column? Although we'll cover how to modify a table in Chapter 7, it's easy enough with the UPDATE statement. For example, to insert "Boss" into John Wood's record (id = 1501), you would use this statement:

```
UPDATE Employees SET title = "Boss" WHERE id = 1501;
```

Deleting Columns

Perhaps your company has ceased international operations, so you can remove the Country column from your database tables. But how do you delete a column?

You can delete a column in a table with this syntax:

```
ALTER TABLE table_name
DROP COLUMN column_name;
```

For example, let's get rid of the title column in the Employees table. That works like this:

```
ALTER TABLE Employees
DROP COLUMN title;
```

And we can confirm the title column is gone with a SELECT * FROM Employees statement.

```
> SELECT * FROM Employees;
+-----------+----------+------------+------------+------------+------+
| firstname | lastname | department | hiredate   | supervisor | id   |
+-----------+----------+------------+------------+------------+------+
| John      | Wood     | Sales      | 2012-01-15 | 1001       | 1501 |
| Mary      | Green    | Sales      | 2012-01-15 | 1501       | 1601 |
| Daniel    | Grant    | Sales      | 2012-01-15 | 1501       | 1602 |
| Nancy     | Jackson  | Accounting | 2012-02-20 | 1501       | 1701 |
| Tom       | Smith    | Accounting | 2012-03-15 | 1701       | 1801 |
| Jessica   | Smith    | Accounting | 2012-03-15 | 1701       | 1901 |
+-----------+----------+------------+------------+------------+------+
6 rows in set (0.00 sec)
```

Renaming a Table

Perhaps you've got a Groceries table, but now you want to expand into hardware as well as groceries. How would you rename your table to something like Products?

Renaming a table is simple. Just use the ALTER TABLE statement with the RENAME clause:

```
ALTER TABLE table_name
RENAME TO new_table_name;
```

For example, if you wanted to rename your Employees table to the Hires table, it would look like this:

```
ALTER TABLE Employees
RENAME TO Hires;
```

Deleting a Table

Want to delete a table? Just use the DROP TABLE statement like this:

```
DROP TABLE table_name;
```

For example, to delete the Employees table, you would execute this statement (don't do this if you're following along—we'll need the Employees table throughout the book):

```
DROP TABLE Employees;
```

And that's it. Now you know all about creating tables, adding data to them, modifying columns, adding columns, deleting columns, renaming tables, and deleting tables. You're a SQL table meister and ready to go on to Chapter 3.

The Least You Need to Know

- You can use the CREATE TABLE statement to create tables.
- Each column in a table gets its own data type.
- You can use constraints to bound the values in a column.
- You use the INSERT statement to insert data into tables.
- You can modify a column's data type with the ALTER TABLE statement's MODIFY clause.
- You can use the ALTER TABLE statement's ADD clause to add columns to a table.
- You can use the ALTER TABLE statement's DROP clause to delete columns from a table.

Retrieving Your Data

In This Chapter

- Getting into the SELECT statement
- Becoming an expert on the FROM clause
- Retrieving data from a table
- Retrieving a single column from a table
- Retrieving selected columns from a table
- Using SQL expressions when specifying what columns to retrieve

This chapter is about retrieving data from database tables. Here, we're going to review the statement you'll use most frequently in SQL—the SELECT statement.

You need more than just the SELECT statement, however; you need to use at least one clause to go with it, and this chapter focuses on the FROM clause, which returns whole columns of data:

```
SELECT xxx FROM yyy
```

There are more clauses you can use with the SELECT statement, of course, and you see them in depth in coming chapters. For example, the FROM clause lets you retrieve data columns. The WHERE clause lets you retrieve individual records.

So there's no end to the ways you can get data out of tables using SQL, and this chapter starts us off by retrieving columns using the SELECT statement with the FROM clause.

Retrieving Columns from a Table

In this chapter, the guinea pig table we use is the table we created in the previous chapter: the Employees table in the Corporation database, which looks like the following:

```
-----------------------------------------------------------------------
| firstname | lastname | department | hiredate   | supervisor | id   |
-----------------------------------------------------------------------
| John      | Wood     | Sales      | 2012-01-15 | 1001       | 1501 |
| Mary      | Green    | Sales      | 2012-01-15 | 1501       | 1601 |
| Daniel    | Grant    | Sales      | 2012-01-15 | 1501       | 1602 |
| Nancy     | Jackson  | Accounting | 2012-02-20 | 1501       | 1701 |
| Tom       | Smith    | Accounting | 2012-03-15 | 1701       | 1801 |
| Jessica   | Smith    | Accounting | 2012-03-15 | 1701       | 1901 |
-----------------------------------------------------------------------
```

SQL TIP

If you didn't follow along and create the Employees table in the previous chapter, you can get the SQL to copy and paste into your DBMS to create that table from createtable.txt in the code for this book, found at www.completeidiotsguides.com. Or, of course, you can type in the SQL to create this table from Chapter 2.

To extract data from this table, we're going to use the *SELECT statement*, the most common statement people use in all SQL. The SELECT statement retrieves data from tables.

The SELECT statement always comes with at least the *FROM clause*, which tells you which table or tables you want to retrieve your data from.

DEFINITION

You use the **SELECT statement** to get data from tables. It's always used with the FROM clause.

You use the **FROM clause** to specify which table or tables you want to retrieve data from in a SELECT statement.

So the syntax is:

```
SELECT [specifier] FROM table_name;
```

Here, *specifier* indicates what columns you want to retrieve from *table_name*.

SQL TIP

The *table_name* expression can stand for more than one table because it's possible to retrieve data from multiple tables at the same time. To do that, you use the JOIN clause with the SELECT statement, as you'll see later.

We start with the broadest specifier of all—the *asterisk (*)* wildcard, which lets you retrieve all the columns in a table. So this statement will recover all the data from the Employees table:

```
SELECT * FROM Employees;
```

DEFINITION

In SQL, the **asterisk (*)** is a wildcard and matches anything appropriate to where it appears in an SQL statement.

You can see how using the * wildcard works where we start by making the Corporation database the default and then retrieving all data from the Employees table in the following way:

```
> use Corporation;
Database changed
> SELECT * FROM Employees;
+-----------+----------+------------+------------+------------+------+
| firstname | lastname | department | hiredate   | supervisor | id   |
+-----------+----------+------------+------------+------------+------+
| John      | Wood     | Sales      | 2012-01-15 | 1001       | 1501 |
| Mary      | Green    | Sales      | 2012-01-15 | 1501       | 1601 |
| Daniel    | Grant    | Sales      | 2012-01-15 | 1501       | 1602 |
| Nancy     | Jackson  | Accounting | 2012-02-20 | 1501       | 1701 |
| Tom       | Smith    | Accounting | 2012-03-15 | 1701       | 1801 |
| Jessica   | Smith    | Accounting | 2012-03-15 | 1701       | 1901 |
+-----------+----------+------------+------------+------------+------+
6 rows in set (0.03 sec)
```

As you might notice here, the DBMS returns the Employees table sorted on the primary key. If the results from your DBMS appear in a different order, don't worry. A DBMS is not obligated to return data in any particular sort order unless you explicitly specify a sort order.

As you can see, you get the whole table with one SELECT statement and the use of the SQL * wildcard. That's a fair bit of data; looking ahead to filtering our data, don't forget that we can use the WHERE clause to retrieve just the rows we want. For example, to get just the rows for employees whose last name is Smith, you'd do this:

```
> SELECT * FROM Employees WHERE (lastname = 'Smith');
+-----------+----------+------------+------------+------------+------+
| firstname | lastname | department | hiredate   | supervisor | id   |
+-----------+----------+------------+------------+------------+------+
| Tom       | Smith    | Accounting | 2012-03-15 | 1701       | 1801 |
| Jessica   | Smith    | Accounting | 2012-03-15 | 1701       | 1901 |
+-----------+----------+------------+------------+------------+------+
2 rows in set (0.02 sec)
```

SQL TIP

We end SQL statements with a semicolon (;) because many DBMSes require that. However, there's another use for the semicolon. You can use it to separate multiple SQL statements on the same line. So USE Corporation; followed by SELECT * FROM Employees; could all have been entered on the same line as USE Corporation; SELECT * FROM Employees;. Just remember, if you're going to enter multiple SQL statements on the same line, separating them with semicolons is mandatory.

What about retrieving single columns of data?

Retrieving Single Columns

To retrieve a single column of data, you specify that column's name in the SELECT statement this way:

```
SELECT column_name FROM table_name;
```

For example, to retrieve the firstname column from the Employees table, you'd use this syntax:

```
SELECT firstname FROM Employees;
```

Here's what it looks like:

```
> SELECT firstname FROM Employees;
+-----------+
| firstname |
+-----------+
| John      |
| Mary      |
| Daniel    |
| Nancy     |
| Tom       |
| Jessica   |
+-----------+
6 rows in set (0.00 sec)
```

As you can see, just the firstname column was returned. How about getting the lastname column? No problem:

```
> SELECT lastname FROM Employees;
+----------+
| lastname |
+----------+
| Wood     |
| Green    |
| Grant    |
| Jackson  |
| Smith    |
| Smith    |
+----------+
6 rows in set (0.00 sec)
```

That's fine. We've been able to retrieve the firstname and the last-name columns separately. So what if we wanted to retrieve both of those columns at the same time?

Retrieving Multiple Columns

To retrieve multiple columns, you specify those columns' names separated by commas in the SELECT statement this way:

```
SELECT column_1, column_2, ... column_n FROM table_name;
```

For example, to retrieve both the firstname and the lastname columns, you would use this:

```
SELECT firstname, lastname FROM Employees;
```

Here's how it looks:

```
> SELECT firstname, lastname FROM Employees;
+-----------+-----------+
| firstname | lastname  |
+-----------+-----------+
| John      | Wood      |
| Mary      | Green     |
| Daniel    | Grant     |
| Nancy     | Jackson   |
| Tom       | Smith     |
| Jessica   | Smith     |
+-----------+-----------+
6 rows in set (0.00 sec)       .
```

The columns are returned in the same order in which they appear in the table. What if you asked for lastname first? You'd get the last-name column followed by the firstname column, and it would look like this:

```
> SELECT lastname, firstname FROM Employees;
+-----------+-----------+
| lastname  | firstname |
+-----------+-----------+
| Wood      | John      |
| Green     | Mary      |
| Grant     | Daniel    |
| Jackson   | Nancy     |
| Smith     | Tom       |
| Smith     | Jessica   |
+-----------+-----------+
6 rows in set (0.00 sec)
```

As you can see, it's the order you request the columns that determines the order in which they are returned to you, not the order in which they appear in the table.

The columns you retrieve need not be adjacent, of course. Take a look at this, where we retrieve the first, third, and fifth columns:

```
> SELECT firstname, department, supervisor FROM Employees;
+-----------+------------+------------+
| firstname | department | supervisor |
+-----------+------------+------------+
| John      | Sales      | 1001       |
| Mary      | Sales      | 1501       |
| Daniel    | Sales      | 1501       |
| Nancy     | Accounting | 1501       |
```

```
| Tom       | Accounting | 1701      |
| Jessica   | Accounting | 1701      |
+-----------+------------+-----------+
6 rows in set (0.06 sec)
```

Using Expressions

Besides giving just the names of columns to retrieve with the SELECT statement, it's also legal to use *SQL expressions* when telling SQL what columns you want to retrieve. Expressions include:

- **Function calls:** These are calls to built-in functions.

- **System values:** These include the time, the database user, and so on.

- **Special constructs:** These are special cases that we'll become more familiar with in time.

- **Numeric or string operators:** These operators include + and – for numeric values, and so on.

DEFINITION

An **SQL expression** is a term that SQL can evaluate to return a value.

So in addition to column names and the * wildcard, you can also use SQL expressions to retrieve columns of data. We take a quick look at expressions here to see what they can do for us.

Using Function Calls

SQL comes with many built-in functions (such as SQRT() for taking square roots), and we take a look at them in Chapter 8.

You pass a value to a function by enclosing it in parentheses and the function returns a new value back to you. For example, the LOWER() function takes a text string and returns it in lowercase. LOWER(FIRSTNAME) would return the value firstname. The ABS() function returns the absolute value of a number. ABS(-4) returns 4.

It's legal to use function calls in addition to column names in the SELECT statement when you're indicating what columns you want.

That's great if you want to manipulate the data you get back from a table. Say, for example, that you wanted to list the last name of all employees along with the year they were hired. To get the year, you use the YEAR() SQL function to extract it from the hiredate field like this:

```
> SELECT lastname, YEAR(hiredate) FROM Employees;
+----------+----------------+
| lastname | YEAR(hiredate) |
+----------+----------------+
| Wood     | 2012           |
| Green    | 2012           |
| Grant    | 2012           |
| Jackson  | 2012           |
| Smith    | 2012           |
| Smith    | 2012           |
+----------+----------------+
6 rows in set (0.00 sec)
```

So now in addition to the lastname column, we've created a column, YEAR(hiredate), that gives the year each employee was hired.

Here's another example. What if you want all your employees' full names? Many DBMSes support a CONCAT() function that joins or concatenates text strings. So you can execute this statement to get the full names:

```
> SELECT CONCAT(firstname, ' ', lastname) FROM Employees;
+--------------------------------+
| CONCAT(firstname, ' ', lastname) |
+--------------------------------+
| John Wood                      |
| Mary Green                     |
| Daniel Grant                   |
| Nancy Jackson                  |
| Tom Smith                      |
| Jessica Smith                  |
+--------------------------------+
6 rows in set (0.00 sec)
```

Now we've created a column that holds each employee's full name. So as you see, it's not just column names that can return columns in the result of an SQL query—you can also use expressions like function calls.

Here's another example. If your table listed each employee's salary by year, you could use the MAX() function to return a column with employees' largest salary over all years—for example, you might want to find their maximum salary to help determine their pension. There are endless examples of crunching your data using functions, and you see more of them in Chapter 8.

Using System Values

In SQL, system values are items like the name of the user, the current date, and so on. These values are legal to use in place of column names or with function calls in SELECT statements when you're retrieving data.

Here are the built-in SQL system values:

- USER returns a string holding the current SQL user name.

- SESSION_USER returns a string with the current SQL session user.

- SYSTEM_USER returns a string with the current operating system user.

- CURRENT_DATE returns a date value for the current system date.

- CURRENT_TIME returns a time value for the current system time.

- CURRENT_TIMESTAMP returns a timestamp value for the current system timestamp.

For example, what if you wanted to list the current date and all your employees' hire dates? You can do that like this with the system value CURRENT_DATE, creating a new column that displays the current date:

```
> SELECT firstname, lastname, hiredate, CURRENT_DATE FROM Employees;
+-----------+----------+------------+--------------+
| firstname | lastname | hiredate   | CURRENT_DATE |
+-----------+----------+------------+--------------+
| John      | Wood     | 2012-01-15 | 2014-10-19   |
| Mary      | Green    | 2012-01-15 | 2014-10-19   |
| Daniel    | Grant    | 2012-01-15 | 2014-10-19   |
| Nancy     | Jackson  | 2012-02-20 | 2014-10-19   |
```

```
| Tom       | Smith     | 2012-03-15 | 2014-10-19   |
| Jessica   | Smith     | 2012-03-15 | 2014-10-19   |
+-----------+-----------+------------+--------------+
6 rows in set (0.00 sec)
```

Note that the name of the fourth column is the system value's name, CURRENT_DATE.

SQL TIP

System values are useful if you ever need to access the user's name (for example, if you want to indicate who is publishing a certain report) or the current time (for example, if you want to mark a report with the time and date it was created on).

Using Special Constructs

You'll see special constructs in Chapter 15 on advanced SQL, so they really need not trouble us now—but they're also legal to create columns from SELECT statements. Special constructs are advanced expressions like the CAST construct that changes the data type of data you pass it, the COALESCE construct that returns the first data item you pass to it that's not NULL (good if you want to avoid NULL data), and the CASE construct that lets you test values and return different values based on the results of that test.

For example, say you want all employees' first names, last names, and IDs (unless that ID is NULL, in which case you want the employee's supervisor's ID). That would look like the following with the COALESCE special construct.

```
> SELECT firstname, lastname, COALESCE(id, supervisor) FROM Employees;
+-----------+-----------+--------------------------+
| firstname | lastname  | COALESCE(id, supervisor) |
+-----------+-----------+--------------------------+
| John      | Wood      | 1501                     |
| Mary      | Green     | 1601                     |
| Daniel    | Grant     | 1602                     |
| Nancy     | Jackson   | 1701                     |
| Tom       | Smith     | 1801                     |
| Jessica   | Smith     | 1901                     |
+-----------+-----------+--------------------------+
6 rows in set (0.00 sec)
```

More on special constructs is coming up in Chapter 15.

Using Operators

Finally, SQL also has a set of operators that you can use in SELECT statements. You can use those operators to manipulate the data in a column, not in place of column names like the other SQL expressions. The numeric operators (operators that work on numbers, such as the + operator) are:

- + (Addition)
- – (Subtraction)
- * (Multiplication)
- / (Division)

These operators can be used on the SMALLINT, INT, NUMERIC, DECIMAL, FLOAT, DOUBLE PRECISION, and REAL data types (defined in Table 2.1).

For example, say that all your employees' IDs are being renumbered—1000 needs to be added to each. You could retrieve the employees' names and new ID numbers like this from the current table.

```
> SELECT firstname, lastname, id + 1000 FROM Employees;
+-----------+-----------+-----------+
| firstname | lastname  | id + 1000 |
+-----------+-----------+-----------+
| John      | Wood      | 2501      |
| Mary      | Green     | 2601      |
| Daniel    | Grant     | 2602      |
| Nancy     | Jackson   | 2701      |
| Tom       | Smith     | 2801      |
| Jessica   | Smith     | 2901      |
+-----------+-----------+-----------+
6 rows in set (0.00 sec)
```

Note the new column of data in the results: id + 1000.

SQL TIP

You can also add and subtract dates with + and –, but the results vary wildly by DBMS (some return an INTERVAL data type, some a DATETIME data type, some return the difference in days, some in YYYYMMDD format, etc). So the best thing is to stick with the SQL functions for adding and subtracting dates.

You can also use operators to concatenate (that is, join) text strings, but again, that varies by DBMS. Oracle, for example, uses a || operator to concatenate text strings, while DBMSes like SQL Server uses +. Again, it's best to stick to the SQL functions here.

And that concludes our chapter on retrieving columns of data from tables. In the next chapter, we take a look at how SQL can sort that data for you.

The Least You Need to Know

- You use the SELECT statement with the FROM clause to retrieve columns of data.
- You use the * wildcard to retrieve all columns.
- You can specify the name of a single column to retrieve just that column.
- You can specify the names of multiple columns separated by commas to retrieve multiple columns at the same time.
- You can use expressions (function calls, system values, special constructs, and operators) in place of or with column names when retrieving columns.

Crunching Your Data

In this part, we'll find out more about what SQL can do for you.

First, you examine the options for sorting your data. SQL has a lot of power here, and you'll see how to do sorts, subsorts, reverse sorts, and so on.

Then you'll see how to filter your data, extracting just the data you want. For example, you might want to get just the customer records for customers who live in certain states, or just the employee names with IDs in a certain numeric range. This is the kind of thing that SQL is good at—letting you extract just the data you want—and you'll see how that works in detail.

Sorting Your Data

In This Chapter

- Default sorts
- Sorting on single or multiple columns
- Sorting by position
- Specifying order
- Custom sort orders

Just as the previous chapter focused on one clause in the SELECT statement—the FROM clause—this chapter focuses on another clause, the ORDER BY clause.

The ORDER BY clause is what you use to sort your data and it comes at the very end of SELECT statements:

```
SELECT columns FROM table_name ORDER BY specifiers;
```

Here, we're going to see how you can sort your data, and what goes into the *specifiers* part of the previous statement. You see all kinds of sorts here—single-column sorts, multiple-column sorts, ascending sorts, descending sorts, even totally customized sorts.

Sorting

If you just retrieve your data from a table without specifying the sort order, like the following, the DBMS is not under any obligation to return your data in any particular sorted order.

```
> SELECT * FROM Employees;
+-----------+----------+------------+------------+------------+------+
| firstname | lastname | department | hiredate   | supervisor | id   |
+-----------+----------+------------+------------+------------+------+
| John      | Wood     | Sales      | 2012-01-15 | 1001       | 1501 |
| Mary      | Green    | Sales      | 2012-01-15 | 1501       | 1601 |
| Daniel    | Grant    | Sales      | 2012-01-15 | 1501       | 1602 |
| Nancy     | Jackson  | Accounting | 2012-02-20 | 1501       | 1701 |
| Tom       | Smith    | Accounting | 2012-03-15 | 1701       | 1801 |
| Jessica   | Smith    | Accounting | 2012-03-15 | 1701       | 1901 |
+-----------+----------+------------+------------+------------+------+
6 rows in set (0.00 sec)
```

The database might return records sorted by primary key, date of insertions, the first field, or whatever. There's no restriction on the DBMS to sort records unless you ask for a specific sort order.

That means you can't rely on the sort order of data returned by an SQL statement unless you specify the sort order—so let's find out just how to do that.

SQL CAUTION

There is no defined default sort order for data in SQL, so don't rely on records being in any order. You need to explicitly specify a sort order if you want your records to be sorted.

Sorting on Single Columns

Now we introduce the ORDER BY clause by sorting on a single column. For example, say you wanted to sort by the values in the lastname column. You do that like this:

```
SELECT * FROM Employees ORDER BY lastname;
```

Here's what it looks like when you run it:

```
> SELECT * FROM Employees ORDER BY lastname;
+-----------+----------+------------+------------+------------+------+
| firstname | lastname | department | hiredate   | supervisor | id   |
+-----------+----------+------------+------------+------------+------+
| Daniel    | Grant    | Sales      | 2012-01-15 | 1501       | 1602 |
| Mary      | Green    | Sales      | 2012-01-15 | 1501       | 1601 |
| Nancy     | Jackson  | Accounting | 2012-02-20 | 1501       | 1701 |
```

```
| Tom      | Smith    | Accounting | 2012-03-15 | 1701       | 1801 |
| Jessica  | Smith    | Accounting | 2012-03-15 | 1701       | 1901 |
| John     | Wood     | Sales      | 2012-01-15 | 1001       | 1501 |
+----------+----------+------------+------------+------------+------+
6 rows in set (0.00 sec)
```

Note that this time, the records are in order, sorted by the lastname field. Not bad.

SQL TIP

Each column has a data type, and your DBMS is set up to perform sorts on any column's data type. So you can sort text columns alphabetically, numeric columns numerically, and so on. But one question remains: is lowercase a the same as uppercase A in your sorts? Most DBMSes use *dictionary order* to sort, and in dictionary order, a is the same as A, b the same as B, and so on. However, some DBMSes also have other sort orders that the administrator of your DBMS can select, so if you're not getting the sort results you wanted, that may be why.

Here's what sorting by id looks like:

```
> SELECT * FROM Employees ORDER BY id;
+-----------+----------+------------+------------+------------+------+
| firstname | lastname | department | hiredate   | supervisor | id   |
+-----------+----------+------------+------------+------------+------+
| John      | Wood     | Sales      | 2012-01-15 | 1001       | 1501 |
| Mary      | Green    | Sales      | 2012-01-15 | 1501       | 1601 |
| Daniel    | Grant    | Sales      | 2012-01-15 | 1501       | 1602 |
| Nancy     | Jackson  | Accounting | 2012-02-20 | 1501       | 1701 |
| Tom       | Smith    | Accounting | 2012-03-15 | 1701       | 1801 |
| Jessica   | Smith    | Accounting | 2012-03-15 | 1701       | 1901 |
+-----------+----------+------------+------------+------------+------+
6 rows in set (0.00 sec)
```

You can even sort by dates:

```
> SELECT * FROM Employees ORDER BY hiredate;
+-----------+----------+------------+------------+------------+------+
| firstname | lastname | department | hiredate   | supervisor | id   |
+-----------+----------+------------+------------+------------+------+
| Mary      | Green    | Sales      | 2012-01-15 | 1501       | 1601 |
| Daniel    | Grant    | Sales      | 2012-01-15 | 1501       | 1602 |
| John      | Wood     | Sales      | 2012-01-15 | 1001       | 1501 |
| Nancy     | Jackson  | Accounting | 2012-02-20 | 1501       | 1701 |
| Tom       | Smith    | Accounting | 2012-03-15 | 1701       | 1801 |
| Jessica   | Smith    | Accounting | 2012-03-15 | 1701       | 1901 |
+-----------+----------+------------+------------+------------+------+
6 rows in set (0.00 sec)
```

The column you sort on does not need to be returned by the SELECT query. Here, we display the firstname and lastname columns, but sort on the id column:

```
> SELECT firstname, lastname FROM Employees ORDER BY id;
+-----------+----------+
| firstname | lastname |
+-----------+----------+
| John      | Wood     |
| Mary      | Green    |
| Daniel    | Grant    |
| Nancy     | Jackson  |
| Tom       | Smith    |
| Jessica   | Smith    |
+-----------+----------+
6 rows in set (0.00 sec)
```

You can sort on the value returned by SQL expressions (introduced in Chapter 3), not just column names. For example, here, we use the MONTH() function call to sort the records according to the month employees were hired:

```
> SELECT * FROM Employees ORDER BY MONTH(hiredate);
+-----------+----------+------------+------------+------------+------+
| firstname | lastname | department | hiredate   | supervisor | id   |
+-----------+----------+------------+------------+------------+------+
| Mary      | Green    | Sales      | 2012-01-15 | 1501       | 1601 |
| Daniel    | Grant    | Sales      | 2012-01-15 | 1501       | 1602 |
| John      | Wood     | Sales      | 2012-01-15 | 1001       | 1501 |
| Nancy     | Jackson  | Accounting | 2012-02-20 | 1501       | 1701 |
| Tom       | Smith    | Accounting | 2012-03-15 | 1701       | 1801 |
| Jessica   | Smith    | Accounting | 2012-03-15 | 1701       | 1901 |
+-----------+----------+------------+------------+------------+------+
6 rows in set (0.00 sec)
```

You see more sorting on values returned by expressions at the end of this chapter, where we sort on values returned by the CASE statement.

Sorting on Multiple Columns

You may have noticed that when we sorted the employee records on lastname, two of the records were still out of order alphabetically, because they had the same last name, Smith, but different first names, which happened to be returned in reverse order—that is, Tom Smith came before Jessica Smith. Here's what the sort looked like:

```
> SELECT * FROM Employees ORDER BY lastname;
+-----------+----------+------------+------------+------------+------+
| firstname | lastname | department | hiredate   | supervisor | id   |
+-----------+----------+------------+------------+------------+------+
| Daniel    | Grant    | Sales      | 2012-01-15 | 1501       | 1602 |
| Mary      | Green    | Sales      | 2012-01-15 | 1501       | 1601 |
| Nancy     | Jackson  | Accounting | 2012-02-20 | 1501       | 1701 |
| Tom       | Smith    | Accounting | 2012-03-15 | 1701       | 1801 |
| Jessica   | Smith    | Accounting | 2012-03-15 | 1701       | 1901 |
| John      | Wood     | Sales      | 2012-01-15 | 1001       | 1501 |
+-----------+----------+------------+------------+------------+------+
6 rows in set (0.00 sec)
```

To fix this, you can perform a multiple-column sort, sorting on lastname and then firstname. To do a multiple-column sort, you specify the columns to sort on, separated by commas. SQL will sort on the columns in the order you give them. Thus, this SQL statement sorts on lastname first, then on firstname:

```
> SELECT * FROM Employees ORDER BY lastname, firstname;
+-----------+----------+------------+------------+------------+------+
| firstname | lastname | department | hiredate   | supervisor | id   |
+-----------+----------+------------+------------+------------+------+
| Daniel    | Grant    | Sales      | 2012-01-15 | 1501       | 1602 |
| Mary      | Green    | Sales      | 2012-01-15 | 1501       | 1601 |
| Nancy     | Jackson  | Accounting | 2012-02-20 | 1501       | 1701 |
| Jessica   | Smith    | Accounting | 2012-03-15 | 1701       | 1901 |
| Tom       | Smith    | Accounting | 2012-03-15 | 1701       | 1801 |
| John      | Wood     | Sales      | 2012-01-15 | 1001       | 1501 |
+-----------+----------+------------+------------+------------+------+
6 rows in set (0.00 sec)
```

As you can see, Jessica Smith now appears in the table before Tom Smith.

Sorting by Column Position

You can also sort by column position, where the first column returned is column 1; the second, column 2; and so on. So if you were retrieving the firstname and the lastname columns, you could sort by lastname column by sorting on column 2 (because lastname is the second column retrieved).

```
> SELECT firstname, lastname FROM Employees ORDER BY 2;
+-----------+----------+
| firstname | lastname |
+-----------+----------+
| Daniel    | Grant    |
| Mary      | Green    |
| Nancy     | Jackson  |
| Tom       | Smith    |
| Jessica   | Smith    |
| John      | Wood     |
+-----------+----------+
6 rows in set (0.00 sec)
```

If you retrieve all the columns in a table, they're numbered in the order in which they're returned. So you can sort on the lastname column this way:

```
> SELECT * FROM Employees ORDER BY 2;
+-----------+----------+------------+------------+------------+------+
| firstname | lastname | department | hiredate   | supervisor | id   |
+-----------+----------+------------+------------+------------+------+
| Daniel    | Grant    | Sales      | 2012-01-15 | 1501       | 1602 |
| Mary      | Green    | Sales      | 2012-01-15 | 1501       | 1601 |
| Nancy     | Jackson  | Accounting | 2012-02-20 | 1501       | 1701 |
| Tom       | Smith    | Accounting | 2012-03-15 | 1701       | 1801 |
| Jessica   | Smith    | Accounting | 2012-03-15 | 1701       | 1901 |
| John      | Wood     | Sales      | 2012-01-15 | 1001       | 1501 |
+-----------+----------+------------+------------+------------+------+
6 rows in set (0.00 sec)
```

And of course, you can sort on multiple columns also by giving column positions:

```
> SELECT * FROM Employees ORDER BY 2, 3;
+-----------+----------+------------+------------+------------+------+
| firstname | lastname | department | hiredate   | supervisor | id   |
+-----------+----------+------------+------------+------------+------+
| Daniel    | Grant    | Sales      | 2012-01-15 | 1501       | 1602 |
| Mary      | Green    | Sales      | 2012-01-15 | 1501       | 1601 |
| Nancy     | Jackson  | Accounting | 2012-02-20 | 1501       | 1701 |
| Tom       | Smith    | Accounting | 2012-03-15 | 1701       | 1801 |
| Jessica   | Smith    | Accounting | 2012-03-15 | 1701       | 1901 |
| John      | Wood     | Sales      | 2012-01-15 | 1001       | 1501 |
+-----------+----------+------------+------------+------------+------+
6 rows in set (0.00 sec)
```

Sorting by column position is convenient when you don't want to have to type column names over again. But there are two drawbacks: you might use the wrong column position, and you can't sort on a column that isn't returned by your query (that is, you can only sort on columns present in the results of your query).

Specifying Sort Order

The default sort order in SQL is ascending—that is, A, B, C, D, and so on, and 1, 2, 3, 4, and so on. But you might want to display your data in descending order. For example, if you're looking for a job and have a table full of prospective jobs, you might want to sort them so the jobs with the largest salaries are at the top of the list. You can convert any sort from the default ascending sort order to descending sort order with the DESC keyword.

For example, if you just sort by hiredate, you get this:

```
> SELECT * FROM Employees ORDER BY hiredate;
+-----------+----------+------------+------------+------------+------+
| firstname | lastname | department | hiredate   | supervisor | id   |
+-----------+----------+------------+------------+------------+------+
| Mary      | Green    | Sales      | 2012-01-15 | 1501       | 1601 |
| Daniel    | Grant    | Sales      | 2012-01-15 | 1501       | 1602 |
| John      | Wood     | Sales      | 2012-01-15 | 1001       | 1501 |
| Nancy     | Jackson  | Accounting | 2012-02-20 | 1501       | 1701 |
| Tom       | Smith    | Accounting | 2012-03-15 | 1701       | 1801 |
| Jessica   | Smith    | Accounting | 2012-03-15 | 1701       | 1901 |
+-----------+----------+------------+------------+------------+------+
6 rows in set (0.00 sec)
```

But you may want to order your employee records by the most recently hired first (for example, in case you have to fire those with the least seniority); you could use DESC to perform a descending sort like the following.

```
> SELECT * FROM Employees ORDER BY hiredate DESC;
+-----------+----------+------------+------------+------------+------+
| firstname | lastname | department | hiredate   | supervisor | id   |
+-----------+----------+------------+------------+------------+------+
| Tom       | Smith    | Accounting | 2012-03-15 | 1701       | 1801 |
| Jessica   | Smith    | Accounting | 2012-03-15 | 1701       | 1901 |
| Nancy     | Jackson  | Accounting | 2012-02-20 | 1501       | 1701 |
| Mary      | Green    | Sales      | 2012-01-15 | 1501       | 1601 |
| Daniel    | Grant    | Sales      | 2012-01-15 | 1501       | 1602 |
| John      | Wood     | Sales      | 2012-01-15 | 1001       | 1501 |
+-----------+----------+------------+------------+------------+------+
6 rows in set (0.00 sec)
```

Now the records appear in descending order of hire date.

The keyword for an ascending sort is ASC, although since it's the default, you don't have to use it. You can use ASC and DESC freely throughout the ORDER BY clause like this, where you sort on ascending last name and descending first name:

```
> SELECT * FROM Employees ORDER BY lastname ASC, firstname DESC;
+-----------+----------+------------+------------+------------+------+
| firstname | lastname | department | hiredate   | supervisor | id   |
+-----------+----------+------------+------------+------------+------+
| Daniel    | Grant    | Sales      | 2012-01-15 | 1501       | 1602 |
| Mary      | Green    | Sales      | 2012-01-15 | 1501       | 1601 |
| Nancy     | Jackson  | Accounting | 2012-02-20 | 1501       | 1701 |
| Tom       | Smith    | Accounting | 2012-03-15 | 1701       | 1801 |
| Jessica   | Smith    | Accounting | 2012-03-15 | 1701       | 1901 |
| John      | Wood     | Sales      | 2012-01-15 | 1001       | 1501 |
+-----------+----------+------------+------------+------------+------+
6 rows in set (0.00 sec)
```

Advanced Sorts

You can even specify a custom sort order if you use a CASE statement. We saw the CASE statement briefly in Chapter 3. This statement lets you return different values depending on what a test value is equal to.

For example, say you wanted to sort on first name using a custom sorting order. You might want to sort on the basis of how well you know each person, or their height, or something else, not just alphabetic. You can do that by setting up a CASE statement that indicates you are testing values in the firstname column of the current record

and returning values 0 through 5 for the various first names (so the
record that returns 0 will come first, the record that returns 1 comes
next, and so on). It looks like this:

```
> SELECT * FROM Employees ORDER BY CASE firstname
    -> WHEN 'Daniel' THEN 0
    -> WHEN 'Tom' THEN 1
    -> WHEN 'John' THEN 2
    -> WHEN 'Mary' THEN 3
    -> WHEN 'Nancy' THEN 4
    -> WHEN 'Jessica' THEN 5
    -> END;
+-----------+----------+------------+------------+------------+------+
| firstname | lastname | department | hiredate   | supervisor | id   |
+-----------+----------+------------+------------+------------+------+
| Daniel    | Grant    | Sales      | 2012-01-15 | 1501       | 1602 |
| Tom       | Smith    | Accounting | 2012-03-15 | 1701       | 1801 |
| John      | Wood     | Sales      | 2012-01-15 | 1001       | 1501 |
| Mary      | Green    | Sales      | 2012-01-15 | 1501       | 1601 |
| Nancy     | Jackson  | Accounting | 2012-02-20 | 1501       | 1701 |
| Jessica   | Smith    | Accounting | 2012-03-15 | 1701       | 1901 |
+-----------+----------+------------+------------+------------+------+
6 rows in set (0.00 sec)
```

So as you can see, you can create a custom sort on first names in this
order:

- Daniel

- Tom

- John

- Mary

- Nancy

- Jessica

You can also use comparison operators like < (less than) in CASE
statements, so you can perform custom sorts like this, where you sort
on id in a custom way (note that this is a multiple-column sort—first
on id, then on lastname).

```
> SELECT * FROM Employees ORDER BY CASE id
    -> WHEN id < 1600 THEN 1
    -> WHEN id < 1700 THEN 2
    -> WHEN id < 2000 THEN 3
    -> END, lastname;
+-----------+----------+------------+------------+------------+------+
| firstname | lastname | department | hiredate   | supervisor | id   |
+-----------+----------+------------+------------+------------+------+
| John      | Wood     | Sales      | 2012-01-15 | 1001       | 1501 |
| Daniel    | Grant    | Sales      | 2012-01-15 | 1501       | 1602 |
| Mary      | Green    | Sales      | 2012-01-15 | 1501       | 1601 |
| Nancy     | Jackson  | Accounting | 2012-02-20 | 1501       | 1701 |
| Tom       | Smith    | Accounting | 2012-03-15 | 1701       | 1801 |
| Jessica   | Smith    | Accounting | 2012-03-15 | 1701       | 1901 |
+-----------+----------+------------+------------+------------+------+
6 rows in set (0.00 sec)
```

Now you can perform your own custom sorts.

The Least You Need to Know

- You use the SELECT statement with the ORDER BY clause to sort data from tables.

- You use the ORDER BY *column* clause to sort on a single column.

- You use the ORDER BY *column_1, column_2, ... column_n* clause to sort on multiple columns.

- You can sort on column position if you use the position of the returned column(s) you want to sort on. So to sort on the returned column 1, you would use the ORDER BY 1 clause, to sort on the returned column 2, you would use the ORDER BY 2 clause, and so on.

- You can specify descending sorts using the DESC keyword and ascending sorts using the ASC keyword (although you don't have to use ASC since it's the default). So to sort on a particular column in descending order, you would use ORDER BY *column* DESC.

- You can use the CASE statement to create your own custom sorts.

Filtering Your Data

In This Chapter

- The WHERE clause
- Employing comparison operators
- Using BETWEEN to specify a range
- Using IN and NOT IN
- Using LIKE and NOT LIKE to match wildcards
- Using SIMILAR TO to test regular expressions

This chapter is all about retrieving records from database tables in general. In this chapter, you fetch a row or rows according to selection criteria, which is called filtering your data. For example, you might want to select only people who've used their bank account in the last 30 days, or customers who haven't made purchases in the previous three years.

Let's take a look at an example. You might want to retrieve just the records of your employees with the last name Smith, which you can do using the WHERE clause:

```
SELECT * FROM Employees WHERE lastname = 'Smith';
```

Here's what you get when you run this query:

```
> SELECT * FROM Employees WHERE lastname = 'Smith';
+-----------+----------+------------+------------+------------+------+
| firstname | lastname | department | hiredate   | supervisor | id   |
+-----------+----------+------------+------------+------------+------+
| Tom       | Smith    | Accounting | 2012-03-15 | 1701       | 1801 |
| Jessica   | Smith    | Accounting | 2012-03-15 | 1701       | 1901 |
+-----------+----------+------------+------------+------------+------+
2 rows in set (0.00 sec)
```

This chapter (and the next one) are about the WHERE clause, which lets you select specific records in a table. Note that together with Chapter 2 on selecting columns with the FROM clause, you'll be able to retrieve just the fields you want from a table. For example, say you want just the first name, last name, and ID of the Smiths. You could do that like this:

```
> SELECT firstname, lastname, id FROM Employees WHERE lastname = 'Smith'
+-----------+----------+------+
| firstname | lastname | id   |
+-----------+----------+------+
| Tom       | Smith    | 1801 |
| Jessica   | Smith    | 1901 |
+-----------+----------+------+
2 rows in set (0.02 sec)
```

When you use the WHERE clause, you give one or more specifiers to tell SQL exactly what rows you want:

```
SELECT column[s] FROM table WHERE specifiers;
```

Let's look at what specifiers you can use with the WHERE clause to zero in on just the rows you want.

Using Comparison Operators

The first specifiers we'll use in the WHERE clause involve these comparison operators:

- = (Equality)
- <> or != (Not equal to)
- < (Less than)

- <= (Less than or equal to)

- !< (Not less than)

- > (Greater than)

- >= (Greater than or equal to)

- !> (Not greater than)

We saw an example using the equality operator, =, when we asked for all rows where the lastname field is Smith, giving us this result:

```
> SELECT * FROM Employees WHERE lastname = 'Smith';
+-----------+----------+------------+------------+------------+------+
| firstname | lastname | department | hiredate   | supervisor | id   |
+-----------+----------+------------+------------+------------+------+
| Tom       | Smith    | Accounting | 2012-03-15 | 1701       | 1801 |
| Jessica   | Smith    | Accounting | 2012-03-15 | 1701       | 1901 |
+-----------+----------+------------+------------+------------+------+
2 rows in set (0.00 sec)
```

The comparison operators are powerful for letting you specify exactly what rows you want. For example, what if you wanted to find only the employees who had been hired after 1/16/2012? You can use the following SQL statement:

```
> SELECT * FROM Employees WHERE hiredate > "20120116";
+-----------+----------+------------+------------+------------+------+
| firstname | lastname | department | hiredate   | supervisor | id   |
+-----------+----------+------------+------------+------------+------+
| Nancy     | Jackson  | Accounting | 2012-02-20 | 1501       | 1701 |
| Tom       | Smith    | Accounting | 2012-03-15 | 1701       | 1801 |
| Jessica   | Smith    | Accounting | 2012-03-15 | 1701       | 1901 |
+-----------+----------+------------+------------+------------+------+
3 rows in set (0.01 sec)
```

Or you might want to see all your employees who are not in Sales. You can do that with the inequality operator, != (or <>), like in the following:

```
> SELECT * FROM Employees WHERE department != 'Sales';
+-----------+----------+------------+------------+------------+------+
| firstname | lastname | department | hiredate   | supervisor | id   |
+-----------+----------+------------+------------+------------+------+
| Nancy     | Jackson  | Accounting | 2012-02-20 | 1501       | 1701 |
| Tom       | Smith    | Accounting | 2012-03-15 | 1701       | 1801 |
| Jessica   | Smith    | Accounting | 2012-03-15 | 1701       | 1901 |
+-----------+----------+------------+------------+------------+------+
3 rows in set (0.00 sec)
```

Using BETWEEN

You can use the BETWEEN clause to specify a range of data. For
example, say you want to select only employees with IDs between
1601 and 1801. You can do this with the BETWEEN and AND
keywords:

```
> SELECT * FROM Employees WHERE id BETWEEN 1601 AND 1801;
+-----------+----------+------------+------------+------------+------+
| firstname | lastname | department | hiredate   | supervisor | id   |
+-----------+----------+------------+------------+------------+------+
| Mary      | Green    | Sales      | 2012-01-15 | 1501       | 1601 |
| Daniel    | Grant    | Sales      | 2012-01-15 | 1501       | 1602 |
| Nancy     | Jackson  | Accounting | 2012-02-20 | 1501       | 1701 |
| Tom       | Smith    | Accounting | 2012-03-15 | 1701       | 1801 |
+-----------+----------+------------+------------+------------+------+
4 rows in set (0.00 sec)
```

Here's another example where you can find all records with hire
dates between 3/1/2012 and 3/15/2012:

```
> SELECT * FROM Employees WHERE hiredate BETWEEN "20120301" AND "20120315";
+-----------+----------+------------+------------+------------+------+
| firstname | lastname | department | hiredate   | supervisor | id   |
+-----------+----------+------------+------------+------------+------+
| Tom       | Smith    | Accounting | 2012-03-15 | 1701       | 1801 |
| Jessica   | Smith    | Accounting | 2012-03-15 | 1701       | 1901 |
+-----------+----------+------------+------------+------------+------+
2 rows in set (0.00 sec)
```

You can use BETWEEN with character, number, bit, date, and time
data. For example, if you wanted to retrieve all employee records in
which the lastname field is between helicopter and starling alphabetically, that would look like the following:

```
> SELECT * FROM Employees WHERE lastname BETWEEN 'helicopter' AND
  ➡ 'starling';
+------------+-----------+------------+------------+------------+------+
| firstname | lastname | department | hiredate   | supervisor | id   |
+------------+-----------+------------+------------+------------+------+
| Nancy     | Jackson  | Accounting | 2012-02-20 | 1501       | 1701 |
| Tom       | Smith    | Accounting | 2012-03-15 | 1701       | 1801 |
| Jessica   | Smith    | Accounting | 2012-03-15 | 1701       | 1901 |
+------------+-----------+------------+------------+------------+------+
3 rows in set (0.00 sec)
```

SQL TIP

Does the range include the endpoints (the values at either end of the range) when you use BETWEEN and AND? The answer is yes.

Checking for NULL

As you know, uninitialized cells in a table contain a NULL value, meaning "nothing" or "I don't know." Because NULL stands for an unknown value, you can't check for NULL with the comparison operators. For example, this SQL statement would not work:

```
SELECT *
FROM Employees
WHERE id = NULL;
```

SQL doesn't do comparisons involving NULL, not even equality. So you can't check if a cell in a table contains NULL by asking if = NULL is true.

Instead, you use the IS NULL test. Those are special keywords you can use in the WHERE clause. Thus, the previous SQL should be written as:

```
SELECT *
FROM Employees
WHERE id IS NULL;
```

You can also test for IS NOT NULL. For example, we'll retrieve all rows from our table where the ID value IS NOT NULL:

```
> SELECT * FROM Employees WHERE id IS NOT NULL;
+------------+-----------+------------+------------+------------+------+
| firstname | lastname | department | hiredate   | supervisor | id   |
+------------+-----------+------------+------------+------------+------+
| John      | Wood     | Sales      | 2012-01-15 | 1001       | 1501 |
```

```
| Mary      | Green    | Sales      | 2012-01-15 | 1501     | 1601 |
| Daniel    | Grant    | Sales      | 2012-01-15 | 1501     | 1602 |
| Nancy     | Jackson  | Accounting | 2012-02-20 | 1501     | 1701 |
| Tom       | Smith    | Accounting | 2012-03-15 | 1701     | 1801 |
| Jessica   | Smith    | Accounting | 2012-03-15 | 1701     | 1901 |
+-----------+----------+------------+------------+----------+------+
6 rows in set (0.00 sec)
```

SQL CAUTION

The fact that you can't use the comparison operator with NULL values has one more consequence—you will run into trouble if you compare any column that has a NULL value to any other value, or any two columns (for example, WHERE id = supervisor) if there is a NULL in either or both columns. If so, the result of the comparison will be indeterminate—that is, it will be unknown, because one or more of the fields are NULL. So although the NULL value has its place in SQL, note that using it can lead to some sticky issues when comparing values in columns.

Using IN and NOT IN

You can specify a set of allowed data values to match with the WHERE clause if you use the IN or NOT IN keywords. You use the IN keyword to see if data items are in a set of values you give, and NOT IN to see if they're not.

For example, if you wanted only records where the employee's last name is Green, Grant, or Smith, it would look like this:

```
> SELECT * FROM Employees WHERE lastname IN ('Green', 'Grant', 'Smith');
+-----------+----------+------------+------------+------------+------+
| firstname | lastname | department | hiredate   | supervisor | id   |
+-----------+----------+------------+------------+------------+------+
| Mary      | Green    | Sales      | 2012-01-15 | 1501       | 1601 |
| Daniel    | Grant    | Sales      | 2012-01-15 | 1501       | 1602 |
| Tom       | Smith    | Accounting | 2012-03-15 | 1701       | 1801 |
| Jessica   | Smith   '| Accounting | 2012-03-15 | 1701       | 1901 |
+-----------+----------+------------+------------+------------+------+
4 rows in set (0.00 sec)
```

That's the way it works: you create a set by giving a comma-separated list of values enclosed in parentheses. A set can also be made up of numbers, as here, where we're looking only for specific ID numbers 1501, 1601, 1701, and 1901:

```
> SELECT * FROM Employees WHERE id IN (1501, 1601, 1701, 1901);
+-----------+----------+------------+------------+------------+------+
| firstname | lastname | department | hiredate   | supervisor | id   |
+-----------+----------+------------+------------+------------+------+
| John      | Wood     | Sales      | 2012-01-15 | 1001       | 1501 |
| Mary      | Green    | Sales      | 2012-01-15 | 1501       | 1601 |
| Nancy     | Jackson  | Accounting | 2012-02-20 | 1501       | 1701 |
| Jessica   | Smith    | Accounting | 2012-03-15 | 1701       | 1901 |
+-----------+----------+------------+------------+------------+------+
4 rows in set (0.00 sec)
```

You can use IN with character, number, bit, date, and time data.

You can also use NOT IN to exclude the members of a set. For example, what if we were looking for records whose ID values were *not* in the set 1501, 1601, 1701, and 1901? We could perform that search like this:

```
> SELECT * FROM Employees WHERE id NOT IN (1501, 1601, 1701, 1901)
+-----------+----------+------------+------------+------------+------+
| firstname | lastname | department | hiredate   | supervisor | id   |
+-----------+----------+------------+------------+------------+------+
| Daniel    | Grant    | Sales      | 2012-01-15 | 1501       | 1602 |
| Tom       | Smith    | Accounting | 2012-03-15 | 1701       | 1801 |
+-----------+----------+------------+------------+------------+------+
2 rows in set (0.00 sec)
```

Here's how you can get all employees whose last name is not Grant or Wood:

```
> SELECT * FROM Employees WHERE lastname NOT IN ('Wood', 'Grant');
+-----------+----------+------------+------------+------------+------+
| firstname | lastname | department | hiredate   | supervisor | id   |
+-----------+----------+------------+------------+------------+------+
| Mary      | Green    | Sales      | 2012-01-15 | 1501       | 1601 |
| Nancy     | Jackson  | Accounting | 2012-02-20 | 1501       | 1701 |
| Tom       | Smith    | Accounting | 2012-03-15 | 1701       | 1801 |
| Jessica   | Smith    | Accounting | 2012-03-15 | 1701       | 1901 |
+-----------+----------+------------+------------+------------+------+
4 rows in set (0.14 sec)
```

Using LIKE and NOT LIKE

Can you use wildcards with the WHERE clause? Yes, if you use the LIKE or NOT LIKE keywords and the following wildcards:

- Underscore (_) stands for any one character (you might be used to the ? wildcard that does this in other contexts).

- Percent (%) stands for any one or more characters (you might be used to the * wildcard that does this in other contexts).

For example, what if you wanted to find all employees whose first names had four characters? You could search for matches to '____' this way:

```
> SELECT * FROM Employees WHERE firstname LIKE '____';
+-----------+----------+------------+------------+------------+------+
| firstname | lastname | department | hiredate   | supervisor | id   |
+-----------+----------+------------+------------+------------+------+
| John      | Wood     | Sales      | 2012-01-15 | 1001       | 1501 |
| Mary      | Green    | Sales      | 2012-01-15 | 1501       | 1601 |
+-----------+----------+------------+------------+------------+------+
2 rows in set (0.00 sec)
```

Or perhaps you might want to find all employees whose last names begin with G. You could match 'G%' like this:

```
> SELECT * FROM Employees WHERE lastname LIKE 'G%';
+-----------+----------+------------+------------+------------+------+
| firstname | lastname | department | hiredate   | supervisor | id   |
+-----------+----------+------------+------------+------------+------+
| Mary      | Green    | Sales      | 2012-01-15 | 1501       | 1601 |
| Daniel    | Grant    | Sales      | 2012-01-15 | 1501       | 1602 |
+-----------+----------+------------+------------+------------+------+
2 rows in set (0.00 sec)
```

Or maybe you want to find all employees whose first name has a as the second character. You would search for '_a%' this way:

```
> SELECT * FROM Employees WHERE firstname LIKE '_a%';
+-----------+----------+------------+------------+------------+------+
| firstname | lastname | department | hiredate   | supervisor | id   |
+-----------+----------+------------+------------+------------+------+
| Mary      | Green    | Sales      | 2012-01-15 | 1501       | 1601 |
| Daniel    | Grant    | Sales      | 2012-01-15 | 1501       | 1602 |
| Nancy     | Jackson  | Accounting | 2012-02-20 | 1501       | 1701 |
+-----------+----------+------------+------------+------------+------+
3 rows in set (0.02 sec)
```

As you can see, there's a lot of power here; using wildcards in your searches can give you a lot of flexibility.

SQL TIP

What if you actually wanted to search for terms that included the _ or % characters? It turns out that you can search for the actual characters _ and % with a LIKE clause if you escape those characters. Escaping those characters means putting any character of your choice right in front of _ or % and then telling SQL the character you chose is an escape character like this:

```
SELECT savings
FROM Financials
WHERE savings LIKE '10#%'
ESCAPE '#';
```

This SQL will find matches to '10%'. You can also use a backslash to escape % or _ in SQL:

```
SELECT savings
FROM Financials
WHERE savings LIKE '10\%';
```

Using SIMILAR TO

The SIMILAR TO clause is even more powerful than the LIKE clause, because you can use *regular expressions* with the SIMILAR TO clause.

DEFINITION

In case you're not familiar with them, **regular expressions** form a whole language of characters and symbols that you can use to match to strings. For example, the regular expression [0-9]+ matches one or more digits. With regular expressions, you can find matches to text strings in a sophisticated way. For more on regular expressions, see http://en.wikipedia.org/wiki/Regular_expression.

For example, if you wanted to find only employees whose first names included no y or z characters, you could match the regular expression '^[a-x]+$' (^ specifies the beginning of a string, [a-x]+ one or more characters from a – x, and $ the end of the string) like the following.

```
> SELECT * FROM Employees WHERE firstname SIMILAR TO '^[a-x]+$';
+-----------+----------+------------+------------+------------+------+
| firstname | lastname | department | hiredate   | supervisor | id   |
+-----------+----------+------------+------------+------------+------+
| John      | Wood     | Sales      | 2012-01-15 | 1001       | 1501 |
| Daniel    | Grant    | Sales      | 2012-01-15 | 1501       | 1602 |
| Tom       | Smith    | Accounting | 2012-03-15 | 1701       | 1801 |
| Jessica   | Smith    | Accounting | 2012-03-15 | 1701       | 1901 |
+-----------+----------+------------+------------+------------+------+
4 rows in set (0.02 sec)
```

Note that many DBMSes use REGEXP in place of SIMILAR TO, such as in the following:

```
> SELECT * FROM Employees WHERE firstname REGEXP '^[a-x]+$';
+-----------+----------+------------+------------+------------+------+
| firstname | lastname | department | hiredate   | supervisor | id   |
+-----------+----------+------------+------------+------------+------+
| John      | Wood     | Sales      | 2012-01-15 | 1001       | 1501 |
| Daniel    | Grant    | Sales      | 2012-01-15 | 1501       | 1602 |
| Tom       | Smith    | Accounting | 2012-03-15 | 1701       | 1801 |
| Jessica   | Smith    | Accounting | 2012-03-15 | 1701       | 1901 |
+-----------+----------+------------+------------+------------+------+
4 rows in set (0.02 sec)
```

In fact, there are rumors that SIMILAR TO will be replaced with REGEXP_LIKE at some point in SQL.

As you can see, there's a lot of power in the WHERE clause of SELECT statements. And there's even more power coming up in the next chapter—we're not done with the WHERE clause yet.

The Least You Need to Know

- The WHERE clause lets you select rows.
- Comparison operators in the WHERE clause let you compare values.
- Using BETWEEN lets you specify a range that a value in a field can be in.
- Using IN and NOT IN lets you select items in, or not in, a set.
- Using IS NULL or IS NOT NULL lets you check if values are NULL (the comparison operators won't work for NULL).
- Using LIKE and NOT LIKE lets you use the wildcards _ (to match a single character) and % (to match multiple characters).

Getting More Filtering Power

In This Chapter

- Using ALL, SOME, and ANY
- Checking with EXISTS for returned results
- Handling NULL with DISTINCT
- Checking whether time intervals overlap with OVERLAPS
- Checking individual records with MATCH

In the previous chapter, we saw a number of keywords you can use the WHERE clause to filter out exactly the data you want. In this chapter, we'll filter with keywords that are meant to be used with subqueries.

For example, take a look at this SQL, where SELECT supervisor FROM Employees is the subquery:

```
> SELECT * FROM Employees WHERE id IN (SELECT supervisor
    ➥ FROM Employees);
```

Here, the subquery returns a list of supervisor IDs, and the WHERE clause checks whether the current employee's ID is in the list with the IN keyword. A subquery feeds its results to the larger, enclosing query to be further checked.

The first case we look at is handling subqueries with the ALL keyword.

Checking Every Result with ALL

The ALL keyword makes SQL check all results returned from a subquery.

Say that you want to find all employees whose IDs are greater than any supervisor ID. In this case, use the subquery SELECT supervisor FROM Employees to create a list of supervisor IDs:

```
SELECT supervisor FROM Employees
```

Now that you have a list of supervisor IDs, you can check whether the current employee ID is greater using the ALL keywords:

```
SELECT * FROM Employees WHERE id > ALL (SELECT supervisor FROM
➥  Employees);
```

In this case, you want to check whether an employee ID is greater than all supervisor IDs, so use the ALL keyword to indicate to SQL that you want to compare the value to all results returned from the subquery.

Here's what the ALL example looks like when it runs:

```
> SELECT * FROM Employees WHERE id > ALL (SELECT supervisor FROM
➥  Employees);
+-----------+----------+------------+------------+------------+------+
| firstname | lastname | department | hiredate   | supervisor | id   |
+-----------+----------+------------+------------+------------+------+
| Tom       | Smith    | Accounting | 2012-03-15 | 1701       | 1801 |
| Jessica   | Smith    | Accounting | 2012-03-15 | 1701       | 1901 |
+-----------+----------+------------+------------+------------+------+
2 rows in set (0.00 sec)
```

Checking Any Result with ANY

As discussed, the ALL keyword enables you to compare a value to all results returned from a subquery. In a similar way, the ANY keyword enables you to compare a value to any result from a subquery.

For example, say that you want to find all the supervisors in the Employees table. You can use the subquery to find all the supervisor IDs in the table:

```
SELECT supervisor FROM Employees
```

Now let's use the ANY keyword with the WHERE clause. Because ANY means any result, you can find whether or not the current employee has an ID that matches any supervisor ID in the table:

```
SELECT * FROM Employees WHERE id = ANY (SELECT supervisor FROM
⮕  Employees);
```

The subquery returns all supervisor IDs, and the WHERE clause checks whether the current employee ID matches any of the supervisor IDs.

Although ALL compared a value to *all* results from a subquery, ANY checks whether *any* of the results from a subquery satisfy the condition you specified.

Here's what the ANY example looks like in a DBMS, where all supervisors are in the table:

```
> SELECT * FROM Employees WHERE id = ANY (SELECT supervisor FROM
⮕  Employees);
+-----------+----------+------------+------------+------------+------+
| firstname | lastname | department | hiredate   | supervisor | id   |
+-----------+----------+------------+------------+------------+------+
| John      | Wood     | Sales      | 2012-01-15 | 1001       | 1501 |
| Nancy     | Jackson  | Accounting | 2012-02-20 | 1501       | 1701 |
+-----------+----------+------------+------------+------------+------+
2 rows in set (0.00 sec)
```

SQL TIP

You might notice that using ALL is like saying *comparison_1* AND *comparison_2* AND … *comparison_n* must be true, while using ANY is like saying *comparison_1* OR *comparison_2* OR … *comparison_n* must be true. In fact, there are ALL and OR keywords in SQL that operate in just this way, and we see them at the end of the chapter.

Using SOME in Place of ANY

Note that the ANY keyword is ambiguous. For example, look at the following two uses of ANY.

First, ANY can mean any one of a set. For example:

Can any of you tell me what 5 + 7 is?

This question asks whether there is at least one person in a group that can tell the questioner what the answer is, which is the way we've been using ANY.

On the other hand, look at this usage:

> I'm better than any of you.

Here, ANY is used as a synonym for *all*. Notice what happens when you replace ANY with ALL in the sentence:

> I'm better than all of you.

The creators of SQL must have been dismayed when someone pointed out the double use of ANY to them—that is, ANY could be understood as ANY or as ALL. So they jumped into action and created a new keyword: SOME.

The SOME keyword means the same thing as the ANY keyword. SOME is not a perfect alternate for ANY (a better fit might be SOME_OR_ONE_OF), but there are only so many words in English, after all. Here's how to find employees who are also supervisors using ANY:

```
> SELECT * FROM Employees WHERE id = ANY (SELECT supervisor FROM
➥ Employees);
+-----------+----------+------------+------------+------------+------+
| firstname | lastname | department | hiredate   | supervisor | id   |
+-----------+----------+------------+------------+------------+------+
| John      | Wood     | Sales      | 2012-01-15 | 1001       | 1501 |
| Nancy     | Jackson  | Accounting | 2012-02-20 | 1501       | 1701 |
+-----------+----------+------------+------------+------------+------+
2 rows in set (0.00 sec)
```

You can change the preceding, which found all employees who are also supervisors, to the same thing using the SOME keyword:

```
> SELECT * FROM Employees WHERE id = SOME (SELECT supervisor FROM
➥ Employees);
+-----------+----------+------------+------------+------------+------+
| firstname | lastname | department | hiredate   | supervisor | id   |
+-----------+----------+------------+------------+------------+------+
| John      | Wood     | Sales      | 2012-01-15 | 1001       | 1501 |
| Nancy     | Jackson  | Accounting | 2012-02-20 | 1501       | 1701 |
+-----------+----------+------------+------------+------------+------+
2 rows in set (0.00 sec)
```

SQL TIP

Personally, I use the ANY keyword, because the meaning is clear to me—if any comparison is true, the WHERE clause is satisfied. The SOME keyword always makes me stop and think what it means. But the choice between ANY or SOME is up to you.

Checking Whether Anything Was Returned with EXISTS

The EXISTS keyword checks whether a subquery returns any results. If a subquery returns no results, the EXISTS keyword returns false, but if the subquery returns at least one result, the EXISTS keyword returns true.

For example, say you have tables named Employees in multiple databases, but you only want data from the table where John Wood is recorded. You can check whether his last name exists in the table, and if so, return the rest of the table:

```
> SELECT * FROM Employees WHERE
EXISTS (SELECT lastname FROM Employees
WHERE lastname = "Wood");
+-----------+----------+------------+------------+------------+------+
| firstname | lastname | department | hiredate   | supervisor | id   |
+-----------+----------+------------+------------+------------+------+
| John      | Wood     | Sales      | 2012-01-15 | 1001       | 1501 |
| Mary      | Green    | Sales      | 2012-01-15 | 1501       | 1601 |
| Daniel    | Grant    | Sales      | 2012-01-15 | 1501       | 1602 |
| Nancy     | Jackson  | Accounting | 2012-02-20 | 1501       | 1701 |
| Tom       | Smith    | Accounting | 2012-03-15 | 1701       | 1801 |
| Jessica   | Smith    | Accounting | 2012-03-15 | 1701       | 1901 |
+-----------+----------+------------+------------+------------+------+
6 rows in set (0.01 sec)
```

We just checked for an employee whose last name is Wood. A better check is to make sure his first name is John as well, so let's look ahead to the AND keyword discussed later in this chapter.

```
> SELECT * FROM Employees WHERE
EXISTS (SELECT lastname FROM Employees
WHERE firstname = "John" AND lastname = "Wood");
+-----------+----------+------------+------------+------------+------+
| firstname | lastname | department | hiredate   | supervisor | id   |
+-----------+----------+------------+------------+------------+------+
| John      | Wood     | Sales      | 2012-01-15 | 1001       | 1501 |
| Mary      | Green    | Sales      | 2012-01-15 | 1501       | 1601 |
| Daniel    | Grant    | Sales      | 2012-01-15 | 1501       | 1602 |
| Nancy     | Jackson  | Accounting | 2012-02-20 | 1501       | 1701 |
| Tom       | Smith    | Accounting | 2012-03-15 | 1701       | 1801 |
| Jessica   | Smith    | Accounting | 2012-03-15 | 1701       | 1901 |
+-----------+----------+------------+------------+------------+------+
6 rows in set (0.01 sec)
```

If you run the same query on a table named Employees that doesn't
have an employee named John Wood, you will not get any results
(just the empty set).

If you have a Customers table and record all the purchases a customer made, you can use the EXISTS keyword to find all customers
with existing purchases.

Checking for One-of-a-Kindness with UNIQUE

There are three places you can use the UNIQUE keyword in SQL:
as a field constraint when creating or altering a table (see Chapter
2), in the WHERE clause, and in the SELECT statement itself.
Because the last two uses involve filtering your data, we focus on
them in this chapter.

Using UNIQUE in the WHERE clause

Use UNIQUE in the WHERE clause to return a value of true
if a subquery returns rows that are all unique. For example, the
following returns a value of true if the subquery SELECT lastname FROM Employees returns all unique rows (in fact, we know
it doesn't, because there are two employees with the last name of
Smith).

```
WHERE UNIQUE (SELECT lastname FROM Employees);
```

Using UNIQUE in the SELECT Statement

You can also use the UNIQUE keyword in the SELECT statement directly, where you ask for the unique last names from the Employees table (note that only one of the two Smiths in the table is returned):

```
> SELECT UNIQUE lastname FROM Employees;
+----------+
| lastname |
+----------+
| Wood     |
| Green    |
| Grant    |
| Jackson  |
| Smith    |
+----------+
5 rows in set (0.08 sec)
```

Notice that the purpose of UNIQUE makes sure a SELECT statement returns only rows with unique column values.

Checking for One-of-a-Kindness with DISTINCT

Besides UNIQUE, you can also use DISTINCT in the SELECT statement and the WHERE clause. This gives you another filtering option.

Using DISTINCT in the WHERE Clause

You can also check whether a subquery returns all unique rows with DISTINCT:

```
WHERE DISTINCT (SELECT lastname FROM Employees);
```

If the subquery returns all unique rows, the WHERE DISTINCT clause returns true.

That sounds a lot like WHERE UNIQUE, doesn't it? What's the difference? The difference is in the way WHERE UNIQUE and WHERE DISTINCT treat NULL rows. If the subquery returns two NULL rows, should the WHERE UNIQUE or WHERE DISTINCT clause return true (the rows are unique) or false (the rows are not unique)?

WHERE UNIQUE treats two NULL rows as still unique, while WHERE DISTINCT treats two NULL rows as not unique. It appears that most DBMS creators have opted for WHERE DISTINCT's version, where two NULL rows in the result from a subquery means you're out. As a result, you'll find more WHERE DISTINCT implementations in DBMSes than WHERE UNIQUE implementations.

Using DISTINCT in the SELECT Statement

You can also use DISTINCT in the SELECT statement, where you ask for all last names that are distinct from the Employees table (note that like SELECT UNIQUE, there is only one Smith row):

```
> SELECT DISTINCT lastname FROM Employees;
+----------+
| lastname |
+----------+
| Wood     |
| Green    |
| Grant    |
| Jackson  |
| Smith    |
+----------+
5 rows in set (0.08 sec)
```

The difference between SELECT UNIQUE and SELECT DISTINCT is that SELECT UNIQUE is considered "old" SQL, and your DBMS is more likely to support SELECT DISTINCT.

Checking Time Intervals with OVERLAPS

You can also use the OVERLAPS keyword to check whether two time intervals overlap. You can specify a time interval in two ways: as a start and end time, or as a start time and an interval length. For example, the following returns true, because the two time intervals overlap:

```
(TIME '04:15' , INTERVAL '1' HOUR)
OVERLAPS
(TIME '04:45' , INTERVAL '2' HOUR)
```

On the other hand, the following returns false, because the two time intervals do not overlap:

```
(TIME '04:15' , TIME '6:15')
OVERLAPS
(TIME '08:45' , TIME '9:15')
```

SQL TIP

Support for OVERLAPS is spotty. Some DBMSes use it to determine whether two geometric regions overlap. Other DBMSes don't support it at all.

Checking for Specific Records with MATCH

MATCH lets you match individual records. For example, the MATCH clause returns true if the subquery returns a row with John and Wood as the first and last name.

```
SELECT * FROM Employees
WHERE ('John', 'Wood') MATCH
(SELECT firstname, lastname FROM Employees);
```

MATCH isn't often used, because you can do the same thing with the equality operator (=) and the AND keyword (coming up next):

```
SELECT * FROM Employees
WHERE (firstname = 'John' AND lastname = 'Wood');
```

Where is MATCH useful? You can use it to determine whether a crucial record has been changed.

Insisting All Clauses Be True with AND

The AND keyword is popular to use in the WHERE clause, because it lets you join conditions together by insisting that every clause you join be true.

For example, look at the SQL we just used to find the record of John Wood:

```
SELECT * FROM Employees
WHERE (firstname = 'John' AND lastname = 'Wood');
```

Note the AND, which means that for a record to return true from the WHERE clause, its firstname field must hold John *and* its lastname field must hold Wood.

In other words, both the clause firstname = 'John' *and* the clause lastname = 'Wood' must be true for the whole WHERE clause to be true. The AND keyword insists all clauses you join together with it be true for the overall result to be true.

Here's what the query looks like when it runs:

```
> SELECT * FROM Employees
WHERE (firstname = 'John' AND lastname = 'Wood');
+-----------+----------+------------+------------+------------+------+
| firstname | lastname | department | hiredate   | supervisor | id   |
+-----------+----------+------------+------------+------------+------+
| John      | Wood     | Sales      | 2012-01-15 | 1001       | 1501 |
+-----------+----------+------------+------------+------------+------+
1 row in set (0.05 sec)
```

What if you wanted to find all the employees in Accounting who were hired after 3/1/2012? This query should do the trick:

```
> SELECT * FROM Employees WHERE (department = 'Accounting'
AND hiredate > '20120301');
+-----------+----------+------------+------------+------------+------+
| firstname | lastname | department | hiredate   | supervisor | id   |
+-----------+----------+------------+------------+------------+------+
| Tom       | Smith    | Accounting | 2012-03-15 | 1701       | 1801 |
| Jessica   | Smith    | Accounting | 2012-03-15 | 1701       | 1901 |
+-----------+----------+------------+------------+------------+------+
2 rows in set (0.00 sec)
```

You can use as many AND clauses as you like. For example, if you want to find all the employees in Accounting who were hired after 3/1/2012 and whose IDs are greater than 1900, here's how you'd do it:

```
> SELECT * FROM Employees WHERE (department = 'Accounting'
AND hiredate > '20120301' AND id > 1900);
+-----------+----------+------------+------------+------------+------+
| firstname | lastname | department | hiredate   | supervisor | id   |
+-----------+----------+------------+------------+------------+------+
| Jessica   | Smith    | Accounting | 2012-03-15 | 1701       | 1901 |
+-----------+----------+------------+------------+------------+------+
1 row in set (0.00 sec)
```

Choosing Any Clause with OR

The OR keyword lets you link clauses just like the AND keyword, but here, *any* clause can be true for the overall result to be true; likewise, if no clause is true, the overall result is false.

For example, let's say you want all records where the employee's last name is Green or Grant. Here's the query to do it:

```
> SELECT * FROM Employees WHERE (lastname = 'Green' OR
lastname = 'Grant');
+-----------+----------+------------+------------+------------+------+
| firstname | lastname | department | hiredate   | supervisor | id   |
+-----------+----------+------------+------------+------------+------+
| Mary      | Green    | Sales      | 2012-01-15 | 1501       | 1601 |
| Daniel    | Grant    | Sales      | 2012-01-15 | 1501       | 1602 |
+-----------+----------+------------+------------+------------+------+
2 rows in set (0.00 sec)
```

And you can use as many ORs as you want. For example, to find all employees with the last name Smith as well as Grant and Green, use the following query:

```
> SELECT * FROM Employees WHERE (lastname = 'Green' OR
lastname = 'Grant' OR lastname = 'Smith');
+-----------+----------+------------+------------+------------+------+
| firstname | lastname | department | hiredate   | supervisor | id   |
+-----------+----------+------------+------------+------------+------+
| Mary      | Green    | Sales      | 2012-01-15 | 1501       | 1601 |
| Daniel    | Grant    | Sales      | 2012-01-15 | 1501       | 1602 |
| Tom       | Smith    | Accounting | 2012-03-15 | 1701       | 1801 |
| Jessica   | Smith    | Accounting | 2012-03-15 | 1701       | 1901 |
+-----------+----------+------------+------------+------------+------+
4 rows in set (0.00 sec)
```

You can use AND and OR together as well, and when you do, it's often best to use parentheses to keep things organized. For example, say you wanted to get all employees named Green or Smith in Accounting. You could do that like this:

```
> SELECT * FROM Employees WHERE ((lastname = 'Green'
OR lastname = 'Smith') AND department = 'Accounting');
+-----------+----------+------------+------------+------------+------+
| firstname | lastname | department | hiredate   | supervisor | id   |
+-----------+----------+------------+------------+------------+------+
| Tom       | Smith    | Accounting | 2012-03-15 | 1701       | 1801 |
| Jessica   | Smith    | Accounting | 2012-03-15 | 1701       | 1901 |
+-----------+----------+------------+------------+------------+------+
2 rows in set (0.00 sec)
```

Note that using parentheses around lastname = 'Green' OR lastname = 'Smith' helps make it clear what you mean.

SQL TIP

The default evaluation order for AND and OR is that AND is evaluated first (unless you use parentheses). So SELECT * FROM Employees WHERE ((lastname = 'Green' OR lastname = 'Smith') AND department = 'Accounting'); is evaluated as SELECT * FROM Employees WHERE (lastname = 'Green' OR (lastname = 'Smith' AND department = 'Accounting')); unless you use parentheses to specify the order you want the clauses evaluated. Remember to use parentheses when using AND and OR— don't rely on the default order.

Negating Conditions with NOT

Suppose you want to find all employees whose last names are not Smith. You can try this:

```
> SELECT * FROM Employees WHERE lastname = 'Smith';
+-----------+----------+------------+------------+------------+------+
| firstname | lastname | department | hiredate   | supervisor | id   |
+-----------+----------+------------+------------+------------+------+
| Tom       | Smith    | Accounting | 2012-03-15 | 1701       | 1801 |
| Jessica   | Smith    | Accounting | 2012-03-15 | 1701       | 1901 |
+-----------+----------+------------+------------+------------+------+
2 rows in set (0.00 sec)
```

But that gives you all employees whose last names *are* Smith. No problem. Just use the NOT operator like this to negate the lastname = 'Smith' condition:

```
> SELECT * FROM Employees WHERE NOT lastname = 'Smith';
+-----------+----------+------------+------------+------------+------+
| firstname | lastname | department | hiredate   | supervisor | id   |
+-----------+----------+------------+------------+------------+------+
| John      | Wood     | Sales      | 2012-01-15 | 1001       | 1501 |
| Mary      | Green    | Sales      | 2012-01-15 | 1501       | 1601 |
| Daniel    | Grant    | Sales      | 2012-01-15 | 1501       | 1602 |
| Nancy     | Jackson  | Accounting | 2012-02-20 | 1501       | 1701 |
+-----------+----------+------------+------------+------------+------+
4 rows in set (0.00 sec)
```

Notice that you can negate conditions with the NOT clause, turning true to false and false to true.

SQL TIP

For some reason, early versions of MySQL didn't implement the NOT keyword except for NOT EXISTS. Now all versions of MySQL after version 5.0 use NOT correctly.

The Least You Need to Know

- Using ALL lets you check a value against all results returned from a subquery.
- Using SOME or ANY let you conform that at least one returned result meets your criteria.
- Checking with EXISTS lets you determine whether a subquery returned any row results.
- Using DISTINCT lets you make sure a subquery returns results with completely unique rows.
- OVERLAPS lets you compare time intervals.
- MATCH lets you check whether a record matches the particular field values you specify.

Updating Your Data

In This Chapter

- Updating single columns, multiple columns, and all rows
- Inserting from a query
- Copying from a table
- Deleting data
- Adding a new column and deleting a column
- Creating an index

This chapter is about updating the data in your tables and even updating the tables themselves. We see how to change individual data items, as well as how to change the data in multiple columns all at once.

We learn how to copy data directly from another table, and how to insert the results of a query into a table.

Then we move on to updating table structure itself by adding new columns to include more data. We even see how to delete existing columns, although not all DBMSes let you do that (especially when the column holds data).

Updating Your Data

Let's start by updating individual cells in a table with new data. This is the most basic, and the most frequently used, update of all.

Updating a Single Table Cell with New Data

Say that you look at your Employees table, and you decide that there are entirely too many people in Accounting. You need more people in Sales.

```
> SELECT * FROM Employees;
+-----------+----------+------------+------------+------------+------+
| firstname | lastname | department | hiredate   | supervisor | id   |
+-----------+----------+------------+------------+------------+------+
| John      | Wood     | Sales      | 2012-01-15 | 1001       | 1501 |
| Mary      | Green    | Sales      | 2012-01-15 | 1501       | 1601 |
| Daniel    | Grant    | Sales      | 2012-01-15 | 1501       | 1602 |
| Nancy     | Jackson  | Accounting | 2012-02-20 | 1501       | 1701 |
| Tom       | Smith    | Accounting | 2012-03-15 | 1701       | 1801 |
| Jessica   | Smith    | Accounting | 2012-03-15 | 1701       | 1901 |
+-----------+----------+------------+------------+------------+------+
6 rows in set (0.00 sec)
```

How would you update Tom Smith's department value from Accounting to Sales? Use the *UPDATE* statement:

```
UPDATE table_name SET
column_1 = expression_1
[, column_2 = expression_2]
...
[, column_n = expression_n]
WHERE [specifiers];
```

DEFINITION

You use the **UPDATE** statement to change your data after it's already been stored in a table. In other words, you use this statement to update your data.

You want to update Tom Smith's department value from Accounting to Sales, so say this:

```
UPDATE Employees SET department = 'Sales'...
```

That's not enough, of course, because you need to tell SQL exactly which record you want to update, and you do that with a WHERE clause.

SQL CAUTION

Some DBMSes require that you have administrative privileges to use UPDATE, so if you see an error message mentioning privileges, you need to get a higher level of access to your database than you have now to use UPDATE. This issue is often frustrating, but be prepared for it.

The WHERE clause operates like any other WHERE clause of the type you saw in Chapters 5 and 6. To update just Tom Smith's record, id = 1801, do this:

```
UPDATE Employees SET department = 'Sales' WHERE id = 1801;
```

Make sure you don't omit the WHERE clause by mistake when using UPDATE. An UPDATE statement without a WHERE clause can update all the rows in a table, meaning a lot of data will get overwritten by mistake.

After specifying and executing a particular record to update, you can check to make sure your change is there:

```
> SELECT * FROM Employees;
+-----------+----------+------------+------------+------------+------+
| firstname | lastname | department | hiredate   | supervisor | id   |
+-----------+----------+------------+------------+------------+------+
| John      | Wood     | Sales      | 2012-01-15 | 1001       | 1501 |
| Mary      | Green    | Sales      | 2012-01-15 | 1501       | 1601 |
| Daniel    | Grant    | Sales      | 2012-01-15 | 1501       | 1602 |
| Nancy     | Jackson  | Accounting | 2012-02-20 | 1501       | 1701 |
| Tom       | Smith    | Sales      | 2012-03-15 | 1701       | 1801 |
| Jessica   | Smith    | Accounting | 2012-03-15 | 1701       | 1901 |
+-----------+----------+------------+------------+------------+------+
6 rows in set (0.00 sec)
```

So Tom Smith has indeed been transferred to Sales.

Updating Multiple Cells

Say that when you inform Tom Smith that he's been transferred to Sales, he objects and quits. You hire a new employee named Karen Jones. So now you need to update the firstname and lastname columns in what was Tom Smith's record.

Here's how to do it:

```
UPDATE Employees SET firstname = 'Karen', lastname = 'Jones'
    ➥ WHERE id = 1801;
```

And here's the result:

```
> SELECT * FROM Employees;
+-----------+----------+------------+------------+------------+------+
| firstname | lastname | department | hiredate   | supervisor | id   |
+-----------+----------+------------+------------+------------+------+
| John      | Wood     | Sales      | 2012-01-15 | 1001       | 1501 |
| Mary      | Green    | Sales      | 2012-01-15 | 1501       | 1601 |
| Daniel    | Grant    | Sales      | 2012-01-15 | 1501       | 1602 |
| Nancy     | Jackson  | Accounting | 2012-02-20 | 1501       | 1701 |
| Karen     | Jones    | Sales      | 2012-03-15 | 1701       | 1801 |
| Jessica   | Smith    | Accounting | 2012-03-15 | 1701       | 1901 |
+-----------+----------+------------+------------+------------+------+
6 rows in set (0.00 sec)
```

Note that Tom Smith has been replaced by Karen Jones.

You can replace as many rows as you like. Say that Tom Smith will return if he gets his position in Accounting. That's good, because Karen has decided to quit. So how do you replace the firstname, last-name, and department columns all at once for id = 1801? Use this statement:

```
UPDATE Employees SET firstname = 'Tom', lastname = 'Smith',
    ➥ department = 'Sales' WHERE id = 1801;
```

And the result is that Tom Smith is back:

```
> SELECT * FROM Employees;
+-----------+----------+------------+------------+------------+------+
| firstname | lastname | department | hiredate   | supervisor | id   |
+-----------+----------+------------+------------+------------+------+
| John      | Wood     | Sales      | 2012-01-15 | 1001       | 1501 |
| Mary      | Green    | Sales      | 2012-01-15 | 1501       | 1601 |
| Daniel    | Grant    | Sales      | 2012-01-15 | 1501       | 1602 |
| Nancy     | Jackson  | Accounting | 2012-02-20 | 1501       | 1701 |
| Tom       | Smith    | Accounting | 2012-03-15 | 1701       | 1801 |
| Jessica   | Smith    | Accounting | 2012-03-15 | 1701       | 1901 |
+-----------+----------+------------+------------+------------+------+
6 rows in set (0.00 sec)
```

Updating All Rows with the Same Data

If needed, you can update all the data in an entire column to a single value. That's pretty rare, but you can do it.

For example, say that you want to move everyone to the Sales department. Here's how you can set all department values to Sales. Note that you just omit the WHERE clause:

```
UPDATE Employees SET department = 'Sales';
```

And the result is that everyone is in Sales:

```
> SELECT * FROM Employees;
+-----------+----------+------------+------------+------------+------+
| firstname | lastname | department | hiredate   | supervisor | id   |
+-----------+----------+------------+------------+------------+------+
| John      | Wood     | Sales      | 2012-01-15 | 1001       | 1501 |
| Mary      | Green    | Sales      | 2012-01-15 | 1501       | 1601 |
| Daniel    | Grant    | Sales      | 2012-01-15 | 1501       | 1602 |
| Nancy     | Jackson  | Sales      | 2012-02-20 | 1501       | 1701 |
| Tom       | Smith    | Sales      | 2012-03-15 | 1701       | 1801 |
| Jessica   | Smith    | Sales      | 2012-03-15 | 1701       | 1901 |
+-----------+----------+------------+------------+------------+------+
6 rows in set (0.00 sec)
```

Inserting Data from a Query

You can also update data in a table using data fetched from a query. For example, say that you want to change Jessica Smith's supervisor from Nancy Jackson to Mary Green, as you see in the current table:

```
> SELECT * FROM Employees;
+-----------+----------+------------+------------+------------+------+
| firstname | lastname | department | hiredate   | supervisor | id   |
+-----------+----------+------------+------------+------------+------+
| John      | Wood     | Sales      | 2012-01-15 | 1001       | 1501 |
| Mary      | Green    | Sales      | 2012-01-15 | 1501       | 1601 |
| Daniel    | Grant    | Sales      | 2012-01-15 | 1501       | 1602 |
| Nancy     | Jackson  | Accounting | 2012-02-20 | 1501       | 1701 |
| Tom       | Smith    | Accounting | 2012-03-15 | 1701       | 1801 |
| Jessica   | Smith    | Accounting | 2012-03-15 | 1701       | 1901 |
+-----------+----------+------------+------------+------------+------+
6 rows in set (0.00 sec)
```

You can find Mary Green's ID with a query, and pop the results of the query into Jessica Smith's supervisor field:

```
UPDATE Employees SET
supervisor = (SELECT id FROM Employees WHERE lastname = 'Green')
WHERE id = 1901;
```

And the results are that Jessica Smith's new supervisor is Mary Green:

```
> SELECT * FROM Employees;
+-----------+----------+------------+------------+------------+------+
| firstname | lastname | department | hiredate   | supervisor | id   |
+-----------+----------+------------+------------+------------+------+
| John      | Wood     | Sales      | 2012-01-15 | 1001       | 1501 |
| Mary      | Green    | Sales      | 2012-01-15 | 1501       | 1601 |
| Daniel    | Grant    | Sales      | 2012-01-15 | 1501       | 1602 |
| Nancy     | Jackson  | Accounting | 2012-02-20 | 1501       | 1701 |
| Tom       | Smith    | Accounting | 2012-03-15 | 1701       | 1801 |
| Jessica   | Smith    | Accounting | 2012-03-15 | 1601       | 1901 |
+-----------+----------+------------+------------+------------+------+
6 rows in set (0.00 sec)
```

Inserting Rows from a Query

Do you want to update a table by inserting whole rows returned by a query? No problem, just use the INSERT SELECT statement. This statement lets you specify which columns to fill in a new record in a table, while using the SELECT statement to fetch rows from the same or another table.

For example, to make a duplicate of Daniel Grant's record, you can use INSERT SELECT:

```
INSERT INTO Employees
(firstname, lastname, department, hiredate, supervisor, id)
SELECT * from Employees WHERE lastname = 'Grant';
```

This statement first specifies what columns to be filled, and then the SELECT statement gets the rows to fill the columns.

In this case, you create a duplicate of Daniel Grant's record:

```
> SELECT * FROM Employees;
+-----------+----------+------------+------------+------------+------+
| firstname | lastname | department | hiredate   | supervisor | id   |
+-----------+----------+------------+------------+------------+------+
| John      | Wood     | Sales      | 2012-01-15 | 1001       | 1501 |
| Mary      | Green    | Sales      | 2012-01-15 | 1501       | 1601 |
| Daniel    | Grant    | Sales      | 2012-01-15 | 1501       | 1602 |
| Nancy     | Jackson  | Accounting | 2012-02-20 | 1501       | 1701 |
| Tom       | Smith    | Sales      | 2012-03-15 | 1701       | 1801 |
| Jessica   | Smith    | Accounting | 2012-03-15 | 1701       | 1901 |
| Daniel    | Grant    | Sales      | 2012-01-15 | 1501       | 1602 |
+-----------+----------+------------+------------+------------+------+
7 rows in set (0.00 sec)
```

Usually, you can't insert more than one row with the INSERT statement. The exception to this is INSERT SELECT, which inserts as many rows as the SELECT statement retrieves.

SQL TIP

It turns out that the column names of the columns returned by the SELECT statement are ignored by SQL in an INSERT SELECT statement. So the names of the returned columns do not need to match the column names of the columns the data is going into.

Note that we copied a row from the Employees table because we don't have another sample table at this point, but you can also copy data from another table using INSERT SELECT. For example, the following shows how to retrieve data from a table called Staff:

```
INSERT INTO Employees
(firstname, lastname, department, hiredate, supervisor, id)
SELECT * from Staff WHERE lastname = 'Grant';
```

Inserting Partial Data into a Row

You can also insert just partial data for a new row using INSERT. For example, say you want to create a new row using Jessica Smith's record in the Employees table, but you want only her first name, last name, and ID.

Start with the INSERT statement, indicating which fields you want to fill in the new row:

```
> INSERT into Employees (firstname, lastname, id)
...
```

Then use a SELECT statement to retrieve these fields from the existing record:

```
> INSERT into Employees (firstname, lastname, id)
SELECT firstname, lastname, id
...
```

And finally, indicate the table you want to get the data from, and use a WHERE clause to indicate Jessica Smith's record:

```
> INSERT INTO Employees (firstname, lastname, id)
SELECT firstname, lastname, id
FROM Employees WHERE id = 1901;
```

Now you've added a new record with only Jessica Smith's name and ID. Here's what the result looks like:

```
> SELECT * FROM Employees;
+-----------+----------+------------+------------+------------+------+
| firstname | lastname | department | hiredate   | supervisor | id   |
+-----------+----------+------------+------------+------------+------+
| John      | Wood     | Sales      | 2012-01-15 | 1001       | 1501 |
| Mary      | Green    | Sales      | 2012-01-15 | 1501       | 1601 |
| Daniel    | Grant    | Sales      | 2012-01-15 | 1501       | 1602 |
| Nancy     | Jackson  | Accounting | 2012-02-20 | 1501       | 1701 |
| Tom       | Smith    | Accounting | 2012-03-15 | 1701       | 1801 |
| Jessica   | Smith    | Accounting | 2012-03-15 | 1701       | 1901 |
| Jessica   | Smith    |            |            |            | 1901 |
+-----------+----------+------------+------------+------------+------+
7 rows in set (0.00 sec)
```

As you can see, there's a new record with Jessica Smith's first name, last name, and ID.

SQL TIP

Inserting partial data into a new row is not commonly done, because it leaves NULL fields. But it is useful in two circumstances: when you cobble together a single record from multiple records, or when you have boilerplate data that goes into everybody's record (for example, Company, Division, Country, and so on).

Copying Whole Tables

The INSERT SELECT statement inserts a row or rows into a table. The SELECT INTO statement, on the other hand, creates a new table by copying an old one.

For example, say you want to create a copy of the Employees table named Staff. To make a full copy of the Employees table, start with SELECT *:

```
SELECT *
...
```

Then specify the table name you want to create, which is INTO Staff for us:

```
SELECT *
INTO Staff
...
```

And then specify the source table, which is FROM Employees for us:

```
SELECT *
INTO Staff
FROM Employees;
```

That creates the new Staff table:

```
> SELECT * FROM Staff;
+-----------+----------+------------+------------+------------+------+
| firstname | lastname | department | hiredate   | supervisor | id   |
+-----------+----------+------------+------------+------------+------+
| John      | Wood     | Sales      | 2012-01-15 | 1001       | 1501 |
| Mary      | Green    | Sales      | 2012-01-15 | 1501       | 1601 |
| Daniel    | Grant    | Sales      | 2012-01-15 | 1501       | 1602 |
| Nancy     | Jackson  | Accounting | 2012-02-20 | 1501       | 1701 |
| Tom       | Smith    | Accounting | 2012-03-15 | 1701       | 1801 |
| Jessica   | Smith    | Accounting | 2012-03-15 | 1701       | 1901 |
+-----------+----------+------------+------------+------------+------+
6 rows in set (0.00 sec)
```

MySQL and Oracle use different syntax to do the same thing:

```
CREATE TABBLE Staff AS
SELECT *
FROM Employees;
```

Using SELECT INTO is a great way to make a "test" copy of a table before experimenting with it. It's more useful than you might think when you come up with some complex SQL that might otherwise mess up a table you want kept intact.

> **SQL CAUTION**
>
> Some DBMSes enable you to overwrite existing tables with SELECT INTO. The only way to find out if yours has overwriting capability is to try it or to check your documentation.

Copying Partial Tables

You can also use SELECT INTO to make a partial copy of a table. For example, say that you want to extract just a few columns from a table and make a new table with these columns.

Here's what the Employees table looks like:

```
> SELECT * FROM Employees;
+-----------+----------+------------+------------+------------+------+
| firstname | lastname | department | hiredate   | supervisor | id   |
+-----------+----------+------------+------------+------------+------+
| John      | Wood     | Sales      | 2012-01-15 | 1001       | 1501 |
| Mary      | Green    | Sales      | 2012-01-15 | 1501       | 1601 |
| Daniel    | Grant    | Sales      | 2012-01-15 | 1501       | 1602 |
| Nancy     | Jackson  | Accounting | 2012-02-20 | 1501       | 1701 |
| Tom       | Smith    | Accounting | 2012-03-15 | 1701       | 1801 |
| Jessica   | Smith    | Accounting | 2012-03-15 | 1701       | 1901 |
+-----------+----------+------------+------------+------------+------+
6 rows in set (0.00 sec)
```

To extract the firstname, lastname, and id columns from the Employees table and make a completely new table, use SELECT INTO.

To copy just the firstname, lastname, and id columns into a new table named Staff, specify the columns you want to copy:

```
SELECT firstname, lastname, id
...
```

Then specify the table name to create:

```
SELECT firstname, lastname, id
INTO Staff
...
```

And finally, give the source table:

```
SELECT firstname, lastname, id
INTO Staff
FROM Employees;
```

And the results are as expected:

```
> SELECT * from Staff;
+-----------+----------+------+
| firstname | lastname | id   |
+-----------+----------+------+
| John      | Wood     | 1501 |
| Mary      | Green    | 1601 |
| Daniel    | Grant    | 1602 |
| Nancy     | Jackson  | 1701 |
| Tom       | Smith    | 1801 |
| Jessica   | Smith    | 1901 |
+-----------+----------+------+
6 rows in set (0.00 sec)
```

In MySQL and Oracle, use:

```
CREATE TABLE Staff AS
SELECT firstname, lastname, id
FROM Employees;
```

SQL TIP

Making partial copies is a great way to make subtables from a table. As shown here, you were able to create a subtable of the Employees table, containing just the firstname, lastname, and id columns. So if you have a master table with many columns, keep this technique in mind.

Deleting Rows

Part of updating a table includes deleting rows. For example, following along with the previous partial INSERT SELECT example leaves your table with a partial record.

```
> SELECT * FROM Employees;
+-----------+----------+-------------+------------+------------+------+
| firstname | lastname | department  | hiredate   | supervisor | id   |
+-----------+----------+-------------+------------+------------+------+
| John      | Wood     | Sales       | 2012-01-15 | 1001       | 1501 |
| Mary      | Green    | Sales       | 2012-01-15 | 1501       | 1601 |
| Daniel    | Grant    | Sales       | 2012-01-15 | 1501       | 1602 |
| Nancy     | Jackson  | Accounting  | 2012-02-20 | 1501       | 1701 |
| Tom       | Smith    | Accounting  | 2012-03-15 | 1701       | 1801 |
| Jessica   | Smith    | Accounting  | 2012-03-15 | 1701       | 1901 |
| Jessica   | Smith    |             |            |            | 1901 |
+-----------+----------+-------------+------------+------------+------+
7 rows in set (0.00 sec)
```

How can you delete the record? Because the record you want to delete has three NULL fields, you should tag it that way.

To delete a row, use the DELETE statement with a WHERE clause. To select the row you want to delete, use the following SQL statement:

```
DELETE FROM Employees WHERE supervisor IS NULL;
```

As you can see, the record you want to delete is gone:

```
> SELECT * FROM Employees;
+-----------+----------+-------------+------------+------------+------+
| firstname | lastname | department  | hiredate   | supervisor | id   |
+-----------+----------+-------------+------------+------------+------+
| John      | Wood     | Sales       | 2012-01-15 | 1001       | 1501 |
| Mary      | Green    | Sales       | 2012-01-15 | 1501       | 1601 |
| Daniel    | Grant    | Sales       | 2012-01-15 | 1501       | 1602 |
| Nancy     | Jackson  | Accounting  | 2012-02-20 | 1501       | 1701 |
| Tom       | Smith    | Accounting  | 2012-03-15 | 1701       | 1801 |
| Jessica   | Smith    | Accounting  | 2012-03-15 | 1701       | 1901 |
+-----------+----------+-------------+------------+------------+------+
6 rows in set (0.00 sec)
```

You can also delete multiple rows with the same DELETE statement if the WHERE clause matches multiple rows.

SQL CAUTION

When deleting a single row or specific rows, don't omit the WHERE clause by mistake. Doing so deletes all the rows in your table (see the next topic), which can be a big problem.

To use DELETE, you might need special privileges in your DBMS. If you get a security error, you'll need more security privileges.

Deleting All Rows

You can also delete all rows from a table with the DELETE statement by omitting the WHERE clause. To delete all rows from the Employees table (don't do this unless you want to rebuild the table from scratch), use:

```
DELETE FROM Employees;
```

And all rows are gone.

Note that DELETE only deletes the contents of a table; it doesn't delete the table itself. For that, you need DROP—see the next section.

SQL TIP

Using UPDATE or DELETE can cause serious errors in a table if you aren't careful. To make sure your WHERE clause retrieves just the data you want, try it as a SELECT statement first.

Deleting a Table

Do you want to delete a table? DELETE is already used to delete rows (only), so the creators of SQL needed a new word, and they chose DROP (one gets the impression they wish English had more synonyms).

To delete a table, use the DROP statement:

```
DROP Employees;
```

Don't do this to the same table unless you want to re-create it from scratch.

DROP is useful if you created practice tables to test some SQL, and then don't want the tables cluttering up your database.

SQL TIP

To prevent accidental deletion of important tables, set up a relation between your table and another table. Most DBMSes will not let you delete a table that has a relation with some other table until that relation is removed. There's no other way to mark a table as nondeletable.

Adding a New Column

Add new columns to a table with the ALTER TABLE statement where *column_definition* is the normal column definition you use when creating a table, and includes the column data type followed by any optional specifiers, such as NOT NULL, PRIMARY KEY, DEFAULT [value], and so on:

```
ALTER TABLE table_name
ADD column_1 column_definition [, column_2 column_definition][, ...
    ➡ column_n column_definition];
```

For example, to add a new column to hold telephone extensions to the Employees table, do this:

```
ALTER TABLE Employees
ADD extension INT;
```

This adds a new column named extension:

```
> SELECT * FROM Employees;
+-----------+----------+------------+------------+------------+------+---------+
| firstname | lastname | department | hiredate   | supervisor | id   |extension|
+-----------+----------+------------+------------+------------+------+---------+
| John      | Wood     | Sales      | 2012-01-15 | 1001       | 1501 |         |
| Mary      | Green    | Sales      | 2012-01-15 | 1501       | 1601 |         |
| Daniel    | Grant    | Sales      | 2012-01-15 | 1501       | 1602 |         |
| Nancy     | Jackson  | Accounting | 2012-02-20 | 1501       | 1701 |         |
| Tom       | Smith    | Accounting | 2012-03-15 | 1701       | 1801 |         |
| Jessica   | Smith    | Accounting | 2012-03-15 | 1701       | 1901 |         |
+-----------+----------+------------+------------+------------+------+---------+
6 rows in set (0.00 sec)
```

All DBMSes let you add new columns like this.

Deleting a Column

To delete a column, use ALTER TABLE again:

```
ALTER TABLE table_name
DROP column_1 column_type [, column_2 column_type] [, ...column_n column_type];;
```

To drop the extension column, do this:

```
ALTER TABLE Employees
DROP extension;
```

And here are the results—note the extension column is gone:

```
> SELECT * FROM Employees;
+-----------+----------+------------+------------+------------+------+
| firstname | lastname | department | hiredate   | supervisor | id   |
+-----------+----------+------------+------------+------------+------+
| John      | Wood     | Sales      | 2012-01-15 | 1001       | 1501 |
| Mary      | Green    | Sales      | 2012-01-15 | 1501       | 1601 |
| Daniel    | Grant    | Sales      | 2012-01-15 | 1501       | 1602 |
| Nancy     | Jackson  | Accounting | 2012-02-20 | 1501       | 1701 |
| Tom       | Smith    | Accounting | 2012-03-15 | 1701       | 1801 |
| Jessica   | Smith    | Accounting | 2012-03-15 | 1701       | 1901 |
+-----------+----------+------------+------------+------------+------+
6 rows in set (0.00 sec)
```

SQL CAUTION

Believe it or not, some DBMSes will not let you delete columns from existing tables. Others won't let you delete a column until you delete all data in the column. Design your tables carefully from the beginning so you don't end up deleting columns unintentionally.

Adding a Column with System Date

You can add a column that displays the system date by default. Doing so displays the current date any time you print a table, marking that table with the date.

To add a column with the system date, add a column with DEFAULT CURRENT_DATE in DB2 and PostgreSQL. The following are ways to find the current date in various DBMSes:

- Access Now:()

- DB2: CURRENT_DATE

- MySQL: CURRENT_DATE()

- Oracle: SYSDATE

- PostgreSQL: CURRENT_DATE

Modifying Columns

You can modify the data type and specifiers (such as NOT NULL, DEFAULT [value], and so on) of a column with the ALTER TABLE statement:

```
ALTER TABLE table_name
MODIFY column_name column_definition;
```

For example, to modify the id column from INT to BIGINT data type in the Employees table, do this:

```
ALTER TABLE Employees
MODIFY id BIGINT;
```

Renaming a Table

To rename a table, use ALTER TABLE again:

```
ALTER TABLE old_table_name
RENAME TO new_table_name;
```

For example, here's how you might rename the Employees table to the Staff table:

```
ALTER TABLE Employees
RENAME TO Staff;
```

And you can verify that it worked easily enough:

```
> SELECT * FROM Staff;
+-----------+----------+------------+------------+------------+------+
| firstname | lastname | department | hiredate   | supervisor | id   |
+-----------+----------+------------+------------+------------+------+
| John      | Wood     | Sales      | 2012-01-15 | 1001       | 1501 |
| Mary      | Green    | Sales      | 2012-01-15 | 1501       | 1601 |
| Daniel    | Grant    | Sales      | 2012-01-15 | 1501       | 1602 |
| Nancy     | Jackson  | Accounting | 2012-02-20 | 1501       | 1701 |
| Tom       | Smith    | Accounting | 2012-03-15 | 1701       | 1801 |
| Jessica   | Smith    | Accounting | 2012-03-15 | 1701       | 1901 |
+-----------+----------+------------+------------+------------+------+
6 rows in set (0.00 sec)
```

Adding an Index

To improve filtering and sorting performance, add an *index* to a table.

> **DEFINITION**
>
> An **index** is a presorted version of the data in a column or columns used to speed filtering and sorting on that column or column's data.

Tables are usually kept sorted on their primary keys, so if you filter or sort on the primary key, you're set. But if you want to filter or sort on another column, things can go slowly if that column is long.

That's where indexes come in: they hold a presorted version of the column's data, much like the index of a book. When you want to access a data item, SQL will know just where to look. Indexes speed up filter and sorting operations on a particular column. In fact, you can create multiple column indexes, but they're only useful if you sort or filter the table on the exact columns that appear in the multiple-column index.

An index is associated with a table after you create the index, but it does not appear with the rest of the columns you can fetch with a SELECT statement—it's internal to your DBMS.

> **SQL CAUTION**
>
> Indexes speed filtering and sorting on a column or columns, but they also can drastically slow data insertion or modification in the column, because the data you insert or modify has to be sorted with respect to the entire rest of the column to update the index. So indexes are useful mostly on columns whose data doesn't change. Also, if you only have 100 or fewer items in your column, don't bother creating an index. You won't gain additional speed over the DBMS's normal filtering and sorting operations.

How you create an index varies by DBMS. Here's the usual syntax:

```
CREATE INDEX index_name
ON table_name (column_1 [, column_2] ... [, column_n]);
```

For example, here's how to create an index named lastname_index for the lastname field of the Employees table:

```
CREATE INDEX lastname_index
ON Employees (lastname);
```

This associates an index named lastname_index with the Employees table. You don't see the index, but the DBMS maintains it.

In DBMSes such as MYSQL, you have to specify a data length if you're creating an index on text or BLOB data to indicate how many characters or bits deep you want to sort on like this:

```
CREATE INDEX lastname_index
ON Staff (lastname (20));
```

The Least You Need to Know

- Update data in a single column or multiple columns with the UPDATE statement.
- Use the INSERT SELECT statement to insert data from SQL query.
- Copy over an entire table with the SELECT INTO statement.
- Delete data with the DELETE statement.
- Add new columns with the ALTER TABLE statement and the ADD keyword.
- Delete columns with the ALTER TABLE statement and the DROP keyword.
- Indexes speed filtering and sorting on a column or columns, and you can create an index with the CREATE INDEX statement.

SQL's Built-In Functions

In This Chapter

- SQL mathematical functions
- SQL string functions
- SQL system functions
- Miscellaneous functions

Nearly all computer languages support some built-in functions, and SQL is no exception. The following are SQL functions:

- System functions
- Numeric functions
- String functions

Each function returns a value—sometimes numeric, sometimes a string, sometimes a date, and so on. For example, the string function TRIM() takes a text string and trims off leading and trailing spaces.

This chapter is about the so-called scalar functions in SQL, such as TRIM(). SQL also contains a number of aggregate functions, used for grouping data, and we'll see these in Chapter 10. Scalar functions are great for manipulating data values.

Getting to Know the Built-In Functions

There's a problem with scalar functions, and that problem is that there are actually very few built-in functions in SQL. The rest are added by your DBMS, and that means that the same functionality is known by different names in different DBMSes.

SQL CAUTION

Different names for the same thing is a persistent problem in SQL databases. The situation is much like the early browser wars over JavaScript. Every DBMS manufacturer seems to think it knows the best name for each function. And all that makes SQL difficult to move from DBMS to another DBMS.

For example, look at the names of the DBMS-specific functions used to extract text from a string:

- DB2 uses MID().

- Oracle and PostgreSQL use SQBSTR().

- MySQL, SQL Server, and Sybase use SUBSTRING().

So we begin this chapter by looking at the official built-in functions in SQL (there aren't many), and then looking at the functions added by various other DBMSes, such as SQL Server and MySQL.

We start with the built-in system functions.

Using the System Functions

System functions have to do with times, dates, users, and so on. Here are the built-in system functions:

- CURRENT_DATE returns the current date.

- CURRENT_TIME returns the current time.

- CURRENT_TIMESTAMP returns the current date and the current time.

- CURRENT_USER returns the current user.

- SESSION_USER returns the current Authorization ID.

- SYSTEM_USER returns the current user within the operating system.

Do all the major DBMSes support these functions? Take a look:

- Microsoft SQL Server supports all of them.

- MySQL supports all of them.

- Oracle does not support them, but it supports USER instead of CURRENT_USER and it supports SYSDATE instead of CURRENT_TIMESTAMP.

- PostgreSQL supports all of them except SESSION_USER.

For example, here's how to use CURRENT_TIME():

```
> SELECT CURRENT_TIME();
+----------------+
| CURRENT_TIME() |
+----------------+
| 14:05:34       |
+----------------+
1 row in set (0.00 sec)
```

Using the Numeric Functions

You might be familiar with a rich set of numeric functions if you already use SQL, such as ABS(), COS(), POW(), and so on. These functions are not built into SQL; they've been added by your DBMS manufacturer.

The numeric function list built into SQL turns out to be small:

- BIT_LENGTH(*expression*) returns the number of bits in an expression.

- CHAR_LENGTH(*expression*) returns the number of characters in an expression.

- EXTRACT(*datepart* FROM *expression*) extracts the *datepart* (YEAR, MONTH, DAY, HOUR, MINUTE, SECOND, TIMEZONE_HOUR, or TIMEZONE_MINUTE) from an expression.

- OCTET_LENGTH(*expression*) returns the number of octets in an expression.

- POSITION(*starting_string* IN *search_string*) returns the starting position of a string inside the search string.

Let's look at these functions in more detail.

BIT-LENGTH(), CHAR_LENGTH(), and OCTET_LENGTH()

Oracle and MySQL support BIT_LENGTH(), which returns the number of bits in a value, which can be useful if you're doing bit-level operations with your data, or just want to measure the length of a data item. For example:

```
> SELECT BIT_LENGTH(5)
+---------------+
| BIT_LENGTH(5) |
+---------------+
| 8             |
+---------------+
1 row in set (0.03 sec)
```

Both MySQL and PostgreSQL support CHAR_LENGTH(), which returns the number of characters a value is long. SQL Server gives you the LEN() function, and Oracle has the LENGTH() function.

Here's an example:

```
> SELECT CHAR_LENGTH('Hello there!');
+----------------------------+
| CHAR_LENGTH('Hello there!') |
+----------------------------+
| 12                         |
+----------------------------+
1 row in set (0.00 sec)
```

Here's another example, where we determine the length in characters of everybody's last name from the Employees table:

```
> SELECT lastname, CHAR_LENGTH(lastname) FROM Employees;
+----------+-----------------------+
| lastname | CHAR_LENGTH(lastname) |
+----------+-----------------------+
| Wood     | 4                     |
| Green    | 5                     |
| Grant    | 5                     |
| Jackson  | 7                     |
| Smith    | 5                     |
| Smith    | 5                     |
+----------+-----------------------+
6 rows in set (0.00 sec)
```

Only MySQL and PostgreSQL support the OCTET_LENGTH() function (which returns the same value as BIT_LENGTH divided by 8, rounded up to the nearest positive integer).

Here's an example:

```
> SELECT OCTET_LENGTH(5);
+-----------------+
| OCTET_LENGTH(5) |
+-----------------+
| 1               |
+-----------------+
1 row in set (0.00 sec)
```

EXTRACT()

The EXTRACT() function, which lets you extract parts of dates from datetime values, is only supported under that name by PostgreSQL and MySQL. Oracle uses the TO_CHAR() function, and SQL Server uses the CONVERT() function.

The parts of dates you can extract are the following:

- YEAR
- MONTH
- DAY
- HOUR

- MINUTE
- SECOND
- TIMEZONE_HOUR
- TIMEZONE_MINUTE

For example, to extract all employees' days and months from their hire date, use the following:

```
> SELECT lastname, EXTRACT(DAY FROM hiredate),
EXTRACT(MONTH FROM hiredate) FROM Employees;
+----------+--------------------------+----------------------------+
| lastname | EXTRACT(DAY FROM hiredate) | EXTRACT(MONTH FROM hiredate) |
+----------+--------------------------+----------------------------+
| Wood     | 15                       | 1                          |
| Green    | 15                       | 1                          |
| Grant    | 15                       | 1                          |
| Jackson  | 20                       | 2                          |
| Smith    | 15                       | 3                          |
| Smith    | 15                       | 3                          |
+----------+--------------------------+----------------------------+
6 rows in set (0.00 sec)
```

POSITION()

The POSITION() function returns the location of a string inside another string, which is supported by MySQL and PostgreSQL. Oracle's function to do the same thing is INSTR(), and SQL Server offers the CHARINDEX() function.

Here's an example, where we find the location of the letter a in all employees' last names:

```
> SELECT lastname, POSITION('a' IN lastname) FROM Employees;
+----------+-------------------------+
| lastname | POSITION('a' IN lastname) |
+----------+-------------------------+
| Wood     | 0                       |
| Green    | 0                       |
| Grant    | 3                       |
| Jackson  | 2                       |
| Smith    | 0                       |
| Smith    | 0                       |
+----------+-------------------------+
6 rows in set (0.00 sec)
```

The text search is case-insensitive, as you can see in this example, where we search for the letter a in all employees' departments—note that A matches as well as a:

```
> SELECT department, POSITION('a' IN department) FROM Employees;
+------------+----------------------------+
| department | POSITION('a' IN department) |
+------------+----------------------------+
| Sales      | 2                          |
| Sales      | 2                          |
| Sales      | 2                          |
| Accounting | 1                          |
| Accounting | 1                          |
| Accounting | 1                          |
+------------+----------------------------+
6 rows in set (0.00 sec)
```

Using the String Functions

The built-in SQL string functions operate on text strings, and they are the following:

- CONCATENATE (expression || expression) concatenates one text string with another.

- CONVERT converts a text string, inside the same character set, to a new representation.

- LOWER converts a text string to all lowercase.

- SUBSTRING extracts part of a text string.

- TRANSLATE translates a text string from one character set to another character set.

- TRIM trims leading and trailing spaces from a text string.

- UPPER converts a text string to all uppercase.

Let's look at these functions in more detail.

CONCATENATE()

The CONCATENATE() function appends two text strings together, such as when you extract a person's first and last name from a database and concatenate them to get their full name, but its implementation varies widely.

Both PostgreSQl and Oracle support the "double-pipe" concatenation operator, which like *string_1 || string_2*. SQL Server uses the + concatenation operator, like *string_1 + string_2*.

MySQL has a CONCAT() function that works like the following:

```
CONCAT(string_1, string_2, [,...string_n]);
```

The official SQL syntax uses both the double-pipe operator and the function call:

```
CONCATENATE(string_1 || string_2)
```

For example:

```
> SELECT CONCATENATE('Hello ' || 'there');
+--------------------------------+
| CONCATENATE('Hello ' || 'there') |
+--------------------------------+
| Hello there                      |
+--------------------------------+
1 row in set (0.00 sec)
```

SQL CAUTION

If you concatenate NULL with any string, you end up with NULL.

If you concatenate a number to a text string, the number is first converted into a text string, and then concatenated:

```
> SELECT CONCATENATE('Apollo ' || 11);
+--------------------------+
| CONCATENATE('Apollo ' || 11) |
+--------------------------+
| Apollo 11                |
+--------------------------+
1 row in set (0.00 sec)
```

CONVERT() and TRANSLATE()

CONVERT() and TRANSLATE() are rarely used, and they're not often supported by DBMSes, but we'll include them here to show their proper usage in case your DBMS supports them. CONVERT() enables you to convert text strings to new representations in the same character set. For example, you might change the number of bits used per character. TRANSLATE() alters the characters from one character set to another. For example, you might convert characters from an English character set to Russian or Chinese.

Here's what the SQL syntax looks like:

```
CONVERT (character new_character_set USING use_form old_character);
TRANSLATE(character new_character_set USING translation_name);
```

No DBMS manufacturer supports CONVERT() and TRANSLATE() as they were specified by the creators of SQL except Oracle. For example, MySQL uses CONVERT() to convert numbers between different bases. SQL Server uses CONVERT() to change data types of data items. MySQL and SQL Server do not support TRANSLATE().

Because the use of these functions is so rare, and because the DBMS implementation of them is usually different from the way the functions were defined, we're not going to spend a lot of time on them. If you really want to use these functions, Oracle is the only choice.

LOWER() and UPPER()

LOWER() and UPPER() are easy ones that convert their text string arguments to lowercase or uppercase, respectively. And they're supported in SQL Server, PostgreSQL, MySQL, and Oracle. These functions are great in case you need to change the case of text data.

Here's an example:

```
> SELECT LOWER('SSSH! NOT SO LOUD!');
+----------------------------+
| LOWER('SSSH! NOT SO LOUD!') |
+----------------------------+
| sssh! not so loud!         |
+----------------------------+
1 row in set (0.00 sec)
```

And here's another example:

```
> SELECT UPPER('What? I can\'t hear you!');
+-------------------------------+
| UPPER('What? I can\'t hear you!') |
+-------------------------------+
| WHAT? I CAN'T HEAR YOU!        |
+-------------------------------+
1 row in set (0.00 sec)
```

SQL TIP

You might notice that the string 'What? I can't hear you!' is ambiguous with respect to quotation marks, because it looks like there are three of them (including the apostrophe in the middle). One way to alert SQL of an apostrophe is to escape it: 'What? I can\'t hear you!' Another way is to alternate quotation mark styles: "What? I can't hear you!"

SUBSTRING()

SUBSTRING() lets you extract substrings from other strings. For example, you might want to extract some text from a huge string of text, and SUBSTRING() is perfect for that. Here's how it works:

```
SUBSTRING(string FROM starting_position [FOR length
[COLLATE collation]])
```

Of course, no DBMS implements it exactly this way. SQL Server and PostgreSQL have the following:

```
SUBSTRING(string [FROM starting_position [FOR length]])
```

MySQL and Oracle give you this (SUBSTRING() also works in MySQL):

```
SUBSTR(string, starting_position [, length])
```

Here's an example:

```
> SELECT SUBSTRING('Los Angeles', 5, 5);
+--------------------------------+
| SUBSTRING('Los Angeles', 5, 5) |
+--------------------------------+
| Angel                          |
+--------------------------------+
1 row in set (0.00 sec)
```

Or say you want to create passwords for employees made up of the first three letters of their last name concatenated with their ID. That could look like this:

```
> SELECT firstname, lastname,
CONCATENATE(SUBSTRING(lastname, 1, 3) || id)
FROM Employees;
```

```
+-----------+----------+------------------------------------------------+
| firstname | lastname | CONCATENATE(SUBSTRING(lastname, 1, 3) || id) |
+-----------+----------+------------------------------------------------+
| John      | Wood     | Woo1501                                        |
| Mary      | Green    | Gre1601                                        |
| Daniel    | Grant    | Gra1602                                        |
| Nancy     | Jackson  | Jac1701                                        |
| Tom       | Smith    | Smi1801                                        |
| Jessica   | Smith    | Smi1901                                        |
+-----------+----------+------------------------------------------------+
6 rows in set (0.06 sec)
```

Note that CONCATENATE(SUBSTRING(lastname, 1, 3) || id) is a complicated column name. Note that you can rename columns with the AS keyword (see Chapter 9 for more on this keyword), so let's rename the column as password:

```
> SELECT firstname, lastname,
CONCATENATE(SUBSTRING(lastname, 1, 3) || id)
AS password FROM Employees;
+-----------+----------+----------+
| firstname | lastname | password |
+-----------+----------+----------+
| John      | Wood     | Woo1501  |
| Mary      | Green    | Gre1601  |
| Daniel    | Grant    | Gra1602  |
| Nancy     | Jackson  | Jac1701  |
| Tom       | Smith    | Smi1801  |
| Jessica   | Smith    | Smi1901  |
+-----------+----------+----------+
6 rows in set (0.00 sec)
```

TRIM()

The TRIM() function trims off leading and trailing characters from a text string, usually spaces. This is useful if your text data contains extra spaces. For example, you can use TRIM() to convert ' SQL ' to 'SQL.'

Here's the official syntax (you can pick one from the choices in {LEADING | TRAILING | BOTH}—the default is BOTH):

```
TRIM([[{LEADING | TRAILING | BOTH}] [string_to_remove] FROM ]
string [COLLATE collation])
```

Surprisingly, Oracle, PostgreSQL, and MySQL support this syntax. Microsoft SQL Server supports LTRIM() for trimming spaces from the left, and RTRIM() for trimming spaces from the right.

Here's an example:

```
> SELECT TRIM('     SQL    ');
+---------------------+
| TRIM('     SQL    ') |
+---------------------+
| SQL                 |
+---------------------+
1 row in set (0.02 sec)
```

Here's an example of what you're trimming:

```
> SELECT TRIM('x' FROM 'xxxxxxxSQLxxxxx');
+--------------------------------+
| TRIM('x' FROM 'xxxxxxxSQLxxxxx') |
+--------------------------------+
| SQL                            |
+--------------------------------+
1 row in set (0.00 sec)
```

Here's how you can trim leading characters:

```
> SELECT TRIM(LEADING 'x' FROM 'xxxxxxxSQLxxxxx');
+------------------------------------------+
| TRIM(LEADING 'x' FROM 'xxxxxxxSQLxxxxx') |
+------------------------------------------+
| SQLxxxxx                                 |
+------------------------------------------+
1 row in set (0.00 sec)
```

And here's how you can trim trailing characters:

```
> SELECT TRIM(TRAILING 'x' FROM 'xxxxxxxSQLxxxxx');
+-------------------------------------------+
| TRIM(TRAILING 'x' FROM 'xxxxxxxSQLxxxxx') |
+-------------------------------------------+
| xxxxxxxSQL                                |
+-------------------------------------------+
1 row in set (0.00 sec)
```

DBMS-Specific Functions

Each DBMS extends the built-in SQL function, and we look at what's available, starting with Oracle.

Oracle

You can find some popular Oracle-specific functions in Table 8.1.

Table 8.1   Oracle-Specific Functions

Function	Means
ABS(*number*)	Returns the absolute value of *number*.
ACOS(*number*)	Returns the arccosine of *number*.
ADD_MONTHS(*date, integer*)	Returns the date plus *integer* months.
ASCII(*string*)	Returns the ASCII value of the first character of *string*.
ASIN(*number*)	Returns the arcsine of *number*.
ATAN(*number*)	Returns the arctangent of *number*.
ATAN2(*number1, number2*)	Returns the arctangent of *number1* and *number2*.
AVG([DISTINCT] *expression*)	Returns the average value of *expression*.
BFILENAME(*directory,filename*)	Returns a BFILE locator for a physical binary file.
CEIL(*number*)	Returns the smallest integer greater than or equal to a number.
CONCAT(*string1, string2*)	Returns *string1* concatenated to *string2*.
COS(*number*)	Returns the cosine of *number*.
COSH(*number*)	Returns the hyperbolic cosine of *number*.
COUNT	Returns the number of rows returned by a query.
DEREF(*expression*)	Returns the object reference of *expression*.
EXP(*number*)	Returns the natural log base, e, raised to *number*.
FIRST_VALUE(*expression*)	Returns the first value in a set.

continues

Table 8.1 Oracle-Specific Functions (continued)

Function	Means
FLOOR(*number*)	Returns the largest integer equal to or less than *number*.
INITCAP(*string*)	Returns *string*, with the first letter of each word capitalized.
INSTR(*string1, string2, start, occurrence*)	Searches one character string for another.
LAST_DAY(*date*)	Returns the date of the last day of the month in which is *date*.
LENGTH(*string*)	Returns the length of *string*.
LN(*number*)	Returns the natural log of *number*.
LOG(*base, number*)	Returns the log to base of *number*.
LOWER(*string*)	Returns *string* with all characters lowercase.
LTRIM(*string*[, *remove_set*])	Removes all characters in *remove_set* (default is one space) from the left of *string*.
MAX([DISTINCT] *expression*)	Returns the maximum value of *expression*.
MIN([DISTINCT] *expression*)	Returns the minimum value of *expression*.
MOD(*dividend, divider*)	Returns the remainder of *dividend* divided by *divider*.
MONTHS_BETWEEN(*date1, date2*)	Returns the number of months between *date1* and *date2*.
POWER(*number, power*)	Returns *number* raised to power *power*.
REPLACE(*string, search_string* [, *replacement*])	Returns *string* with all occurrences of *search_string* replaced by *replacement*.
ROUND(*number, decimal*)	Returns *number* rounded to *decimal* places.
ROUND(*date* [, *format*])	Returns *date* rounded to the unit given by *format*.

Function	Means
RTRIM(*string*[, *remove_set*])	Removes all characters in *remove_set* (default is one space) from the right of *string*.
SIGN(*number*)	Returns the sign of *number*.
SIN(*number*)	Returns the sine of *number*.
SINH(*number*)	Returns the hyperbolic sine of *number*.
SQRT(*number*)	Returns square root of *number*.
SUBSTR(*string* [FROM *start*] [FOR *length*])	Extracts a substring from *string* starting at *start*, of *length*.
SUM([DISTINCT] *expression*)	Returns sum of values of *expression*.
SYSDATE	Returns current date and time.
TAN(*number*)	Returns the tangent of *number*.
TANH(*number*)	Returns the hyperbolic tangent of *number*.
TO_DATE(*string* [, *format* [, '*nls_parameter*']])	Converts *string* to a date.
TO_NUMBER(*string* [, *format* [, '*nls_parameter*']])	Converts *string* to a number.
TRIM([[LEADING I TRAILING I BOTH] *char* } FROM *string*})	Trims leading or trailing *char* characters from *string*.
UPPER(*string*)	Returns *string* with all letters in uppercase.
USER	Returns the name of the user.
USERENV(*option*)	Returns data about the current session.

SQL Server

You can find some popular SQL Server–specific functions in Table 8.2.

Table 8.2   SQL Server–Specific Functions

Function	Means
ABS(*number*)	Returns absolute value of *number*.
ACOS(*number*)	Returns arccosine of *number*.
APP_NAME	Returns the name of the application.
ASCII(*character*)	Converts *character* to an ASCII code.
ASIN(*number*)	Returns arcsine of *number*.
ATAN(*number*)	Returns arctangent of *number*.
AVG([ALL| DISTINCT] *expression*)	Computes average of *expression*.
CAST(*expression* as *type*)	Converts *expression* to the given datatype.
CEILING(*number*)	Returns the smallest integer greater than or equal to *number*.
CHAR(*number*)	Converts an ASCII code to a character.
COALESCE(*expression* [,...n])	Returns the first non-NULL value from a list.
COL_LENGTH(*table, column*)	Returns a column's length.
COL_NAME(*table, column*)	Returns a column's name.
CONVERT(*data_type* [(*length*)], *expression* [, *style*])	Converts from one datatype to another.
COS(*number*)	Returns cosine of *number*.
COT(number)	Returns cotangent of *number*.
COUNT(([ALL | DISTINCT] *expression*]| *))	Counts the rows in *expression*.
COUNT(DISTINCT *expression*)	Returns the number of distinct non-NULL values in *expression*.

Function	Means
COUNT(*expression*)	Returns the number of non-NULL values in *expression*.
CURRENT_TIMESTAMP	Returns current date and time.
CURRENT_USER	Returns the current user name.
DATALENGTH(*expression*)	Returns number of bytes in a character string.
DATEADD(*datepart, number, date*)	Adds number of dateparts such as DAYS to *date*.
DATEDIFF(*datepart, start, end*)	Returns the difference between two datetimes.
DAY(*date*)	Returns the day of *date*.
DB_ID('[*database_name*]')	Returns the database ID.
DB_NAME(*database_id*)	Returns the database name.
DEGREES(*number*)	Converts radians to degrees.
EXP(*number*)	Returns e, the natural log base, raised to the power of *number*.
FLOOR(*number*)	Returns the largest integer less than or equal to *number*.
FILE_ID(*filename*)	Returns the file ID for *filename*.
FILE_NAME(*file_id*)	Returns the filename for *file_id*.
GETDATE	Returns the current date and time.
GETUTCDATE	Returns the current Universal Time Coordinate (UTC) date.
HOST_ID	Returns the host ID.
HOST_NAME	Returns the host name.
ISDATE(*expression*)	Returns true if *expression* is a date value.
ISNULL(*expression, alternate*)	Returns *expression* if it is not NULL; otherwise, returns *alternate*.
ISNUMERIC(*expression*)	Returns true if *expression* is a number.

continues

Table 8.2   SQL Server–Specific Functions (continued)

Function	Means
LEFT(*expression*, *left*)	Returns part of *expression*, starting at *left* characters from the left.
LEN(*string*)	Returns the number of characters in *string*.
LOG(*expression*)	Returns natural log of *expression*.
LOG10(*expression*)	Returns base-10 log of *expression*.
LOWER(*string*)	Converts string to lowercase.
LTRIM(*string*)	Trims leading space characters from *string*.
MAX([ALL | DISTINCT] *expression*)	Returns maximum value in *expression*.
MIN([ALL | DISTINCT] *expression*)	Returns minimum value in *expression*.
MONTH(*date*)	Returns month of *date*.
NULLIF(*expression1*, *expression2*)	Returns NULL if the two expressions are equal.

MySQL

You can find some popular MySQL-specific functions in Table 8.3.

Table 8.3   MySQL-Specific Functions

Function	Means
ABS(*number*)	Returns the absolute value of *number*.
ACOS(*number*)	Returns the arccosine of *number*.
ASCII(*string*)	Returns the ASCII code of the first character of *string*.
ASIN(*number*)	Returns the arcsine of *number*.
ATAN(*number*)	Returns the arctangent of *number*.
AVG(*expression*)	Returns the average value of *expression*.

Function	Means
BINARY(*string*)	Casts *string* to binary.
BIT_COUNT(*number*)	Returns the number of bits that are set in *number.*
BIT_AND(*number*)	Returns the bitwise AND of all bits in *number.*
BIT_OR(*number*)	Returns the bitwise OR of all bits in *number.*
CEILING(*number*)	Returns the smallest integer value not less than *number.*
COALESCE(*expression*)	Returns first non-NULL element in *expression.*
CONCAT(*string1, string2, ...*)	Returns *string1* concatenated to *string2.*
CONV(*number, from_base, to_base*)	Converts a number from one base to another.
COS(*number*)	Returns the cosine of *number.*
COT(*number*)	Returns the cotangent of *number.*
COUNT(DISTINCT *expression1,* [*expression2...*])	Returns a count of the number of different values in the expression(s).
COUNT(*expression*)	Returns a count of the number of non-NULL values in *expression.*
CURDATE( )	Returns today's date.
CURTIME( )	Returns the current time.
DATABASE( )	Returns the database name.
DATE_FORMAT(*date, format*)	Formats *date* value according to *format.*
DAYNAME(*date*)	Returns the name of the day of the week for *date.*
DAYOFMONTH(*date*)	Returns the day of the month for *date.*
DAYOFYEAR(*date*)	Returns the day of the year for *date.*
DEGREES(*number*)	Returns *number* in degrees.

continues

Table 8.3 MySQL-Specific Functions (continued)

Function	Means
EXP(*number*)	Returns e, the base of natural logarithms, raised to the power of *number*.
FIND_IN_SET(*string, stringlist*)	Returns 1 to *n* if *string* is in the list *stringlist* consisting of *n* strings.
FLOOR(*number*)	Returns the largest integer value not greater than *number*.
GREATEST(*value1, value2,...*)	Returns the greatest argument.
HOUR(*time*)	Returns the hour for *time*.
IF(*expression1, expression2, expression3*)	If *expression1* is true, then IF( ) returns *expression2*, or else it returns *expression3*.
IFNULL(*expression1, expression2*)	If *expression1* is not NULL, IFNULL( ) returns *expression1*; otherwise, it returns *expression2*. IFNULL( ) returns a numeric or string value, depending on the context in which it is used.
ISNULL(*expression*)	If *expression* is NULL, it returns 1; otherwise, it returns 0.
INSTR(*string, substring*)	Returns the position of the first occurrence of *substring* in *string*.
LCASE(*string*) LOWER(*string*)	Returns *string* in lowercase.
LEAST(*value1, value2,...*)	Returns the smallest argument.
LEFT(*string, length*)	Returns the leftmost *length* characters from *string*.
LENGTH(*string*)	Returns the length of *string*.
LOAD_FILE(*file_name*)	Returns the file contents as a string.
LOCATE(*substring, string*) POSITION(*substring* IN *string*)	Returns the position of the first occurrence of *substring* in *string*.
LOG(*number*)	Returns the natural log of *number*.
LOG10(*number*)	Returns the base-10 log of *number*.

Function	Means
LTRIM(*string*)	Returns *string* with leading space characters trimmed.
MIN(*expression*) MAX(*expression*)	Returns the minimum or maximum value of *expression*.
MINUTE(*time*)	Returns the minute for *time*.
MOD(*dividend, divider*)	Returns the remainder of *dividend* divided by *divider*.
MONTH(*date*)	Returns the month for *date*.
MONTHNAME(*date*)	Returns the name of the month for *date*.
NULLIF(*expression1, expression2*)	If *expression1* = *expression2*, returns NULL; otherwise, returns *expression1*.
PASSWORD(*string*)	Returns a password string from the plain-text *string*.
POW(*x,y*) POWER(*x,y*)	Returns *x* raised to the power *y*.
RADIANS(*number*)	Returns *number* in radians.
REPLACE(*string, from_string, to_string*)	Returns *string* with all occurrences of *from_string* replaced with *to_string*.
REVERSE(*string*)	Returns *string* with the characters reversed.
ROUND(*number*)	Returns *number* rounded to an integer.
RTRIM(*string*)	Returns *string* with trailing space characters trimmed.
SECOND(*time*)	Returns the seconds for *time*.
SIGN(*number*)	Returns the sign of *number*.
SIN(*number*)	Returns the sine of *number*.
SPACE(*number*)	Returns a string consisting of *number* spaces.
SQRT(*number*)	Returns the square root of *number*.

continues

Table 8.3 **MySQL-Specific Functions** (continued)

Function	Means
STRCMP(*expression1*, *expression2*)	Returns 0 if the expressions are the same, −1 if the first expression is smaller than the second, and 1 otherwise.
SUBSTRING(*string, position*) SUBSTRING(*string* FROM *position*)	Returns the substring from *string* starting at *position*.
SUM(*expression*)	Returns the sum of *expression*.
TAN(*number*)	Returns the tangent of *number*.
TRIM([[BOTH | LEADING | TRAILING] [*remove*] FROM] *string*)	Trims *remove* from *string*.
TRUNCATE(*number, digits*)	Returns *number*, truncated to *digits* decimal places.
UCASE(*string*) UPPER(*string*)	Returns *string* with all characters in uppercase.
USER( ) SYSTEM_USER( ) SESSION_USER( )	Return the current MySQL user name.
VERSION()	Returns the MySQL server version.
WEEKDAY(*date*)	Returns the weekday for *date*.
YEAR(*date*)	Returns the year for *date*.

PostgreSQL

You can find some popular PostgreSQL-specific functions in Table 8.4.

Table 8.4 **PostgreSQL-Specific Functions**

Function	Means
ABS(*number*)	Returns absolute value of *number*.
ACOS(*number*)	Returns arccosine of *number*.
ASIN(*number*)	Returns arcsine of *number*.
ATAN(*number*)	Returns arctangent of *number*.

Function	Means
CBRT(*number*)	Returns cube root of *number*.
CHAR_LENGTH(*string*) CHARACTER_LENGTH(*string*)	Returns length of *string*.
COALESCE(*expression*)	Returns the first non-NULL value in *expression*.
COS(*number*)	Returns cosine of *number*.
COT(*number*)	Returns cotangent of *number*.
DEGREES (*number*)	Converts *number* radians to degrees.
EXP(*number*)	Raises e to *number*.
FLOAT(*int*)	Converts *int* to floating point number.
INITCAP(*string*)	Converts the first character of each word to uppercase.
INTEGER(*number*)	Converts floating point *number* to integer.
INTERVAL(*expression*)	Converts *expression* to an interval.
LN(*number*)	Returns the natural log of *number*.
LOG(*number*)	Returns the base-10 log of *number*.
LOWER(string)	Converts *string* to lowercase.
LTRIM(*string, remove*)	Returns *string* with any *remove* characters trimmed from the left.
NULLIF(*expression1, expression2*)	Returns NULL if *expression1* = *expression2*; otherwise, returns *expression1*.
POW(*number, power*)	Returns *number* raised to the power of *power*.
RADIANS(*number*)	Returns *number* converted to radians.
ROUND(*number*)	Rounds *number* to the nearest integer.
RTRIM(*string, remove*)	Returns *string* with any *remove* characters trimmed from the right.
SIN(*number*)	Returns the sine of *number*.

continues

Table 8.4 PostgreSQL-Specific Functions (continued)

Function	Means
SQRT(*number*)	Returns the square root of *number*.
SUBSTRING(*string* [FROM *int*] [FOR *int*])	Returns the specified substring.
TAN(*number*)	Returns the tangent of *number*.
TEXTPOS(*string1, string2*)	Returns the position of *string2* in *string1*.
TRIM([LEADING | TRAILING | BOTH] [*characters*] FROM *string*)	Trims *characters* from *string*.
UPPER(*string*)	Returns *string* in uppercase.

The Least You Need to Know

- SQL comes with some built-in mathematical functions such as EXTRACT().
- SQL comes with some built-in string functions such as SUBSTRING().
- SQL also includes some built-in system functions such as CURRENT_USER().
- Most DBMSes add many DBMS-specific functions.

In-Depth Data Handling

In this part, you see SQL at work in more depth, starting with joining tables together.

As your database gets bigger, you'll find that it's more convenient to store data in multiple tables with different columns, rather than try to pack everything into one table. When you start using multiple tables, you can connect them so that, for example, you can find an employee's current record in one table and information about the employee's supervisor in another table in a record linked to the first table by the employee's ID.

You also take a look at how SQL lets you group data inside one table. For example, you might have employees in both the Sales and Accounting departments, and want to find who was hired first in both departments. You can group your data into subtables, one for Sales and one for Accounting, and search those subtables independently.

Joining Tables

In This Chapter

- Understanding joins
- Creating joins
- Using different types of joins
- Working with aliases
- Inner joins and outer joins

This chapter focuses on using multiple databases at the same time. You connect those databases with joins, and that means you can relate the data in one table to another. This is an exceptionally powerful technique, so let's dig in immediately.

Using Joins

Sometimes you need to access information from two different tables. For example, say that you have the Employees table:

```
> SELECT * FROM Employees;
+-----------+----------+------------+------------+------------+------+
| firstname | lastname | department | hiredate   | supervisor | id   |
+-----------+----------+------------+------------+------------+------+
| John      | Wood     | Sales      | 2012-01-15 | 1001       | 1501 |
| Mary      | Green    | Sales      | 2012-01-15 | 1501       | 1601 |
| Daniel    | Grant    | Sales      | 2012-01-15 | 1501       | 1602 |
| Nancy     | Jackson  | Accounting | 2012-02-20 | 1501       | 1701 |
| Tom       | Smith    | Accounting | 2012-03-15 | 1701       | 1801 |
| Jessica   | Smith    | Accounting | 2012-03-15 | 1701       | 1901 |
+-----------+----------+------------+------------+------------+------+
6 rows in set (0.00 sec)
```

How do you get the phone extension of Mary Green's supervisor to commend her on a good job when the supervisor phone extensions are stored in a different table, such as the following Supervisors table?

```
> SELECT * FROM Supervisors;
+-----------+----------+------+-----------+
| firstname | lastname | id   | extension |
+-----------+----------+------+-----------+
| George    | Edwards  | 1001 | 231       |
| John      | Wood     | 1501 | 244       |
| Nancy     | Jackson  | 1701 | 255       |
+-----------+----------+------+-----------+
3 rows in set (0.00 sec)
```

You can connect the Employees and the Supervisors table to get a table that displays your employees and their supervisor's phone numbers like this:

```
+-----------+----------+-----------+
| firstname | lastname | extension |
+-----------+----------+-----------+
| John      | Wood     | 231       |
| Mary      | Green    | 244       |
| Daniel    | Grant    | 244       |
| Nancy     | Jackson  | 244       |
| Tom       | Smith    | 255       |
| Jessica   | Smith    | 255       |
+-----------+----------+-----------+
```

Because this table takes data from two different tables, it's known as a *join*.

 DEFINITION

A **join** is an SQL statement that takes data from two or more tables.

So how do you create a join to take data from two different tables, the Employees table and the Supervisors table?

Creating a Join

In this case, you want to display an employee's first name and last name from the Employees table and then look up the supervisor's phone extension from the Supervisors extension.

If you're following along, you can create the Supervisors table this way:

```
> CREATE TABLE Supervisors
(firstname VARCHAR(20),
lastname VARCHAR(20),
id INT,
extension INT);
Query OK, 0 rows affected (0.00 sec)
```

And then stock it with data this way:

```
> INSERT INTO Supervisors VALUES ('George', 'Edwards', 1001, 231);
Query OK, 1 row affected (0.03 sec)
> INSERT INTO Supervisors VALUES ('John', 'Wood', 1501,  244);
Query OK, 1 row affected (0.03 sec)
> INSERT INTO Supervisors VALUES ('Nancy', 'Jackson', 1701, 255);
Query OK, 1 row affected (0.02 sec)
```

Now you have the Supervisors table in addition to the Employees table:

```
> SELECT * FROM Supervisors;
+-----------+----------+------+-----------+
| firstname | lastname | id   | extension |
+-----------+----------+------+-----------+
| George    | Edwards  | 1001 | 231       |
| John      | Wood     | 1501 | 244       |
| Nancy     | Jackson  | 1701 | 255       |
+-----------+----------+------+-----------+
3 rows in set (0.00 sec)
```

Now you want to display each employee's first and last names, and then get the supervisor's phone number. Let's look at one particular employee, Daniel Grant. You get his first name and last name from the Employees table:

```
+-----------+----------+------------+------------+------------+------+
| firstname | lastname | department | hiredate   | supervisor | id   |
+-----------+----------+------------+------------+------------+------+
| John      | Wood     | Sales      | 2012-01-15 | 1001       | 1501 |
| Mary      | Green    | Sales      | 2012-01-15 | 1501       | 1601 |
| Daniel    | Grant    | Sales      | 2012-01-15 | 1501       | 1602 |
| Nancy     | Jackson  | Accounting | 2012-02-20 | 1501       | 1701 |
| Tom       | Smith    | Accounting | 2012-03-15 | 1701       | 1801 |
| Jessica   | Smith    | Accounting | 2012-03-15 | 1701       | 1901 |
+-----------+----------+------------+------------+------------+------+
```

Now look up his supervisor in the Supervisors table. Check the value in Daniel Grant's supervisor column, which is 1501. Then find out who in the Supervisor's table has the ID 1501, and retrieve the phone extension like this:

```
+-----------+----------+------------+------------+------------+------+
| firstname | lastname | department | hiredate   | supervisor | id   |
+-----------+----------+------------+------------+------------+------+
| John      | Wood     | Sales      | 2012-01-15 | 1001       | 1501 |
| Mary      | Green    | Sales      | 2012-01-15 | 1501       | 1601 |
| Daniel    | Grant    | Sales      | 2012-01-15 | 1501       | 1602 |
| Nancy     | Jackson  | Accounting | 2012-02-20 |            | 1701 |
| Tom       | Smith    | Accounting | 2012-03-15 |            | 1801 |
| Jessica   | Smith    | Accounting | 2012-03-15 |            | 1901 |
+-----------+----------+------------+------------+------------+------+
                                                        |
                        +-----------+----------+----|--+-----------+
                        | firstname | lastname | id |  | extension |
                        +-----------+----------+----|--+-----------+
                        | George    | Edwards  |  V |  | 231       |
                        | John      | Wood     | 1501--->244      |
                        | Nancy     | Jackson  | 1701 | 255        |
                        +-----------+----------+------+-----------+
```

Now you need to find the record in the Supervisors table whose ID matches the supervisor value in the Employees record. To recover fields from two tables, use a join—that is, a SELECT statement that ties two tables together.

Begin with the SELECT keyword, selecting the columns you want to display—the firstname, lastname, and extension columns:

```
SELECT firstname, lastname, extension
  ...
```

Note that you're already faced with an issue that often appears when you create joins—column names that are the same in the two tables. In this case, both the Employees table and the Supervisors table have columns named firstname and lastname, so SQL will have a problem knowing which one you want returned.

To make it clear to SQL that the firstname and lastname columns you want come from the Employees table, not the Supervisors table, qualify the firstname and lastname names as Employees.firstname and Employees.lastname:

```
SELECT Employees.firstname, Employees.lastname, extension
...
```

Now you indicate from which tables you want to take data. In this case, that's the Employees table and Supervisors table, which you indicate with a FROM clause:

```
SELECT Employees.firstname, Employees.lastname, extension
FROM Employees, Supervisors
...
```

Now you have to indicate, for each Employees record, which record in the Supervisors table you want. For a particular Employees table record, you want to find the record in the Supervisors table such as Employees.supervisor = Supervisors.id. You can alert SQL with a WHERE clause:

```
SELECT Employees.firstname, Employees.lastname, extension
FROM Employees, Supervisors
WHERE Employees.supervisor = Supervisors.id;
```

This creates the first join. Running this join gives you the following result:

```
> SELECT Employees.firstname, Employees.lastname, extension
FROM Employees, Supervisors
WHERE Employees.supervisor = Supervisors.id;
+-----------+-----------+-----------+
| firstname | lastname  | extension |
+-----------+-----------+-----------+
| John      | Wood      | 231       |
| Mary      | Green     | 244       |
| Daniel    | Grant     | 244       |
| Nancy     | Jackson   | 244       |
| Tom       | Smith     | 255       |
| Jessica   | Smith     | 255       |
+-----------+-----------+-----------+
6 rows in set (0.00 sec)
```

Now you have each employee's first name, last name, and the phone extension of the supervisor.

Why Joins?

Joins are important in SQL because if you have a lot of data, it's not practical to store it all in one table. And when you have your data distributed across multiple tables, you need a join to retrieve data from these tables all at once.

For example, look at the Employees table:

```
+-----------+----------+------------+------------+------------+------+
| firstname | lastname | department | hiredate   | supervisor | id   |
+-----------+----------+------------+------------+------------+------+
| John      | Wood     | Sales      | 2012-01-15 | 1001       | 1501 |
| Mary      | Green    | Sales      | 2012-01-15 | 1501       | 1601 |
| Daniel    | Grant    | Sales      | 2012-01-15 | 1501       | 1602 |
| Nancy     | Jackson  | Accounting | 2012-02-20 | 1501       | 1701 |
| Tom       | Smith    | Accounting | 2012-03-15 | 1701       | 1801 |
| Jessica   | Smith    | Accounting | 2012-03-15 | 1701       | 1901 |
+-----------+----------+------------+------------+------------+------+
```

There's a lot of data, but the phone extensions of the supervisors are not included. Because there are six employees and only three supervisors, listing the supervisors' extensions for each employee creates duplicated fields. For example, Mary Green, Daniel Grant, and Nancy Jackson all have the same supervisor, which would list the same supervisor's extension three times.

It's best to avoid data duplication not only for better storage and simplicity, but also to make updating the data easier. If you only have to update it in one place, not three, the chances are that the update process will go smoother.

So store the supervisors' extensions in a separate table, the Supervisors table, where there is no duplication:

```
+-----------+----------+------+-----------+
| firstname | lastname | id   | extension |
+-----------+----------+------+-----------+
| George    | Edwards  | 1001 | 231       |
| John      | Wood     | 1501 | 244       |
| Nancy     | Jackson  | 1701 | 255       |
+-----------+----------+------+-----------+
```

But now you have distributed the data over two tables, and you need to relate the two. To do this, read the supervisor value in the Employees table and find the ID value that matches in the

Supervisors table, thus creating a join. The join condition is
Employees.supervisor = Supervisors.id.

Inner Joins

The kind of join you've been using so far, where the join condition is
an equality, is called an inner join (or sometimes called an equijoin):

```
SELECT Employees.firstname, Employees.lastname, extension
FROM Employees, Supervisors
WHERE Employees.supervisor = Supervisors.id;
```

You can use this syntax to create an inner join:

```
> SELECT Employees.firstname, Employees.lastname, extension
FROM Employees INNER JOIN Supervisors
ON Employees.supervisor = Supervisors.id;
+-----------+-----------+-----------+
| firstname | lastname  | extension |
+-----------+-----------+-----------+
| John      | Wood      | 231       |
| Mary      | Green     | 244       |
| Daniel    | Grant     | 244       |
| Nancy     | Jackson   | 244       |
| Tom       | Smith     | 255       |
| Jessica   | Smith     | 255       |
+-----------+-----------+-----------+
6 rows in set (0.00 sec)
```

Note that the results are the same, but the syntax is different. Either
way works.

SQL TIP

What's the correct syntax—listing the two tables in an inner join separated by commas, or using INNER JOIN? According to the ANSI SQL
standard, the correct syntax is INNER JOIN.

Joining Multiple Tables

Can you join more than two tables at the same time? Yes, you can,
by separating the table names with commas and using AND clauses.

For example, say you have three tables: Employees, Supervisors, and Salaries (which lists the ID and salary of every employee) and want to create a table showing each employee's first and last name, salary, and extension. You can create such a table like this:

```
SELECT Employees.firstname, Employees.lastname, salary, extension,
FROM Employees, Supervisors, Salaries
WHERE Employees.supervisor = Supervisors.id
AND Employees.id = Salaries.id;
```

And here's what the result of running this query might look like:

```
>SELECT Employees.firstname, Employees.lastname, salary, extension,
FROM Employees, Supervisors, Salaries
WHERE Employees.supervisor = Supervisors.id
AND Employees.id = Salaries.id;
+-----------+----------+-----------+----------+
| firstname | lastname | extension | salary   |
+-----------+----------+-----------+----------+
| John      | Wood     | 231       | 84000    |
| Mary      | Green    | 244       | 62000    |
| Daniel    | Grant    | 244       | 62000    |
| Nancy     | Jackson  | 244       | 75000    |
| Tom       | Smith    | 255       | 41000    |
| Jessica   | Smith    | 255       | 41000    |
+-----------+----------+-----------+----------+
6 rows in set (0.00 sec)
```

SQL CAUTION

What's the maximum number of tables you can join? There is no limit according to SQL itself, but most DBMSes have their own limits. This is one of those cases where you have to check your DBMSes docs. Note that the more tables you join, the more work the DBMS has to do, so don't be surprised if things slow down considerably after you join four or more tables.

Using Aliases

You can refer to column names and table names with a different name in SQL, which is called using an alias. For example, look at the following SQL, which concatenates each employee's first and last name:

```
> SELECT CONCATENATE(Employees.firstname, Employees.lastname),
extension
FROM Employees INNER JOIN Supervisors
ON Employees.supervisor = Supervisors.id;
+-------------------------------------------------------+----------+
| CONCATENATE(Employees.firstname, Employees.lastname)  | extension |
+-------------------------------------------------------+----------+
| JohnWood                                              | 231      |
| MaryGreen                                             | 244      |
| DanielGrant                                           | 244      |
| NancyJackson                                          | 244      |
| TomSmith                                              | 255      |
| JessicaSmith                                          | 255      |
+-------------------------------------------------------+----------+
6 rows in set (0.00 sec)
```

CONCATENATE(Employees.firstname, Employees.lastname) is a complicated column name. To change it to a simpler name, use an AS name clause. While you're at it, rename the extension column to supervisor extension:

```
> SELECT CONCATENATE(Employees.firstname, ' ',
Employees.lastname) AS name,
extension as 'supervisor extension'
FROM Employees INNER JOIN Supervisors
ON Employees.supervisor = Supervisors.id;
+---------------+----------------------+
| name          | supervisor extension |
+---------------+----------------------+
| John Wood     | 231                  |
| Mary Green    | 244                  |
| Daniel Grant  | 244                  |
| Nancy Jackson | 244                  |
| Tom Smith     | 255                  |
| Jessica Smith | 255                  |
+---------------+----------------------+
6 rows in set (0.00 sec)
```

Note that the columns have been renamed to read as you want them.

You can also rename table names, which comes in handy when creating joins where you have to refer to table names multiple times. For example, look at the following syntax.

```
> SELECT E.firstname, E.lastname, extension
FROM Employees AS E INNER JOIN Supervisors AS S
ON E.supervisor = S.id;
+-----------+----------+-----------+
| firstname | lastname | extension |
+-----------+----------+-----------+
| John      | Wood     | 231       |
| Mary      | Green    | 244       |
| Daniel    | Grant    | 244       |
| Nancy     | Jackson  | 244       |
| Tom       | Smith    | 255       |
| Jessica   | Smith    | 255       |
+-----------+----------+-----------+
6 rows in set (0.00 sec)
```

Here, you aliased the Employees table as E and Supervisors table as S, which makes it easier to enter names and makes self joins, the next topic, possible.

SQL CAUTION

Oracle doesn't support the AS keyword. If you're using Oracle, use the previous syntax for aliases, but omit the AS.

Using Different Joins

In addition to inner joins, there are other types of joins you can make, and we look at some of them in the next section.

Self Joins

To use joins on the same table, you must alias the table name so that it looks like you're doing a standard join on two different tables to SQL.

For example, say you want the first name of every employee whose last name matches at least one last name on the same table. You can do a self join like the following:

```
> SELECT E1.firstname
FROM Employees AS E1, Employees AS E2
WHERE E1.lastname = E2.lastname;
+-----------+
| firstname |
+-----------+
| John      |
| Mary      |
| Daniel    |
| Nancy     |
| Tom       |
| Jessica   |
| Tom       |
| Jessica   |
+-----------+
8 rows in set (0.00 sec)
```

Note that all employees appear in the results table at least once, because each employee has a last name that matches at least one last name in the same table—and Tom and Jessica Smith appear twice because they both have the last name Smith.

Natural Joins

What's a natural join? Each inner join has two columns that usually share the same values (the columns you join on). A natural join has only one, at most, of these columns in the result.

That is, a natural join is an inner join where each column is unique. Here's an example of a join that is not a natural join, because it lists the supervisor ID from both the Employees table and the Supervisors table for each employee:

```
> SELECT Employees.firstname, Employees.lastname,
Employees.supervisor, Supervisors.id AS 'supervisor id'
FROM Employees, Supervisors
WHERE Employees.supervisor = Supervisors.id;
+-----------+----------+------------+---------------+
| firstname | lastname | supervisor | supervisor id |
+-----------+----------+------------+---------------+
| John      | Wood     | 1001       | 1001          |
| Mary      | Green    | 1501       | 1501          |
| Daniel    | Grant    | 1501       | 1501          |
| Nancy     | Jackson  | 1501       | 1501          |
| Tom       | Smith    | 1701       | 1701          |
| Jessica   | Smith    | 1701       | 1701          |
+-----------+----------+------------+---------------+
6 rows in set (0.00 sec)
```

To call something a natural join, just omit duplicate columns:

```
> SELECT Employees.firstname, Employees.lastname,
Supervisors.id AS 'supervisor id'
FROM Employees, Supervisors
WHERE Employees.supervisor = Supervisors.id;
+-----------+----------+---------------+
| firstname | lastname | supervisor id |
+-----------+----------+---------------+
| John      | Wood     | 1001          |
| Mary      | Green    | 1501          |
| Daniel    | Grant    | 1501          |
| Nancy     | Jackson  | 1501          |
| Tom       | Smith    | 1701          |
| Jessica   | Smith    | 1701          |
+-----------+----------+---------------+
6 rows in set (0.00 sec)
```

Outer Joins

We've discussed inner joins, which are the standard SQL join. Now we look at outer joins. Please note that outer joins must be considered advanced SQL, and as such, you can skip this section if you like. Understanding outer joins is a little tricky.

You've seen how inner joins work; outer joins include all rows from a table, whether or not they meet the join condition.

Here's an example. To get the first name, last name, and phone extension of all employees from the Employees table who are also supervisors, use the following inner join:

```
> SELECT Employees.firstname, Employees.lastname, extension
FROM Employees INNER JOIN Supervisors
ON Employees.id = Supervisors.id;
+-----------+----------+-----------+
| firstname | lastname | extension |
+-----------+----------+-----------+
| John      | Wood     | 244       |
| Nancy     | Jackson  | 255       |
+-----------+----------+-----------+
2 rows in set (0.00 sec)
```

Now say you want to include all employees from the Employees table in the result table but just give NULL phone extensions to those who are not supervisors. You can do that with an OUTER JOIN, which you can make copy all rows from the Employees table (the left table in the outer join, as specified below with the keywords LEFT OUTER JOIN), and which puts a NULL into columns for fields from rows where the JOIN condition wasn't true:

```
> SELECT Employees.firstname, Employees.lastname, extension
FROM Employees LEFT OUTER JOIN Supervisors
ON Employees.id = Supervisors.id;
+-----------+----------+-----------+
| firstname | lastname | extension |
+-----------+----------+-----------+
| John      | Wood     | 244       |
| Mary      | Green    | NULL      |
| Daniel    | Grant    | NULL      |
| Nancy     | Jackson  | 255       |
| Tom       | Smith    | NULL      |
| Jessica   | Smith    | NULL      |
+-----------+----------+-----------+
6 rows in set (0.00 sec)
```

Now all employees appear in the table, and it's easy to pick out which ones are also supervisors, because they have numbers, not NULL, in their extension field.

Note that an outer join includes all rows from the table to the left of the OUTER JOIN keywords or the table to the right of OUTER JOIN (your choice), and includes NULLs for fields that don't match the join condition.

A right outer join displays all rows from the Supervisors table, because that's the table you've specified to the right of the OUTER JOIN keywords. This join leaves NULL any fields where the join condition was false—that is, for supervisors not listed in the Employees table (note that a NULL value translates into an empty string for the test fields firstname and lastname). Here's what the right join looks like:

```
> SELECT Employees.firstname, Employees.lastname, extension
FROM Employees RIGHT OUTER JOIN Supervisors
ON Employees.id = Supervisors.id;
+-----------+----------+-----------+
| firstname | lastname | extension |
+-----------+----------+-----------+
|           |          | 231       |
| John      | Wood     | 244       |
| Nancy     | Jackson  | 255       |
+-----------+----------+-----------+
3 rows in set (0.00 sec)
```

Note that supervisor George Edward's name is not listed, because although he appears in the Supervisors table, he doesn't appear in the Employees table.

The Least You Need to Know

- Joins let you recover data from multiple tables.
- You create an inner join by listing the tables from which you want to recover data separated by commas, and a WHERE clause specifying the join condition, or by using the INNER JOIN syntax and ON in place of WHERE.
- Using aliases enables you to rename columns and tables on the fly.
- Outer joins include all rows from either joined table (your choice) with NULL or empty string values for fields from the second table where the join condition was not met.

Aggregating and Grouping Data

In This Chapter

- Returning the average value with AVG()
- Returning the number of rows with COUNT()
- Returning the largest and smallest value with MAX() and MIN()
- Returning the sum with SUM()
- Filtering aggregate results
- Creating groups with GROUP BY

This chapter is about summarizing and grouping data. We summarize data with the aggregate functions, which average your data, count items, and so on. And we group data with the GROUP BY clause to organize longer tables.

Let's start with the aggregating functions.

Using the Aggregating Functions

As we saw in Chapter 8, SQL comes with some built-in functions, and most DBMSes add to that list. SQL also comes with some built-in aggregating functions, which let you handle many data items at the same time, counting them, averaging them, and so on. We start with the AVG() function, which averages data items.

AVG() Returns the Average Value

The AVG() function averages values. Look at the Employees table:

```
> SELECT * FROM Employees;
+-----------+----------+------------+------------+------------+------+
| firstname | lastname | department | hiredate   | supervisor | id   |
+-----------+----------+------------+------------+------------+------+
| John      | Wood     | Sales      | 2012-01-15 | 1001       | 1501 |
| Mary      | Green    | Sales      | 2012-01-15 | 1501       | 1601 |
| Daniel    | Grant    | Sales      | 2012-01-15 | 1501       | 1602 |
| Nancy     | Jackson  | Accounting | 2012-02-20 | 1501       | 1701 |
| Tom       | Smith    | Accounting | 2012-03-15 | 1701       | 1801 |
| Jessica   | Smith    | Accounting | 2012-03-15 | 1701       | 1901 |
+-----------+----------+------------+------------+------------+------+
6 rows in set (0.01 sec)
```

The only real candidates we have for the AVG() function are the supervisor values and the ID values. We demonstrate how to use AVG() on the ID values:

```
> SELECT AVG(id) FROM Employees;
+-----------+
| AVG(id)   |
+-----------+
| 1684.5000 |
+-----------+
1 row in set (0.00 sec)
```

And that's all it takes. Just use SELECT AVG(id) FROM Employees, and you get the average value of the employees' IDs.

> **SQL TIP**
>
> NULL values are ignored by the AVG() function. Because NULL is an indeterminate value, SQL can't assign a value to it to use in the AVG() function.

COUNT() Returns the Number of Rows

The COUNT() function does just that—it counts items. For example, we can count how many records we have in the Employees table, like the following:

```
> SELECT COUNT(*) FROM Employees;
+----------+
| COUNT(*) |
+----------+
| 6        |
+----------+
1 row in set (0.02 sec)
```

You can also get a count of the non-NULL number of records in the table by counting the number of entries in a column. In the following example, we count the number of firstname entries in the Employees table:

```
> SELECT COUNT(firstname) FROM Employees;
+----------+
| COUNT(*) |
+----------+
| 6        |
+----------+
1 row in set (0.02 sec)
```

If you don't like the results returned as COUNT(*), use an alias instead, like the following:

```
> SELECT COUNT(*) AS 'Number of Employees' FROM Employees;
+---------------------+
| Number of Employees |
+---------------------+
| 6                   |
+---------------------+
1 row in set (0.02 sec)
```

SQL TIP

NULL values are ignored by the COUNT() function if you specify a column name, but not if you specify the * wildcard.

You can also use filtering (that is, a WHERE clause) with aggregate functions, as here, where we count all employees whose last names are not Smith:

```
> SELECT COUNT(*) FROM Employees WHERE lastname != 'Smith'
+----------+
| COUNT(*) |
+----------+
| 4        |
+----------+
1 row in set (0.02 sec)
```

MAX() and MIN() Return the Largest and Smallest Value

The MAX() and MIN() functions return the maximum and minimum values in a column, respectively. You have to use these functions with column names or MAX(*) or MIN(*) doesn't work.

For example, you can find the maximum ID value in the Employees table:

```
> SELECT MAX(id) FROM Employees;
+---------+
| MAX(id) |
+---------+
| 1901    |
+---------+
1 row in set (0.00 sec)
```

Or you can find the minimum ID value in the Employees table:

```
> SELECT MIN(id) FROM Employees;
+---------+
| MIN(id) |
+---------+
| 1501    |
+---------+
1 row in set (0.00 sec)
```

To find which employee has the highest ID value, use a subquery the following way:

```
> SELECT firstname, lastname FROM Employees
WHERE id = (SELECT MAX(id) FROM Employees);
+-----------+----------+
| firstname | lastname |
+-----------+----------+
| Jessica   | Smith    |
+-----------+----------+
1 row in set (0.00 sec)
```

You can even use MAX() and MIN() on non-numeric values (not all DBMSes support this). In the following example, we find who has the maximum last name in terms of alphanumeric sort order:

```
> SELECT MAX(lastname) FROM Employees;
+---------------+
| MAX(lastname) |
+---------------+
| Wood          |
+---------------+
1 row in set (0.00 sec)
```

SQL TIP

NULL values are ignored by the MAX() and MIN() functions. So if you have NULL values in your tables, be careful about using MAX() and MIN().

SUM() Returns the Sum

The SUM() aggregate function returns the sum of a column of values. Here's an example where we add up everybody's ID values:

```
> SELECT SUM(id) FROM Employees;
+---------+
| SUM(id) |
+---------+
| 10107   |
+---------+
1 row in set (0.00 sec)
```

You can also use SUM() in combination with other functions, of course. Here's how we use SUM() and COUNT() to find the average ID value:

```
> SELECT SUM(id) / COUNT(id) AS 'Average ID' FROM Employees;
+------------+
| Average ID |
+------------+
| 1684.5000  |
+------------+
1 row in set (0.02 sec)
```

Although I say to use functions like MIN(), MAX(), or AVG() on single columns, the truth is that you are using these functions on single *values*. So as long as you feed these functions a set of single values, they won't complain. That means you actually can use these functions on multiple columns if you end up with a single value for each row. For example, you can find the sum of everyone's ID values plus their Supervisor ID values, like the following:

```
> SELECT SUM(supervisor + id) FROM Employees;
+----------------------+
| SUM(supervisor + id) |
+----------------------+
| 19013                |
+----------------------+
1 row in set (0.02 sec)
```

NULL values are ignored by the SUM() function, so if you have any NULL values, they will not be added to the sum.

Aggregating on Distinct Values

You might notice that we have two employees with the same last name in the Employees table—Tom Smith and Jessica Smith:

```
> SELECT * FROM Employees;
+-----------+----------+------------+------------+------------+------+
| firstname | lastname | department | hiredate   | supervisor | id   |
+-----------+----------+------------+------------+------------+------+
| John      | Wood     | Sales      | 2012-01-15 | 1001       | 1501 |
| Mary      | Green    | Sales      | 2012-01-15 | 1501       | 1601 |
| Daniel    | Grant    | Sales      | 2012-01-15 | 1501       | 1602 |
| Nancy     | Jackson  | Accounting | 2012-02-20 | 1501       | 1701 |
| Tom       | Smith    | Accounting | 2012-03-15 | 1701       | 1801 |
| Jessica   | Smith    | Accounting | 2012-03-15 | 1701       | 1901 |
+-----------+----------+------------+------------+------------+------+
6 rows in set (0.00 sec)
```

We can get a count of all last names in the Employees table with the COUNT() function:

```
> SELECT COUNT(lastname) AS 'All Last Names' FROM Employees;
+----------------+
| All Last Names |
+----------------+
| 6              |
+----------------+
1 row in set (0.00 sec)
```

In fact, COUNT(lastname) is short for COUNT(ALL lastname), where the ALL means select all non-NULL values. So this is the same thing as COUNT(lastname):

```
> SELECT COUNT(ALL lastname) AS 'All Last Names' FROM Employees;
+----------------+
| All Last Names |
+----------------+
| 6              |
+----------------+
1 row in set (0.00 sec)
```

ALL is the default, so you don't have to include it when using an aggregate function, but there's another option: DISTINCT. When you use DISTINCT, you get only unique values, which means that only one "Smith" last name will be counted, giving you only 5 unique last names, as you see here:

```
> SELECT COUNT(DISTINCT lastname) AS 'Distinct Last Names' FROM Employees;
+---------------------+
| Distinct Last Names |
+---------------------+
| 5                   |
+---------------------+
1 row in set (0.02 sec)
```

Creating Groups

In the Employees table, you find there's a good bit of data:

```
> SELECT * FROM Employees;
+-----------+----------+------------+------------+------------+------+
| firstname | lastname | department | hiredate   | supervisor | id   |
+-----------+----------+------------+------------+------------+------+
| John      | Wood     | Sales      | 2012-01-15 | 1001       | 1501 |
| Mary      | Green    | Sales      | 2012-01-15 | 1501       | 1601 |
| Daniel    | Grant    | Sales      | 2012-01-15 | 1501       | 1602 |
| Nancy     | Jackson  | Accounting | 2012-02-20 | 1501       | 1701 |
| Tom       | Smith    | Accounting | 2012-03-15 | 1701       | 1801 |
| Jessica   | Smith    | Accounting | 2012-03-15 | 1701       | 1901 |
+-----------+----------+------------+------------+------------+------+
6 rows in set (0.00 sec)
```

It might be helpful to work with subsets of that data—for example, all employees in the Sales department, or all employees in the accounting department.

That's what groups are for—using groups, you can work with a subset of a table's data.

You create groups with the GROUP BY statement like the following, where we create groups of records where each group has the same department value with a GROUP BY department clause:

```
> SELECT department
FROM Employees GROUP BY department;
+------------+
| department |
+------------+
| Accounting |
| Sales      |
+------------+
2 rows in set (0.00 sec)
```

What happened? That result doesn't look useful. All it tells you is that there are two groups of records: one that has department set to "Sales" and one that has department set to "Accounting."

In fact, now that we created some groups, you can use aggregate functions on those groups. Take a look at the next section.

Using Aggregate Functions on Groups

You can also use aggregate functions on groups. For example, after you create groups, you can refer to all the members of a group with the * wildcard. So, for example, to count the number of members in each of the two groups, you can ask to see COUNT(*):

```
> SELECT department, COUNT(*) AS number
FROM Employees GROUP BY department;
+------------+--------+
| department | number |
+------------+--------+
| Accounting | 3      |
| Sales      | 3      |
+------------+--------+
2 rows in set (0.02 sec)
```

Now we know that there are three records in the Accounting group and three records in the Sales group.

You can use any of the aggregate functions on groups. For example, to find the average ID value in the Accounting group and in the Sales group, use AVG(*):

```
> SELECT department, COUNT(*), AVG(id) AS number
FROM Employees GROUP BY department;
+------------+----------+-----------+
| department | COUNT(*) | number    |
+------------+----------+-----------+
| Accounting | 3        | 1801.0000 |
| Sales      | 3        | 1568.0000 |
+------------+----------+-----------+
2 rows in set (0.03 sec)
```

And that's the power of groups. You can group data into subsets and then run aggregate functions such as AVG() or MAX() and MIN() on the subgroup.

You can also use aggregate functions on individual columns like the following, where we find the maximum ID value in the Sales and Accounting groups:

```
> SELECT department, MAX(id)
FROM Employees GROUP BY department;
+------------+---------+
| department | MAX(id) |
+------------+---------+
| Accounting | 1901    |
| Sales      | 1602    |
+------------+---------+
2 rows in set (0.01 sec)
```

SQL TIP

Many DBMSes do not allow grouping based on variable-length fields.

Nesting Groups

How about nesting groups? You can also specify multiple columns in which to group. SQL groups by the first column, then by the second, then the third, and so on.

For example, you can group the Employees table by department, then by supervisor ID to find how many employees have which supervisor in which department:

```
> SELECT department, supervisor, COUNT(*)
FROM Employees GROUP BY department, supervisor;
+------------+------------+----------+
| department | supervisor | COUNT(*) |
+------------+------------+----------+
| Accounting | 1501       | 1        |
| Accounting | 1701       | 2        |
| Sales      | 1001       | 1        |
| Sales      | 1501       | 2        |
+------------+------------+----------+
4 rows in set (0.00 sec)
```

Filtering Groups

You can also filter groups, retaining only the groups that meet your filtering criteria. To filter groups, you can use the HAVING clause. For example, you might want to view only groups by department and supervisor where each group has more than one member. That looks like the following:

```
> SELECT department, supervisor, COUNT(*)
FROM Employees GROUP BY department, supervisor
HAVING COUNT(*) > 1;
+------------+------------+----------+
| department | supervisor | COUNT(*) |
+------------+------------+----------+
| Accounting | 1701       | 2        |
| Sales      | 1501       | 2        |
+------------+------------+----------+
2 rows in set (0.00 sec)
```

SQL TIP

Why do you have to use a HAVING clause to filter groups? Why not a WHERE clause? The reason is that you can also use WHERE clauses with the SELECT statement when you create groups; the GROUP BY clause must come after the WHERE clause and before HAVING clauses.

Grouping and Sorting

Want to sort your groups? No trouble at all—just use an ORDER BY clause.

For example, to sort department groups by supervisor ID, use an ORDER BY clause like the following:

```
> SELECT department, supervisor, COUNT(*)
FROM Employees GROUP BY department, supervisor
HAVING COUNT(*) > 1
ORDER BY supervisor;
+------------+------------+----------+
| department | supervisor | COUNT(*) |
+------------+------------+----------+
| Sales      | 1501       | 2        |
| Accounting | 1701       | 2        |
+------------+------------+----------+
2 rows in set (0.02 sec)
```

And that's it for aggregate functions and groups.

The Least You Need to Know

- The AVG() aggregate function returns the average value of a set of values.
- The COUNT() aggregate function returns the number of rows in a set of values.
- The MAX() and MIN() aggregate functions return the largest and smallest value in a set.
- The SUM() aggregate function returns the sum of a set of values.
- Create groups with the GROUP BY clause, which groups together records based on one or more columns' values.
- You can filter, nest, and sort groups.

Views, Unions, and Variables

In This Chapter

- Working with views
- Creating some views
- Employing views to simplify joins
- Creating views and calculated fields
- Working with variables

Views are virtual tables that don't hold data. They just hold a query. Every time you want to access a view, the query underlying the view is run and you can work with the results of that query as though they made up an actual table.

There are several reasons for using views. For example, you can use views to break up complex SQL statements into easier handled shorter queries. We look at how that works first.

We'll also take a look at unions in this chapter; unions let you overlap tables in ways that are useful. And we'll also take a look at working with variables in SQL here. Variables work in SQL just as they do in other languages—they act as named memory locations where you can store your data, allowing you to write more complex procedures.

Understanding Views

As mentioned, views are virtual tables created with a dynamically executed SQL statement. For example, say you have a complex SQL statement like the following, which generates a table with employees' first names, last names, department, and the phone extension of their supervisor (from the Supervisors table we constructed in Chapter 9):

```
> SELECT E.firstname, E.lastname, E.department, S.extension
AS 'supervisor extension'
FROM Employees AS E INNER JOIN Supervisors AS S
ON E.supervisor = S.id;
+-----------+----------+------------+---------------------+
| firstname | lastname | department | supervisor extension |
+-----------+----------+------------+---------------------+
| John      | Wood     | Sales      | 231                 |
| Mary      | Green    | Sales      | 244                 |
| Daniel    | Grant    | Sales      | 244                 |
| Nancy     | Jackson  | Accounting | 244                 |
| Tom       | Smith    | Accounting | 255                 |
| Jessica   | Smith    | Accounting | 255                 |
+-----------+----------+------------+---------------------+
6 rows in set (0.00 sec)
```

Now suppose you want to view just the employees who are in Sales. You can write the whole SQL query all over again and add WHERE E.department = 'Sales':

```
> SELECT E.firstname, E.lastname, E.department, S.extension
FROM Employees AS E INNER JOIN Supervisors AS S
ON E.supervisor = S.id WHERE E.department = 'Sales';
+-----------+----------+------------+-----------+
| firstname | lastname | department | extension |
+-----------+----------+------------+-----------+
| John      | Wood     | Sales      | 231       |
| Mary      | Green    | Sales      | 244       |
| Daniel    | Grant    | Sales      | 244       |
+-----------+----------+------------+-----------+
3 rows in set (0.03 sec)
```

Or you can create an interim table named Phonebook of the results from the SQL query:

```
CREATE VIEW Phonebook AS
SELECT E.firstname, E.lastname, E.department, S.extension
FROM Employees AS E INNER JOIN Supervisors AS S
ON E.supervisor = S.id;
```

And then execute the query SELECT * FROM Phonebook
WHERE E.department = 'Sales':

```
> SELECT * FROM Phonebook WHERE E.department = 'Sales';
+-----------+----------+------------+-----------+
| firstname | lastname | department | extension |
+-----------+----------+------------+-----------+
| John      | Wood     | Sales      | 231       |
| Mary      | Green    | Sales      | 244       |
| Daniel    | Grant    | Sales      | 244       |
+-----------+----------+------------+-----------+
3 rows in set (0.03 sec)
```

The interim table, Phonebook, is a view in this case. It's not really
a table that exists in the database; it's a query that produces a table,
and having that view available means you don't have to remember the
complex SQL statement to create it again.

Not only are views helpful so that you don't have to use a complex
SQL statement, but they are also used for the following reasons:

- You don't have to keep using a complex SQL statement
  that you make small modifications to every time you use it.
  Instead, you can use the complex SQL statement to create
  a view, a pseudo-table, that you want then apply various fil-
  ters to.

- If you have a large table and only want to work with a small
  subset of it, you can use a view to create what acts like a
  much smaller table containing the subset of data you want.

- Views are also good for security. If you don't want to give
  individuals access to a whole table, you can just give them a
  view, which lets them look only at the part of the table you
  want to show.

- You can do your own calculations—such as finding averages
  or maximums, or performing complex calculations on the
  data in a table—and present the result as a table using views.

Creating Views

Let's look at how to create views now. It's simple: just preface the
SELECT statement with CREATE VIEW *view_name* AS, where
view_name is the name of the view you want to create.

For example, here's how to create a view of only the employees' first and last names from the Employees table, and name the new view names:

```
> CREATE VIEW names AS SELECT firstname, lastname FROM Employees;
Query OK, 0 rows affected (0.03 sec)
```

Now you can treat names as you do any table. For example, here's how we select and view all names in the new view:

```
> SELECT * FROM names;
+-----------+----------+
| firstname | lastname |
+-----------+----------+
| John      | Wood     |
| Mary      | Green    |
| Daniel    | Grant    |
| Nancy     | Jackson  |
| Tom       | Smith    |
| Jessica   | Smith    |
+-----------+----------+
6 rows in set (0.02 sec)
```

Views remain in a database until you delete (drop) them.

SQL CAUTION

If you have SQL Server, omit the semicolon (;) from the end of CREATE VIEW statements.

Using Views to Simplify Joins

Let's look at the join we created at the beginning of this chapter, which lists employees' first name, last name, department, and supervisor phone extension:

```
> SELECT E.firstname, E.lastname, E.department, S.extension
AS 'supervisor extension'
FROM Employees AS E INNER JOIN Supervisors AS S
ON E.supervisor = S.id;
+-----------+----------+------------+----------------------+
| firstname | lastname | department | supervisor extension |
+-----------+----------+------------+----------------------+
| John      | Wood     | Sales      | 231                  |
| Mary      | Green    | Sales      | 244                  |
| Daniel    | Grant    | Sales      | 244                  |
```

```
| Nancy     | Jackson  | Accounting | 244                      |
| Tom       | Smith    | Accounting | 255                      |
| Jessica   | Smith    | Accounting | 255                      |
+-----------+----------+------------+----------------------+
6 rows in set (0.00 sec)
```

Every time you want to filter the results, such as viewing the same table for just Sales employees, you have to re-enter everything and add a filtering WHERE clause:

```
> SELECT E.firstname, E.lastname, E.department, S.extension
FROM Employees AS E INNER JOIN Supervisors AS S
ON E.supervisor = S.id WHERE E.department = 'Sales';
+-----------+----------+------------+-----------+
| firstname | lastname | department | extension |
+-----------+----------+------------+-----------+
| John      | Wood     | Sales      | 231       |
| Mary      | Green    | Sales      | 244       |
| Daniel    | Grant    | Sales      | 244       |
+-----------+----------+------------+-----------+
3 rows in set (0.03 sec)
```

So let's create a view named Phonebook instead, which will hold the results of the SQL join query. You create that view the following way:

```
> CREATE VIEW Phonebook AS
SELECT E.firstname, E.lastname, E.department, S.extension
FROM Employees AS E INNER JOIN Supervisors AS S
ON E.supervisor = S.id;
Query OK, 0 rows affected (0.02 sec)
```

That's great. Now we've created a view named Phonebook. We can view the records in Phonebook (note that the records are not really "in" Phonebook, because Phonebook is created dynamically when you reference it), like the following.

```
> SELECT * FROM Phonebook;
+-----------+----------+------------+-----------+
| firstname | lastname | department | extension |
+-----------+----------+------------+-----------+
| John      | Wood     | Sales      | 231       |
| Mary      | Green    | Sales      | 244       |
| Daniel    | Grant    | Sales      | 244       |
| Nancy     | Jackson  | Accounting | 244       |
| Tom       | Smith    | Accounting | 255       |
| Jessica   | Smith    | Accounting | 255       |
+-----------+----------+------------+-----------+
6 rows in set (0.00 sec)
```

Now you don't have to use the complex join statement that created the Phonebook view; you can just use the view as you like.

For example, you can filter just the Sales employees, as mentioned at the beginning of the chapter:

```
> SELECT * FROM Phonebook WHERE department = 'Sales';
+-----------+----------+------------+-----------+
| firstname | lastname | department | extension |
+-----------+----------+------------+-----------+
| John      | Wood     | Sales      | 231       |
| Mary      | Green    | Sales      | 244       |
| Daniel    | Grant    | Sales      | 244       |
+-----------+----------+------------+-----------+
3 rows in set (0.00 sec)
```

Or you might filter only those whose last names are Smith:

```
> SELECT * FROM Phonebook WHERE lastname = 'Smith';
+-----------+----------+------------+-----------+
| firstname | lastname | department | extension |
+-----------+----------+------------+-----------+
| Tom       | Smith    | Accounting | 255       |
| Jessica   | Smith    | Accounting | 255       |
+-----------+----------+------------+-----------+
2 rows in set (0.00 sec)
```

That's an easier query than the following:

```
> SELECT E.firstname, E.lastname, E.department, S.extension
FROM Employees AS E INNER JOIN Supervisors AS S
ON E.supervisor = S.id WHERE E.lastname = 'Smith';
```

Reformatting Retrieved Data

Joins aren't the only kind of query that are so long that you don't want to retype them every time you want to use them. You might also reformat the data you get from a table, and views can be handy here, too.

For example, you might concatenate employees' first name and last name, and then sort the result by ID the following way:

```
> SELECT CONCATENATE(firstname, ' ', lastname) AS name, id
FROM Employees ORDER BY id;
+---------------+------+
| name          | id   |
+---------------+------+
| John Wood     | 1501 |
| Mary Green    | 1601 |
| Daniel Grant  | 1602 |
| Nancy Jackson | 1701 |
| Tom Smith     | 1801 |
| Jessica Smith | 1901 |
+---------------+------+
6 rows in set (0.00 sec)
```

You can make a view out of this named idview and save a lot of typing whenever you want to retrieve this data in the future:

```
> CREATE VIEW idview AS
SELECT CONCAT(firstname, ' ', lastname) AS name, id
FROM Employees ORDER BY id;
Query OK, 0 rows affected (0.02 sec)
```

Now you can look at the whole view:

```
> SELECT * FROM idview;
+---------------+------+
| name          | id   |
+---------------+------+
| John Wood     | 1501 |
| Mary Green    | 1601 |
| Daniel Grant  | 1602 |
| Nancy Jackson | 1701 |
| Tom Smith     | 1801 |
| Jessica Smith | 1901 |
+---------------+------+
6 rows in set (0.00 sec)
```

Or you can filter it for your needs:

```
> SELECT * FROM idview WHERE id > 1601;
+---------------+------+
| name          | id   |
+---------------+------+
| Daniel Grant  | 1602 |
| Nancy Jackson | 1701 |
| Tom Smith     | 1801 |
| Jessica Smith | 1901 |
+---------------+------+
4 rows in set (0.00 sec)
```

As you can see, using views makes it easier to handle the formatted data here. As usual, any time you have a complex SQL statement that generates the result set you want, and you need to modify the result set, views are a good idea.

Filtering Out Unwanted Data

If you look at the Employees table, you can see that there's a lot of data:

```
> SELECT * FROM Employees;
+-----------+----------+------------+------------+------------+------+
| firstname | lastname | department | hiredate   | supervisor | id   |
+-----------+----------+------------+------------+------------+------+
| John      | Wood     | Sales      | 2012-01-15 | 1001       | 1501 |
| Mary      | Green    | Sales      | 2012-01-15 | 1501       | 1601 |
| Daniel    | Grant    | Sales      | 2012-01-15 | 1501       | 1602 |
| Nancy     | Jackson  | Accounting | 2012-02-20 | 1501       | 1701 |
| Tom       | Smith    | Accounting | 2012-03-15 | 1701       | 1801 |
| Jessica   | Smith    | Accounting | 2012-03-15 | 1701       | 1901 |
+-----------+----------+------------+------------+------------+------+
6 rows in set (0.11 sec)
```

How about trimming it down to only the columns you need—say, firstname, lastname, supervisor, and id?

This task is simple with views. Here's all you do:

```
> CREATE VIEW EmployeesShort AS
SELECT firstname, lastname, supervisor, id
FROM Employees;
Query OK, 0 rows affected (0.00 sec)
```

Now you can look at the abbreviated "table":

```
> SELECT * FROM EmployeesShort;
+-----------+----------+------------+------+
| firstname | lastname | supervisor | id   |
+-----------+----------+------------+------+
| John      | Wood     | 1001       | 1501 |
| Mary      | Green    | 1501       | 1601 |
| Daniel    | Grant    | 1501       | 1602 |
| Nancy     | Jackson  | 1501       | 1701 |
| Tom       | Smith    | 1701       | 1801 |
| Jessica   | Smith    | 1701       | 1901 |
+-----------+----------+------------+------+
6 rows in set (0.00 sec)
```

Here's another example of filtering out unwanted data. Look again at the Supervisors table we created in Chapter 9:

```
> SELECT * FROM Supervisors;
+-----------+----------+------+-----------+
| firstname | lastname | id   | extension |
+-----------+----------+------+-----------+
| George    | Edwards  | 1001 | 231       |
| John      | Wood     | 1501 | 244       |
| Nancy     | Jackson  | 1701 | 255       |
+-----------+----------+------+-----------+
3 rows in set (0.03 sec)
```

Say that you want to notify all supervisors of an important meeting with your robo-caller device, so you want to avoid all NULL phone extensions.

As it happens, there are no NULL phone extensions in the Supervisors table but there could be at some future date. And that's the beauty of views—they're dynamic, so the data in them is updated every time you access them. In other words, you don't create a table and fill it with static data that might be outdated. You work with real-time data from the table from which you create a view.

So to create a view of the Supervisors table that contains only records that have a non-NULL phone extension, do the following:

```
> CREATE VIEW SupervisorsOKPhone AS
SELECT * FROM Supervisors
WHERE extension IS NOT NULL;
Query OK, 0 rows affected (0.00 sec)
```

Now you have a new view, SupervisorsOKPhone, where you can count on all phone extensions not NULL, even if you refer to this view at some point in the future.

SQL TIP

Because views are created dynamically, as you access them, they have some advantages over creating subtables from a table. When you access views of a table, the data in those views is always fresh and up-to-date, while the data in subtables made from a table is static and can be out-of-date.

Note that the SupervisorsOKPhone view was created with a WHERE clause (WHERE extension != NULL). Can you still add WHERE clauses when you use it?

Yes. For example, say you only want supervisors with an ID greater than 1500. You can do the following:

```
> SELECT * FROM SupervisorsOKPhone WHERE id > 1500;
+-----------+----------+------+-----------+
| firstname | lastname | id   | extension |
+-----------+----------+------+-----------+
| John      | Wood     | 1501 | 244       |
| Nancy     | Jackson  | 1701 | 255       |
+-----------+----------+------+-----------+
2 rows in set (0.00 sec)
```

The two WHERE clauses—the one in the view and the one in the SELECT statement that uses the view—are combined.

Using Views and Calculated Fields

Views are also good when you have calculated fields. For example, say you want a view of the Employees table that shows employees' first and last names and salary. To keep things simple, let's give everyone the same salary, except John Wood (id = 1501), who gets more than the others.

You can create a view named Salaries that calculates a salary column the following way (note that we're using the SQL CASE statement here; see Chapter 15 for more information on it):

```
> CREATE VIEW Salaries AS
SELECT firstname, lastname, CASE WHEN id = 1501 THEN 60000
ELSE 45000 END
AS salary
FROM Employees;
Query OK, 0 rows affected (0.00 sec)
```

And here's what the contents of the view look like:

```
> SELECT * FROM salaries;
+-----------+----------+--------+
| firstname | lastname | salary |
+-----------+----------+--------+
| John      | Wood     | 60000  |
| Mary      | Green    | 45000  |
| Daniel    | Grant    | 45000  |
| Nancy     | Jackson  | 45000  |
| Tom       | Smith    | 45000  |
| Jessica   | Smith    | 45000  |
+-----------+----------+--------+
6 rows in set (0.00 sec)
```

Here's another example: say that directions have come down from corporate headquarters that everyone's ID value is to be increased by 1000 to avoid conflicting with the new employees coming on board in a corporate merger. You can create a new view named Ids like the following:

```
> CREATE VIEW Ids AS
SELECT firstname, lastname, hiredate, supervisor,
id + 1000 AS id
FROM Employees;
Query OK, 0 rows affected (0.00 sec)
```

Here are the contents of this view:

```
> SELECT * FROM Ids;
+-----------+----------+------------+------------+------+
| firstname | lastname | hiredate   | supervisor | id   |
+-----------+----------+------------+------------+------+
| John      | Wood     | 2012-01-15 | 1001       | 2501 |
| Mary      | Green    | 2012-01-15 | 1501       | 2601 |
| Daniel    | Grant    | 2012-01-15 | 1501       | 2602 |
| Nancy     | Jackson  | 2012-02-20 | 1501       | 2701 |
| Tom       | Smith    | 2012-03-15 | 1701       | 2801 |
| Jessica   | Smith    | 2012-03-15 | 1701       | 2901 |
+-----------+----------+------------+------------+------+
6 rows in set (0.01 sec)
```

Using Unions

Views come in handy when you combine data from two or more tables with the UNION keyword.

UNION lets you join data without creating a join. It adds data in any number of columns from one table to data in the same number of columns from another (or even the same) table.

Let's look at an example to make it clear what UNION does, and how you can use views with unions. Say you want a table showing all employees in your corporation. Start by looking at the Employees table:

```
> SELECT * FROM Employees;
+-----------+----------+------------+------------+------------+------+
| firstname | lastname | department | hiredate   | supervisor | id   |
+-----------+----------+------------+------------+------------+------+
| John      | Wood     | Sales      | 2012-01-15 | 1001       | 1501 |
| Mary      | Green    | Sales      | 2012-01-15 | 1501       | 1601 |
| Daniel    | Grant    | Sales      | 2012-01-15 | 1501       | 1602 |
| Nancy     | Jackson  | Accounting | 2012-02-20 | 1501       | 1701 |
| Tom       | Smith    | Accounting | 2012-03-15 | 1701       | 1801 |
| Jessica   | Smith    | Accounting | 2012-03-15 | 1701       | 1901 |
+-----------+----------+------------+------------+------------+------+
6 rows in set (0.00 sec)
```

Does the table show all your employees? No. There's also George Edwards, who appears only in the Supervisors table:

```
> SELECT * FROM Supervisors;
+-----------+----------+------+-----------+
| firstname | lastname | id   | extension |
+-----------+----------+------+-----------+
| George    | Edwards  | 1001 | 231       |
| John      | Wood     | 1501 | 244       |
| Nancy     | Jackson  | 1701 | 255       |
+-----------+----------+------+-----------+
3 rows in set (0.00 sec)
```

We can add George Edwards to the list of all employees by fetching the first name and last name of all employees from the Employees table, then adding all employees in the Supervisors table who don't appear in the Employees table:

```
SELECT firstname, lastname FROM Employees
UNION
SELECT firstname, lastname FROM Supervisors
WHERE id NOT IN
(SELECT id FROM Employees);
+-----------+----------+
| firstname | lastname |
+-----------+----------+
| John      | Wood     |
| Mary      | Green    |
| Daniel    | Grant    |
| Nancy     | Jackson  |
```

```
| Tom       | Smith     |
| Jessica   | Smith     |
| George    | Edwards   |
+-----------+-----------+
7 rows in set (0.03 sec)
```

And that's it. We are able to pick up George Edwards and add him to the list from another table using a union.

SQL TIP

Note that the two SELECT statements you use to create the union must return the same number of columns so that the resulting table can have the same number of columns.

Unions are a good place to use views, because you don't have to re-create the whole union each time you want to work with it. You only need to work with the view. Here's how to create a view named AllEmployees with a union:

```
> CREATE VIEW AllEmployees AS
SELECT firstname, lastname FROM Employees
UNION
SELECT firstname, lastname FROM Supervisors
WHERE id NOT IN
(SELECT id FROM Employees);
Query OK, 0 rows affected (0.00 sec)
```

And you can confirm that all employees appear in the view the following way.

```
> SELECT * FROM AllEmployees;
+-----------+-----------+
| firstname | lastname  |
+-----------+-----------+
| John      | Wood      |
| Mary      | Green     |
| Daniel    | Grant     |
| Nancy     | Jackson   |
| Tom       | Smith     |
| Jessica   | Smith     |
| George    | Edwards   |
+-----------+-----------+
7 rows in set (0.03 sec)
```

Deleting Views

Want to delete a view? Just drop it like the following:

```
> DROP VIEW Salaries;
Query OK, 0 rows affected (0.00 sec)
```

That's all there is to it.

Understanding Variables

In SQL, you can use variables as well as constants. Variables are just that—data items whose value can vary.

Variables are good when you have values that change, such as the mark-up factor for various products as inflation rises. Rather than updating dozens of constants to get the new prices of your items, you can change the value of a single variable, and all the prices will update automatically.

You can create a variable by declaring it, where *var_name* is the name of the new variable, *type* is the new variable's data type, and *value* is the new variable's optional default value:

```
DECLARE var_name[,...] type [DEFAULT value];
```

> **SQL TIP**
>
> In your DBMS, you might find that you don't have to declare variables before you use them. You can just use them with the SET statement. That's because most DBMSes don't require (or don't allow) you to declare variables when you use them outside stored procedures (see Chapter 12).

You can set the value stored in a variable with the SET statement like this, where we set a variable named a to 5 (if your DBMS doesn't allow you to declare variables outside stored procedures, don't declare them. Just start with the SET statement):

```
> SET a = 5;
Query OK, 0 rows affected (0.00 sec)
```

Some DBMSes let you omit the SET keyword:

```
> a = 5;
Query OK, 0 rows affected (0.00 sec)
```

If you omit the SET keyword, some DBMSes require you to use :=
as the assignment operator for variables:

```
> a := 5;
Query OK, 0 rows affected (0.00 sec)
```

Use := for the assignment here, not =, because otherwise SQL might
get confused and think you're using an equality operator, which is
also =.

Now you can check the value in the variable with a SELECT
statement:

```
> SELECT a;
+------+
| @a   |
+------+
| 5    |
+------+
1 row in set (0.01 sec)
```

Some DBMSes, like SQL Server and MySQL, require an @ as the
first character in all variable names:

```
> SET @a = 5;
Query OK, 0 rows affected (0.00 sec)

> SELECT @a;
+------+
| @a   |
+------+
| 5    |
+------+
1 row in set (0.01 sec)
```

You can reassign the values in variables at any time:

```
> SET a = 6;
Query OK, 0 rows affected (0.00 sec)

> SELECT a;
+------+
| @a   |
+------+
| 6    |
+------+
1 row in set (0.00 sec)
```

You can assign values to variables in SELECT statements if you want. Say that we assigned 1 to a:

```
> SET a = 1;
Query OK, 0 rows affected (0.00 sec)
```

Assign 2 to b:

```
> SET b = 2;
Query OK, 0 rows affected (0.02 sec)
```

Then you can create a third variable, c, on the fly, assigning it the value a + b like the following in a SELECT statement:

```
> SELECT a, b, c := a + b;
+------+------+---------------+
| @a   | @b   | @c := @a + @b |
+------+------+---------------+
| 1    | 2    | 3             |
+------+------+---------------+
1 row in set (0.00 sec)
```

Here's how you might put a variable to use when retrieving data from a table. Start by declaring a variable named id1:

```
> SET id1 = 1901;
Query OK, 0 rows affected (0.00 sec)
```

Then find all employees whose IDs are equal to id1:

```
> SELECT * FROM Employees WHERE id = id1;
+-----------+----------+------------+------------+------------+------+
| firstname | lastname | department | hiredate   | supervisor | id   |
+-----------+----------+------------+------------+------------+------+
| Jessica   | Smith    | Accounting | 2012-03-15 | 1701       | 1901 |
+-----------+----------+------------+------------+------------+------+
1 row in set (0.00 sec)
```

Can you create a view using a variable like the following?

```
> CREATE VIEW t AS
SELECT firstname, lastname, id + @a AS id
FROM Employees;
```

Nope, views won't accept variables. You can, however, use variables like this when retrieving data from stored procedures, as we see in Chapter 12. We have a lot more to say about variables when we start discussing stored procedures.

The Least You Need to Know

- Views are virtual tables that don't hold data, only SQL statements. Those statements are executed each time the view is accessed.
- Create a view with the CREATE VIEW As statement.
- Views can simplify joins and formatted fields.
- Unions let you add rows from the same or different tables together, as long as the rows all have the same number of columns.
- Variables hold values that you can change.
- You can use variables in many SQL statements.

Power Techniques

The final part is about SQL power techniques. Here, you see how to put your SQL code into stored procedures which, when called, execute code. So if you have long SQL scripts that you need to execute often, this is what you need to learn.

Next, you see how to use SQL transactions so that you can "undo" operations on a database. When you execute SQL inside a transaction, you can undo or roll back those operations to some earlier savepoint.

Finally, you'll see how to use constraints and triggers. These let you guard what happens to your data, letting you make sure that only data you approve of is inserted or updated in tables.

Stored Procedures and Cursors

In This Chapter

- Working with procedures
- Creating and passing data to procedures
- Working with cursors
- Putting cursors to work

In this chapter, we look at creating stored procedures—that is, collections of SQL statements that you can run by calling them, just like the procedures you find in other programming languages.

Creating stored procedures is great if you have several SQL statements you need to execute often. For example, say that you have a stored procedure that updates the prices of various products in a table. You can call the procedure daily to make sure your table is always up-to-date.

We also look at working with cursors in this chapter. A cursor is a location in the result set of an SQL query, and you can move cursors up and down in results sets, fetching records from various locations at will.

Let's get started with procedures.

Understanding Procedures

Say that you have 25 lines of SQL that you have to enter every day to refresh the data in your databases—for example, with new inventory count.

SQL CAUTION

Please note that different DBMSes will act differently here. If you're using PHPAdmin, for example, switch to using the MySQL command line here.

You can continue to type those 25 lines of SQL code every day, but that's a pretty error-prone proposition. Sooner or later, you'll make a mistake. Not to mention getting tired of typing all the SQL every day.

It's better to pack all the SQL into a procedure, and then just run the procedure every day—no fuss, no muss. There is just one simple line to be entered as opposed to 25 lines.

Procedures can take several lines of code, store them, and then run them on command. They're useful for collecting large SQL scripts into a single, callable routine, and making it easier to handle changes to that SQL by storing it all in one place.

For example, you can run a procedure in these cases:

- To create backups of all your tables automatically

- As a procedure you pass data to and that returns data back to you

- As a procedure that works much like a view, returning a result set of customers ordered by city, for example, but which you can also pass data to select the cities you're interested in (you can't pass data to views)

We look at how to create procedures here next.

Creating a Procedure

There is no standard ANSI SQL syntax to for creating procedures, which means every DBMS has its own syntax. For example, you might want a simple procedure that just returns a value of 5. That looks like the following in Oracle:

```
CREATE PROCEDURE simple (OUT param1 INT)
AS
BEGIN
  param1 := 5;
END
```

Or this in SQL Server:

```
CREATE PROCEDURE simple @param1 INT
AS
  @param1 = 5;
  RETURN @param1;
```

Or this in MySQL:

```
CREATE PROCEDURE simple (OUT param1 INT)
BEGIN
  SET param1 = 5;
END
```

As you can see, the syntax is more or less similar. You always have a CREATE PROCEDURE line, then usually enclose your SQL inside BEGIN and END.

So although it's possible to discuss creating stored procedures in general, you might have to look at your DBMS's documentations for the specifics.

SQL CAUTION

As we develop stored procedures, bear in mind that procedure syntax varies by DBMS, and you might have to customize the code for your own DBMS.

Executing SQL from Procedures

Here's an example that creates and executes a stored procedure. In the Employees table, say that you want to move Tom Smith into the Sales department.

```
> SELECT * FROM Employees;
+-----------+----------+------------+------------+------------+------+
| firstname | lastname | department | hiredate   | supervisor | id   |
+-----------+----------+------------+------------+------------+------+
| John      | Wood     | Sales      | 2012-01-15 | 1001       | 1501 |
| Mary      | Green    | Sales      | 2012-01-15 | 1501       | 1601 |
| Daniel    | Grant    | Sales      | 2012-01-15 | 1501       | 1602 |
| Nancy     | Jackson  | Accounting | 2012-02-20 | 1501       | 1701 |
| Tom       | Smith    | Accounting | 2012-03-15 | 1701       | 1801 |
| Jessica   | Smith    | Accounting | 2012-03-15 | 1701       | 1901 |
+-----------+----------+------------+------------+------------+------+
6 rows in set (0.06 sec)
```

When entering a stored procedure in your DBMS, you have to create that procedure first—and that involves entering many lines of SQL that end with semicolons (;)—and when the DBMS sees a semicolon, it tries to execute that line of SQL immediately.

To avoid that, it's common to change the end-of-line marker, or delimiter, from a semicolon to something else like // when you create a new stored procedure.

To change the end-of-line delimiter, use the following line:

```
> DELIMITER //
```

Now create a new procedure named updatetable like the following:

```
> CREATE PROCEDURE updatetable()
...
```

SQL TIP

The parentheses following the word updatetable is used when we start passing data to procedures. They won't be used in this example, but you still need them to create procedures in most DBMSes.

Now add the BEGIN and END keywords:

```
> CREATE PROCEDURE updatetable()
BEGIN
 ...
END
```

And finally, add the SQL you want to execute between BEGIN and END (there can be as many lines of SQL between BEGIN and END as you need):

```
> CREATE PROCEDURE updatetable( )
BEGIN
  UPDATE Employees SET department = 'Sales' WHERE id =1801;
END
```

To complete the procedure, enter the // delimiter:

```
> CREATE PROCEDURE updatetable( )
BEGIN
  UPDATE Employees SET department = 'Sales' WHERE id =1801;
END
//
Query OK, 0 rows affected (0.00 sec)
```

That creates the new procedure; now you can change the end-of-line delimiter back to a semicolon:

```
> DELIMITER ;
```

To execute the procedure, you can use the CALL statement:

```
> CALL updatetable( );
Query OK, 1 row affected (0.00 sec)
```

Then check the Employees table to make sure the change was made. As you can see, Tom Smith was moved to Sales:

```
> SELECT * FROM Employees;
+-----------+----------+------------+------------+------------+------+
| firstname | lastname | department | hiredate   |supervisor  | id   |
+-----------+----------+------------+------------+------------+------+
| John      | Wood     | Sales      | 2012-01-15 | 1001       | 1501 |
| Mary      | Green    | Sales      | 2012-01-15 | 1501       | 1601 |
| Daniel    | Grant    | Sales      | 2012-01-15 | 1501       | 1602 |
| Nancy     | Jackson  | Accounting | 2012-02-20 | 1501       | 1701 |
| Tom       | Smith    | Sales      | 2012-03-15 | 1701       | 1801 |
| Jessica   | Smith    | Accounting | 2012-03-15 | 1701       | 1901 |
+-----------+----------+------------+------------+------------+------+
6 rows in set (0.00 sec)
```

Returning Data from Procedures

Procedures can also return data. For example, you can build a procedure to start that just returns a value of 5.

First, set the end-of-line delimiter to //:

```
> DELIMITER //
```

Then create a new procedure named return5():

```
> CREATE PROCEDURE return5 (OUT param1 INT)
  ...
```

Note the contents of the parentheses here: OUT param1 INT. The OUT keyword indicates that the data we store in param1 will be returned by the procedure, and the INT keyword gives the type of the data (which could have been FLOAT, VARCAHR[20], and so on).

Now add the BEGIN and END:

```
> CREATE PROCEDURE return5 (OUT param1 INT)
BEGIN
  ...
END
//
Query OK, 0 rows affected (0.05 sec)
```

To return a value of 5, we just set the OUT variable param1 to 5 this way:

```
> CREATE PROCEDURE return5 (OUT param1 INT)
BEGIN
  SET param1 = 5;
END
//
Query OK, 0 rows affected (0.05 sec)
```

Now you can change the end-of-line delimiter back to a semicolon:

```
> DELIMITER ;
```

And you can use the return5 procedure, passing it a variable, @a, inside the parentheses (bear in mind that your DBMS may not require an at sign [@] in front of variable names):

```
> CALL return5(@a);
Query OK, 0 rows affected (0.00 sec)
```

The procedure sets the passed variable, @a, to 5, which you can confirm with a SELECT statement:

```
> SELECT @a;
+------+
| @a   |
+------+
| 5    |
+------+
1 row in set (0.00 sec)
```

Here's another one. In this case, you want to return the number of rows in the Employees table. Start by setting the end-of-line delimiter to //:

```
> DELIMITER //
```

Then create a procedure named counter():

```
> CREATE PROCEDURE counter (OUT param1 INT)
BEGIN
  ...
END;
```

To get the number of rows from Employees into the param1 variable, we can use the SQL SET param1 = SELECT COUNT(*) FROM Employees, but let's use the following alternate syntax:

```
> CREATE PROCEDURE counter (OUT param1 INT)
BEGIN
  SELECT COUNT(*) INTO param1 FROM Employees;
END;
//
Query OK, 0 rows affected (0.00 sec)
```

The SELECT statement here stores the count in param1. Now you can change the end-of-line delimiter back to a semicolon:

```
> DELIMITER ;
```

And you can call counter, putting the count into a variable named @a this way:

```
> CALL counter(@a);
Query OK, 0 rows affected (0.00 sec)
```

You can confirm that @a holds the count like the following.

```
> SELECT @a;
+------+
| @a   |
+------+
| 6    |
+------+
1 row in set (0.00 sec)
```

Passing Data to Procedures

You can also pass data to procedures. For example, say that you want to change Nancy Jackson's supervisor ID from 1501 to 1001:

```
> SELECT * FROM Employees;
+-----------+----------+------------+------------+------------+------+
| firstname | lastname | department | hiredate   | supervisor | id   |
+-----------+----------+------------+------------+------------+------+
| John      | Wood     | Sales      | 2012-01-15 | 1001       | 1501 |
| Mary      | Green    | Sales      | 2012-01-15 | 1501       | 1601 |
| Daniel    | Grant    | Sales      | 2012-01-15 | 1501       | 1602 |
| Nancy     | Jackson  | Accounting | 2012-02-20 | 1501       | 1701 |
| Tom       | Smith    | Accounting | 2012-03-15 | 1701       | 1801 |
| Jessica   | Smith    | Accounting | 2012-03-15 | 1701       | 1901 |
+-----------+----------+------------+------------+------------+------+
6 rows in set (0.00 sec)
```

To do that, we can create a new procedure named updater():

```
> CREATE PROCEDURE updater(IN new_supervisor INT)
...
```

To pass the new supervisor ID to this procedure, you declare a parameter named new_supervisor as an IN parameter of type INT.

You can update the table with the new supervisor ID like the following:

```
> CREATE PROCEDURE updater(IN new_supervisor INT)
BEGIN
  UPDATE Employees SET supervisor = new_supervisor WHERE id = 1701;
END
//
Query OK, 0 rows affected (0.13 sec)
```

You can call updater(), passing it the new supervisor ID, 1001, this way:

```
> CALL updater(1001);
Query OK, 1 row affected (0.02 sec)
```

And finally, check the Employees table to make sure Nancy Jackson's supervisor's ID updated properly:

```
> SELECT * FROM Employees;
+-----------+----------+------------+------------+------------+------+
| firstname | lastname | department | hiredate   | supervisor | id   |
+-----------+----------+------------+------------+------------+------+
| John      | Wood     | Sales      | 2012-01-15 | 1001       | 1501 |
| Mary      | Green    | Sales      | 2012-01-15 | 1501       | 1601 |
| Daniel    | Grant    | Sales      | 2012-01-15 | 1501       | 1602 |
| Nancy     | Jackson  | Accounting | 2012-02-20 | 1001       | 1701 |
| Tom       | Smith    | Accounting | 2012-03-15 | 1701       | 1801 |
| Jessica   | Smith    | Accounting | 2012-03-15 | 1701       | 1901 |
+-----------+----------+------------+------------+------------+------+
6 rows in set (0.01 sec)
```

It worked, as you can see.

You can pass as many parameters to procedures, and get as many back as you like. For example, you might pass two parameters to a procedure named updater2()—the employee ID and the employee's new supervisor ID:

```
> CREATE PROCEDURE updater2(IN emp_id INT,IN new_supervisor INT)
BEGIN
  UPDATE Employees SET supervisor = new_supervisor WHERE id = emp_id;
END
//
Query OK, 0 rows affected (0.00 sec)
```

Note that you just have to separate multiple parameters with commas when declaring them inside the parentheses.

You can change Nancy Jackson's (id = 1701) supervisor's ID back to 1501 by calling updater2() the following way. Note that the two parameters we pass to updater2() are separated by a comma:

```
> CALL updater2(1701, 1501);
Query OK, 1 row affected (0.00 sec)
```

And you can check that Nancy Jackson's supervisor's ID is back to
1501:

```
> SELECT * FROM Employees;
+-----------+----------+------------+------------+------------+------+
| firstname | lastname | department | hiredate   | supervisor | id   |
+-----------+----------+------------+------------+------------+------+
| John      | Wood     | Sales      | 2012-01-15 | 1001       | 1501 |
| Mary      | Green    | Sales      | 2012-01-15 | 1501       | 1601 |
| Daniel    | Grant    | Sales      | 2012-01-15 | 1501       | 1602 |
| Nancy     | Jackson  | Accounting | 2012-02-20 | 1501       | 1701 |
| Tom       | Smith    | Accounting | 2012-03-15 | 1701       | 1801 |
| Jessica   | Smith    | Accounting | 2012-03-15 | 1701       | 1901 |
+-----------+----------+------------+------------+------------+------+
6 rows in set (0.00 sec)
```

Here's a procedure that both takes data and returns data. You pass
the adder() procedure two numbers to add, and it returns the sum.
To create this procedure, you pass it two numbers (a and b) and it
returns a + b (as parameter c):

```
> CREATE PROCEDURE adder(IN a INT, IN b INT, OUT c INT)
BEGIN
  SET c = a + b;
END
//
Query OK, 0 rows affected (0.00 sec)
```

You can use adder() to add 3 + 4:

```
> CALL adder(3, 4, @c);
Query OK, 0 rows affected (0.00 sec)
```

And you end up with 7:

```
> SELECT @c;
+------+
| @c   |
+------+
| 7    |
+------+
1 row in set (0.00 sec)
```

Using Local Variables

You might want to use variables inside a procedure, and such variables defined and used inside a procedure are called *local variables*.

For example, you might declare and use a local variable named temp in a procedure named adder2() like the following:

```
> CREATE PROCEDURE adder2(IN a INT, IN b INT, OUT c INT)
BEGIN
  DECLARE temp INT;
  SELECT a + b INTO temp;
  SELECT temp INTO c;
END
//
Query OK, 0 rows affected (0.00 sec)
```

Now you can try adding 4 + 11:

```
> CALL adder2(4, 11, @a);
Query OK, 0 rows affected (0.02 sec)
```

And we can check the answer, which, sure enough, is 15:

```
> SELECT @a;
+------+
| @a   |
+------+
| 15   |
+------+
1 row in set (0.00 sec)
```

Calling Procedures from Procedures

You can also call procedures from inside procedures. For example, this procedure calls the adder2() procedure we just wrote to add two numbers:

```
> CREATE PROCEDURE caller(IN p1 INT, IN p2 INT, OUT p3 INT)
BEGIN
  CALL adder2(p1, p2, p3);
END
//
Query OK, 0 rows affected (0.00 sec)
```

Let's try adding 1 + 2 with this new procedure:

```
> CALL caller(1, 2, @a);
Query OK, 0 rows affected (0.00 sec)
```

And sure enough, you get the right answer:

```
> SELECT @a;
+------+
| @a   |
+------+
| 3    |
+------+
1 row in set (0.00 sec)
```

Dropping Procedures

To delete a stored procedure, just drop it.

Here's an example:

```
DROP PROCEDURE createtable;
```

> **SQL TIP**
>
> Note that you don't include the parentheses that usually follow a procedure's name when dropping it.

Note that once a procedure has been dropped, it's gone—you can't undo it.

Understanding Cursors

Cursors point at particular records in the result set of an SQL query and allow you to fetch those records.

For example, when you open a new cursor corresponding to a result set of records from an SQL query, that cursor points at the first record:

```
+-----------+----------+------------+------------+------------+------+
| firstname | lastname | department | hiredate   | supervisor | id   |
+-----------+----------+------------+------------+------------+------+
--> | John    | Wood     | Sales      | 2012-01-15 | 1001       | 1501 |
| Mary        | Green    | Sales      | 2012-01-15 | 1501       | 1601 |
| Daniel      | Grant    | Sales      | 2012-01-15 | 1501       | 1602 |
| Nancy       | Jackson  | Accounting | 2012-02-20 | 1501       | 1701 |
| Tom         | Smith    | Accounting | 2012-03-15 | 1701       | 1801 |
| Jessica     | Smith    | Accounting | 2012-03-15 | 1701       | 1901 |
+-----------+----------+------------+------------+------------+------+
```

You can use the cursor to fetch data from the first record. After you do, the cursor automatically moves to the next record:

```
+-----------+----------+------------+------------+------------+------+
| firstname | lastname | department | hiredate   | supervisor | id   |
+-----------+----------+------------+------------+------------+------+
| John        | Wood     | Sales      | 2012-01-15 | 1001       | 1501 |
--> | Mary    | Green    | Sales      | 2012-01-15 | 1501       | 1601 |
| Daniel      | Grant    | Sales      | 2012-01-15 | 1501       | 1602 |
| Nancy       | Jackson  | Accounting | 2012-02-20 | 1501       | 1701 |
| Tom         | Smith    | Accounting | 2012-03-15 | 1701       | 1801 |
| Jessica     | Smith    | Accounting | 2012-03-15 | 1701       | 1901 |
+-----------+----------+------------+------------+------------+------+
```

And you're ready to fetch data from the second row.

In other words, cursors point to the location at which the next FETCH command will retrieve data from a result set. After fetching data, the cursor moves on to the next record. Some DBMSes enable you to position cursors as you like; some DBMSes just let you fetch the first record, then the next, then the next, and so on.

Fetching Data with Cursors

Here's an example showing how to fetch data using a cursor. In this case, you just fetch some data from the first record of the Employees table.

You start by creating a new procedure:

```
> CREATE PROCEDURE cursorproc(OUT p VARCHAR(20))
...
```

Then declare the new cursor with a DECLARE CURSOR statement. Note that you associate a result set of records with the cursor
right away when declaring it by using a FOR SELECT firstname
FROM employees clause:

```
> CREATE PROCEDURE cursorproc(OUT p VARCHAR(20))
BEGIN
  DECLARE cur_1 CURSOR FOR SELECT firstname FROM employees;
...
```

Then open the cursor, which makes it ready for use:

```
> CREATE PROCEDURE cursorproc(OUT p VARCHAR(20))
BEGIN
  DECLARE cur_1 CURSOR FOR SELECT firstname FROM employees;
  OPEN cur_1;
...
```

Next, you fetch the first first name from the Employees table into
the OUT parameter p, and close the cursor:

```
> CREATE PROCEDURE cursorproc(OUT p VARCHAR(20))
BEGIN
  DECLARE cur_1 CURSOR FOR SELECT firstname FROM employees;
  OPEN cur_1;
  FETCH cur_1 INTO p;
  CLOSE cur_1;
END
//
Query OK, 0 rows affected (0.01 sec)
```

Okay, now let's run the procedure:

```
> CALL cursorproc(@a);
Query OK, 0 rows affected (0.08 sec)
```

And then check whether we got the first name:

```
> SELECT @a;
+------+
| @a   |
+------+
| John |
+------+
1 row in set (0.00 sec)
```

Perfect. Things worked as planned.

Moving to the Next Record with Cursors

Now we show how cursors automatically move from one record to the next after each data fetch. Instead of just fetching the first first name from the Employees table, we use FETCH three times in a new procedure:

```
> CREATE PROCEDURE cursorproc2(OUT p VARCHAR(20))
BEGIN
  DECLARE cur_1 CURSOR FOR SELECT firstname FROM Employees;
  OPEN cur_1;
  FETCH cur_1 INTO p;
  FETCH cur_1 INTO p;
  FETCH cur_1 INTO p;
  CLOSE cur_1;
END
//
Query OK, 0 rows affected (0.01 sec)
```

Then we call the new procedure:

```
> CALL cursorproc2(@a);
Query OK, 0 rows affected (0.08 sec)
```

Did it work? We can check the value of the parameter we passed to the procedure like the following:

```
> SELECT @a;
+--------+
| @a     |
+--------+
| Daniel |
+--------+
1 row in set (0.00 sec)
```

And that's correct—Daniel is the first name stored in the third record in the Employees table.

In some DBMSes, you can move the cursor at will with the ABSOLUTE keyword like the following, which moves the cursor to the fourth record:

```
CREATE PROCEDURE cursorproc3(OUT p VARCHAR(20))
BEGIN
  DECLARE cur_1 SCROLL CURSOR FOR SELECT firstname FROM Employees;
  OPEN cur_1;
  FETCH ABSOLUTE 4 cur_1 INTO p;
  CLOSE cur_1;
END
//
```

In some DBMSes, you can also use keywords like NEXT, PRIOR, FIRST, and LAST to move the cursor.

The Least You Need to Know

- Procedures are lists of SQL statements that get executed when you call the procedure.
- You can pass data to procedures by using parameters with the IN keyword.
- You can return data from procedures by using parameters with the OUT keyword.
- You can declare local variables inside procedures.
- Cursors point to specific locations in results sets from SQL queries.
- After you fetch data from the current cursor position, cursors will move automatically to the next record in the result set.

Using Transactions

In This Chapter

- Working with transactions
- Creating a transaction
- Handling savepoints
- Rolling back transactions
- Committing transactions

In this chapter we look at transactions, which are sets of SQL statements that you can undo if there is some kind of error.

Your data might be sensitive to errors. For example, you might own a bank and want to make sure that every operation or transaction with your database system is error-free. That's what transaction processing is about; it says that a particular (usually multi-SQL-statement) transaction must complete without error, or it should be completely undone so that no part of it affects your database.

In other words, transaction processing is all about protecting your data's integrity. If some problem occurs in the database, transaction processing allows you to wipe the whole transaction out—not leave it partially completed—so you can start from scratch.

We start by taking a look at an example of a transaction that can benefit from transaction processing, and then we perform a few transactions in DBMSes directly to see how they work.

Understanding Transactions

There you are, the president of the First National SQL Bank, and you want to transfer money from Mary's account to Sam's.

To do this, you remove the money from Mary's account by updating the balance in her record in your database, then adding the amount to Sam's account by updating his record.

You call a stored procedure, passing it the account numbers and the amount to transfer. The procedure starts by removing the money from Mary's account. But then, zap, there's a power spike, which causes an internal error in your DBMS. The money is never credited to Sam's account.

SQL CAUTION

Unfortunately, transaction processing syntax varies strongly from DBMS to DBMS. We'll discuss the major DBMSes in this chapter.

When things go wrong or errors occur with this kind of (usually multistep) SQL transaction, transaction handling comes in handy.

Here, you start a transaction, and if an error occurs at some point, you can *roll back* the transaction, which undoes it in its entirety.

If the transaction finishes without error, you can *commit* the transaction, which means you write the changes to your database.

DEFINITION

When you **roll back** a transaction, you undo it. **Committing** a transaction writes all its changes to the underlying database.

So that's the story: you start a transaction, then either roll it back or commit it. Let's look at doing this with real DBMSes.

Performing Transactions

Some DBMSes require that you mark the beginning of transactions. For example, you start a transaction in SQL Server this way:

```
BEGIN TRANSACTION;
```

In MySQL, you start transactions like this:

```
START TRANSACTION;
```

In PostgreSQL, you use:

```
BEGIN:
```

In Oracle, all changes to data are automatically executed inside a transaction.

Let's start our own transaction now as an example. We start by creating a transaction (if needed in your DBMS):

```
> START TRANSACTION;
Query OK, 0 rows affected (0.00 sec)
```

Take a look at the Employees table:

```
> SELECT * FROM Employees;
+-----------+----------+------------+------------+------------+------+
| firstname | lastname | department | hiredate   | supervisor | id   |
+-----------+----------+------------+------------+------------+------+
| John      | Wood     | Sales      | 2012-01-15 | 1001       | 1501 |
| Mary      | Green    | Sales      | 2012-01-15 | 1501       | 1601 |
| Daniel    | Grant    | Sales      | 2012-01-15 | 1501       | 1602 |
| Nancy     | Jackson  | Accounting | 2012-02-20 | 1501       | 1701 |
| Tom       | Smith    | Accounting | 2012-03-15 | 1701       | 1801 |
| Jessica   | Smith    | Accounting | 2012-03-15 | 1701       | 1901 |
+-----------+----------+------------+------------+------------+------+
6 rows in set (0.00 sec)
```

Let's change Nancy Jackson's department from Accounting to Sales:

```
> UPDATE Employees SET department = 'Sales' WHERE id = 1701;
Query OK, 1 row affected (0.00 sec)
Rows matched: 1  Changed: 1  Warnings: 0
```

And check the results:

```
> SELECT * FROM Employees;
+-----------+----------+------------+------------+------------+------+
| firstname | lastname | department | hiredate   | supervisor | id   |
+-----------+----------+------------+------------+------------+------+
| John      | Wood     | Sales      | 2012-01-15 | 1001       | 1501 |
| Mary      | Green    | Sales      | 2012-01-15 | 1501       | 1601 |
| Daniel    | Grant    | Sales      | 2012-01-15 | 1501       | 1602 |
| Nancy     | Jackson  | Sales      | 2012-02-20 | 1501       | 1701 |
| Tom       | Smith    | Accounting | 2012-03-15 | 1701       | 1801 |
| Jessica   | Smith    | Accounting | 2012-03-15 | 1701       | 1901 |
+-----------+----------+------------+------------+------------+------+
6 rows in set (0.00 sec)
```

Okay, the change was made. Because we're using transactions, let's experiment with rolling back the transaction next.

Using Rollbacks

To roll back a transaction—that is, undo it—you only have to use the ROLLBACK statement.

In the previous section, we began a transaction and updated a cell in the Employees table:

```
> START TRANSACTION;
Query OK, 0 rows affected (0.00 sec)

> UPDATE Employees SET department = 'Sales' WHERE id = 1701;
Query OK, 1 row affected (0.00 sec)
Rows matched: 1  Changed: 1  Warnings: 0
```

Confirm that the change was made in the table:

```
> SELECT * FROM Employees;
+-----------+----------+------------+------------+------------+------+
| firstname | lastname | department | hiredate   | supervisor | id   |
+-----------+----------+------------+------------+------------+------+
| John      | Wood     | Sales      | 2012-01-15 | 1001       | 1501 |
| Mary      | Green    | Sales      | 2012-01-15 | 1501       | 1601 |
| Daniel    | Grant    | Sales      | 2012-01-15 | 1501       | 1602 |
| Nancy     | Jackson  | Sales      | 2012-02-20 | 1501       | 1701 |
| Tom       | Smith    | Accounting | 2012-03-15 | 1701       | 1801 |
| Jessica   | Smith    | Accounting | 2012-03-15 | 1701       | 1901 |
+-----------+----------+------------+------------+------------+------+
6 rows in set (0.00 sec)
```

Now you can undo the update by rolling back the transaction with ROLLBACK:

```
> ROLLBACK;
Query OK, 0 rows affected (0.02 sec)
```

That undoes the transaction. To verify, you can look at the Employees table:

```
> SELECT * FROM Employees;
+-----------+----------+------------+------------+------------+------+
| firstname | lastname | department | hiredate   | supervisor | id   |
+-----------+----------+------------+------------+------------+------+
| John      | Wood     | Sales      | 2012-01-15 | 1001       | 1501 |
| Mary      | Green    | Sales      | 2012-01-15 | 1501       | 1601 |
| Daniel    | Grant    | Sales      | 2012-01-15 | 1501       | 1602 |
| Nancy     | Jackson  | Accounting | 2012-02-20 | 1501       | 1701 |
| Tom       | Smith    | Accounting | 2012-03-15 | 1701       | 1801 |
| Jessica   | Smith    | Accounting | 2012-03-15 | 1701       | 1901 |
+-----------+----------+------------+------------+------------+------+
6 rows in set (0.00 sec)
```

As you see, Nancy Jackson is back in Accounting.

Using Commit

The other option besides rolling back a transaction is to commit it. While rolling back a transaction undoes it, committing it writes it to the underlying database. That is, committing a transaction makes its changes in the database.

Here's what a complete transaction looks like in MySQL, from the start to the COMMIT statement, where we're updating Nancy Jackson's department to Sales:

```
>START TRANSACTION;
Query OK, 0 rows affected (0.00 sec)

>UPDATE Employees SET department = 'Sales' WHERE id = 1701;
Query OK, 1 row affected (0.00 sec)
Rows matched: 1  Changed: 1  Warnings: 0

> SELECT * FROM Employees;
+-----------+----------+------------+------------+------------+------+
| firstname | lastname | department | hiredate   | supervisor | id   |
+-----------+----------+------------+------------+------------+------+
| John      | Wood     | Sales      | 2012-01-15 | 1001       | 1501 |
| Mary      | Green    | Sales      | 2012-01-15 | 1501       | 1601 |
| Daniel    | Grant    | Sales      | 2012-01-15 | 1501       | 1602 |
| Nancy     | Jackson  | Sales      | 2012-02-20 | 1501       | 1701 |
| Tom       | Smith    | Accounting | 2012-03-15 | 1701       | 1801 |
| Jessica   | Smith    | Accounting | 2012-03-15 | 1701       | 1901 |
+-----------+----------+------------+------------+------------+------+
6 rows in set (0.00 sec)

>COMMIT;
Query OK, 1 row affected (0.00 sec)
```

Here's what it looks like in SQL Server:

```
>BEGIN TRANSACTION;
>UPDATE Employees SET department = 'Sales' WHERE id = 1701;
>COMMIT TRANSACTION;
```

In Oracle, you just do the following:

```
>UPDATE Employees SET department = 'Sales' WHERE id = 1701;
>COMMIT;
```

In PostgreSQL, you do the following:

```
>BEGIN:
>UPDATE Employees SET department = 'Sales' WHERE id = 1701;
>COMMIT;
```

SQL CAUTION

There might be an error code in your DBMS that you can check before committing. For example, in SQL Server, errors are held in a variable named @@error, so you might use the following code to roll back if there was an error before you commit:

```
        IF @@error <> 0 ROLLBACK;
        COMMIT;
```

In MySQL, the error code is @error.

Using Savepoints

If you have some long, drawn-out transactions, you might want to roll back only part of them, not the whole thing, if something goes wrong. That's the role of *savepoints*. A savepoint in a transaction is a position that you can roll back the transaction to.

DEFINITION

A marked location in a transaction that you can roll back to is a **savepoint.**

Let's see this at work, performing the same transaction as before but this time using savepoints.

Start the transaction (use BEGIN TRANSACTION or whatever
your DBMS requires):

```
> START TRANSACTION;
Query OK, 0 rows affected (0.00 sec)
```

Then create a savepoint:

```
> SAVEPOINT update1;
Query OK, 0 rows affected (0.00 sec)
```

That's how it works in Oracle, PostgreSQL, and MySQL. Here's
how you would create a savepoint in SQL Server:

```
SAVE TRANSACTION update1;
```

Then make the change to the Employees table by updating Nancy
Jackson to Sales:

```
> UPDATE Employees SET department = 'Sales' WHERE id = 1701;
Query OK, 1 row affected (0.00 sec)
Rows matched: 1  Changed: 1  Warnings: 0
```

Check the result:

```
> SELECT * FROM Employees;
+-----------+----------+------------+------------+------------+------+
| firstname | lastname | department | hiredate   | supervisor | id   |
+-----------+----------+------------+------------+------------+------+
| John      | Wood     | Sales      | 2012-01-15 | 1001       | 1501 |
| Mary      | Green    | Sales      | 2012-01-15 | 1501       | 1601 |
| Daniel    | Grant    | Sales      | 2012-01-15 | 1501       | 1602 |
| Nancy     | Jackson  | Sales      | 2012-02-20 | 1501       | 1701 |
| Tom       | Smith    | Accounting | 2012-03-15 | 1701       | 1801 |
| Jessica   | Smith    | Accounting | 2012-03-15 | 1701       | 1901 |
+-----------+----------+------------+------------+------------+------+
6 rows in set (0.00 sec)
```

Now we roll back the change. Here's how you roll back to savepoint
update1 in Oracle, MySQL, and PostgreSQL:

```
> ROLLBACK TO SAVEPOINT update1;
Query OK, 0 rows affected (0.02 sec)
```

And here's how you do it in SQL Server:

```
ROLLBACK TRANSACTION update1;
```

Let's check whether the change was rolled back in the Employees table:

```
> SELECT * FROM Employees;
+-----------+----------+------------+------------+------------+------+
| firstname | lastname | department | hiredate   | supervisor | id   |
+-----------+----------+------------+------------+------------+------+
| John      | Wood     | Sales      | 2012-01-15 | 1001       | 1501 |
| Mary      | Green    | Sales      | 2012-01-15 | 1501       | 1601 |
| Daniel    | Grant    | Sales      | 2012-01-15 | 1501       | 1602 |
| Nancy     | Jackson  | Accounting | 2012-02-20 | 1501       | 1701 |
| Tom       | Smith    | Accounting | 2012-03-15 | 1701       | 1801 |
| Jessica   | Smith    | Accounting | 2012-03-15 | 1701       | 1901 |
+-----------+----------+------------+------------+------------+------+
6 rows in set (0.00 sec)
```

The transaction was rolled back, as expected.

SQL TIP

When you have lengthy transactions, use as many savepoints as you can. Doing so gives you more flexibility and control when rolling back transactions.

As you can see, transactions can be powerful operations, giving you a safety net in case of database error.

The usual form of a transaction is:

- Begin the transaction.
- Perform SQL operations.
- Commit the transaction.

But if there is an error, the transaction goes like the following:

- Begin the transaction.
- Perform SQL operations.
- Roll back the transaction.

The Least You Need to Know

- Transactions are great for maintaining data integrity in case of database errors.
- Transactions are blocks of SQL statements that make changes to the data in a database.
- Rolling back a transaction means undoing the changes to data performed by the SQL statements in the transaction, restoring the data the way it was.
- Committing a transaction means writing the changes it makes to the data in an underlying database to that database. In other words, committing a transaction makes that transaction final in the database.
- Savepoints are marked locations that you can add to transactions that you can roll back to if needed. Using savepoints, you can perform complete or partial rollbacks of transactions.
- The more savepoints you use, the better, because more savepoints gives you more control in undoing your transactions.

Understanding Constraints and Triggers

In This Chapter

- Using primary and foreign keys
- Introducing unique constraints
- Introducing check constraints
- Creating triggers
- Testing triggers

In this chapter, we take an in-depth look at constraints and triggers. We originally introduced constraints in Chapter 2 on creating tables. Here, we take a closer look at what makes them tick, including primary keys and foreign keys.

We also look at triggers in this chapter. Triggers are like constraints in that they check values and take action as needed. Triggers let you specify the condition you want to watch for, and execute SQL when that condition is met or not met (your choice).

Let's start with constraints.

Using Constraints

A constraint is a limitation on the values a table (usually a column in a table) can hold.

You create a table with the SQL CREATE TABLE statement, and in that statement you specify all the columns in the table, which includes each column's name and data type. Here's how it looks formally:

```
CREATE TABLE table_name
(column_1 data_type,
 column_2 data_type,
...
 column_n data_type);
```

But wait, there's more. You can add optional constraints as well:

```
CREATE TABLE table_name
(column_1 data_type [constraint],
 column_2 data_type [constraint],
...
 column_n data_type [constraint]);
```

You usually specify constraints on a column-by-column basis like this when you create each column. Let's look at the kinds of constraints that are available.

Using Primary Keys

Making one column a *primary key* is a constraint that you should add when creating any table.

DEFINITION

A **primary key** for a table is a column whose values are unique and can therefore be used to uniquely specify any row in the table.

Primary keys indicate to the DBMS the primary column to sort on. That is, the primary key gives the DBMS a unique value it can use for every row in a table. The primary key is the main default index for a table.

SQL TIP

By default, DBMSes sort tables on the primary key value, in an ascending sort.

When we created the sample Employees table in Chapter 2, we used the id column as the primary key:

```
CREATE TABLE Employees
(firstname VARCHAR(20),
lastname VARCHAR(20),
department VARCHAR(20),
hiredate DATE,
supervisor INT CHECK (supervisor > 1000 AND supervisor < 2000),
id INT PRIMARY KEY CHECK (id > 1000 AND id < 3000));
```

Then we were able to fill the newly created table with data:

```
> SELECT * FROM Employees;
+-----------+----------+------------+------------+------------+------+
| firstname | lastname | department | hiredate   | supervisor | id   |
+-----------+----------+------------+------------+------------+------+
| John      | Wood     | Sales      | 2012-01-15 | 1001       | 1501 |
| Mary      | Green    | Sales      | 2012-01-15 | 1501       | 1601 |
| Daniel    | Grant    | Sales      | 2012-01-15 | 1501       | 1602 |
| Nancy     | Jackson  | Accounting | 2012-02-20 | 1501       | 1701 |
| Tom       | Smith    | Accounting | 2012-03-15 | 1701       | 1801 |
| Jessica   | Smith    | Accounting | 2012-03-15 | 1701       | 1901 |
+-----------+----------+------------+------------+------------+------+
6 rows in set (0.06 sec)
```

To emphasize that each primary key value must be unique, let's try adding someone new to the table with an already taken ID, 1901. You get an error message something like the following (depending on your DBMS):

```
> INSERT INTO Employees
VALUES
('Cary', 'Grant', 'Acting', '20120615', 1001, 1901)
ERROR 1062 (23000): Duplicate entry '1901' for key 1
```

As you can see, primary keys need to be unique. That's useful to avoid situations like this, where you want to delete Jessica Smith's record, but Tom Smith's record is deleted as well by mistake:

```
DELETE FROM Employees WHERE lastname = 'Smith';
```

You can make this safer by sticking to the primary key in DELETE statements:

```
DELETE FROM Employees WHERE id = 1901;
```

Besides being unique, you can't change a record's primary key. Once you set it, it's set.

For example, look as we try to update an employee with a new ID (the error you get depends on your DBMS):

```
> UPDATE Employees SET id = 1501 WHERE id = 1901;
ERROR 1062 (23000): Duplicate entry '1501' for key 1
```

SQL TIP

Did you create a table and forget to add a primary key? You can always add a primary key to a table that doesn't have one after the table is created with the following:

```
ALTER TABLE Employees ADD CONSTRAINT PRIMARY KEY (id);
```

So how do you know if a column is ready to be used as a primary key? Here are the guidelines:

- Each value in the column must be unique.

- No value in the column can be NULL.

- The values in the column cannot be modified.

- The values in the column cannot be reused.

SQL TIP

Do you really need to change a primary key value for a record? Drop the primary key constraint, update the record, and add the column as a primary key constraint gain. Here's how to drop a column named id as the primary key:

```
ALTER TABLE Orders
DROP PRIMARY KEY id;
```

If that doesn't work in your DBMS, use the following SQL instead:

```
ALTER TABLE Orders
DROP CONSTRAINT PRIMARY KEY id;
```

Using Foreign Keys

Foreign keys are great when you have multiple related tables in a database. A foreign key in a table must appear in a column in another table. So, for example, if one column in the Supervisors table refers to your supervisor's IDs, adding a foreign key constraint means that the values in that column must also appear in the Employees table's id column, enforcing the constraint that all supervisors must also be employees.

DEFINITION

A **foreign key** is a value in one table that must appear in a column you specify in another table.

Foreign keys are great for data integrity by making sure that two tables you think are related *are* actually related, without any gaps.

For example, take the Employees table:

```
> SELECT * FROM Employees;
+-----------+----------+------------+------------+------------+------+
| firstname | lastname | department | hiredate   | supervisor | id   |
+-----------+----------+------------+------------+------------+------+
| John      | Wood     | Sales      | 2012-01-15 | 1001       | 1501 |
| Mary      | Green    | Sales      | 2012-01-15 | 1501       | 1601 |
| Daniel    | Grant    | Sales      | 2012-01-15 | 1501       | 1602 |
| Nancy     | Jackson  | Accounting | 2012-02-20 | 1501       | 1701 |
| Tom       | Smith    | Accounting | 2012-03-15 | 1701       | 1801 |
| Jessica   | Smith    | Accounting | 2012-03-15 | 1701       | 1901 |
+-----------+----------+------------+------------+------------+------+
6 rows in set (0.00 sec)
```

And now look at the Supervisors table we created in Chapter 9:

```
> SELECT * FROM Supervisors;
+-----------+----------+------+-----------+
| firstname | lastname | id   | extension |
+-----------+----------+------+-----------+
| George    | Edwards  | 1001 | 231       |
| John      | Wood     | 1501 | 244       |
| Nancy     | Jackson  | 1701 | 255       |
+-----------+----------+------+-----------+
3 rows in set (0.00 sec)
```

Each supervisor must also be an employee, so we want to make sure that all values in the Supervisors id column also appear in the Employees id column. Here's how that looks for supervisor Nancy Jackson.

```
+-----------+----------+------+-----------+
| firstname | lastname | id   | extension |
+-----------+----------+------+-----------+
| George    | Edwards  | 1001 | 231       |
| John      | Wood     | 1501 | 244       |
| Nancy     | Jackson  | 1701 | 255       |
+-----------+----------+---|--+-----------+
                           |_____
                           |
+-----------+----------+------------+------------+------------+---|--+
| firstname | lastname | department | hiredate   | supervisor |id |  |
+-----------+----------+------------+------------+------------+---|--+
| John      | Wood     | Sales      | 2012-01-15 | 1001       |   |  |
| Mary      | Green    | Sales      | 2012-01-15 | 1501       |   |  |
| Daniel    | Grant    | Sales      | 2012-01-15 | 1501       | V |  |
| Nancy     | Jackson  | Accounting | 2012-02-20 | 1501       | 1701 |
| Tom       | Smith    | Accounting | 2012-03-15 | 1701       | 1801 |
| Jessica   | Smith    | Accounting | 2012-03-15 | 1701       | 1901 |
+-----------+----------+------------+------------+------------+------+
```

So to enforce the constraint that all supervisors must have an ID in
the Employees table, you can create the Supervisors table with the
REFERENCES keyword:

```
> CREATE TABLE Supervisors
(firstname VARCHAR(20),
lastname VARCHAR(20),
id INT REFERENCES Employees(id),
extension INT);
Query OK, 0 rows affected (0.00 sec)
```

That makes the Supervisors table's ID a foreign key whose values
must also appear in the Employees table's id column.

SQL TIP

Foreign keys can also prevent data from accidentally being deleted. In
most databases, if an item is tied to a foreign key, you can't delete it.
However, note that some DBMSes have something called "cascading
delete," which means that if you delete an item that is the foreign key in
other tables, the corresponding rows are deleted in those other tables
as well.

Because the Supervisors table already exists, however, we have to
alter it to add the foreign key constraint. You can add a foreign key
constraint to a table this way:

```
> ALTER TABLE Supervisors
ADD CONSTRAINT
FOREIGN KEY(id) REFERENCES Employees(id);
ERROR 1452 (23000): Cannot add or update a child row: a foreign key constraint
    ⇒ fails ('corporation/#sql-724_1', CONSTRAINT '#sql-724_1_ibfk_1' FOREIGN
    ⇒ KEY ('id') REFERENCES 'employees' ('id'))
```

As you can see, there was an error. Adding the foreign key constraint didn't work. Why not?

The answer is that the first person in the Supervisors table, George Edwards, actually has an ID that doesn't appear in the Employees id column.

We can fix that by giving George Edwards a temporary ID of 1601, which is an ID value that does appear in the Employees table's id column:

```
> UPDATE Supervisors SET id = 1601 WHERE id = 1001;
Query OK, 1 row affected (0.03 sec)
Rows matched: 1  Changed: 1  Warnings: 0
```

Now we can make the id column in the Supervisors table a foreign key without any problem:

```
> ALTER TABLE Supervisors
ADD CONSTRAINT
FOREIGN KEY(id) REFERENCES Employees(id);
Query OK, 3 rows affected (0.02 sec)
Records: 3  Duplicates: 0  Warnings: 0
```

Great; let's test it. Here, we insert a new supervisor into the Supervisors table whose ID (1000) is not in the Employees table:

```
> INSERT INTO Supervisors
VALUES ('Jimmy', 'Stewart', 1000, 256);
ERROR 1452 (23000): Cannot add or update a child row: a foreign key constraint
    ⇒ fails ('corporation/supervisors', CONSTRAINT 'supervisors_ibfk_1' FOREIGN
    ⇒ KEY ('id') REFERENCES 'employees' ('id'))
```

And as you can see, there was an error. The foreign key constraint is working.

SQL TIP

You can drop a foreign key constraint by typing the following:

```
ALTER TABLE Orders
DROP FOREIGN KEY id;
```

If that doesn't work in your DBMS, use the following SQL instead:

```
ALTER TABLE Orders
DROP CONSTRAINT FOREIGN KEY id;
```

Using Unique Constraints

The UNIQUE constraint, as its name implies, constrains items in a column to be unique.

For example, say you're considering some job candidates and want to keep track of them in a table named Candidates. To create that table and keep track of the candidate's first and last names, and to insist that the entries in the lastname column be unique, you can create the Candidates table the following way:

```
> CREATE TABLE Candidates
(
firstname VARCHAR(30),
lastname VARCHAR(30) UNIQUE
);
Query OK, 0 rows affected (0.00 sec)
```

Or this way:

```
> CREATE TABLE Candidates
(
firstname VARCHAR(30),
lastname VARCHAR(30),
CONSTRAINT lastname UNIQUE
);
Query OK, 0 rows affected (0.00 sec)
```

Say that you created the Candidates table but forgot to add the UNIQUE constraint:

```
> CREATE TABLE Candidates
(
firstname VARCHAR(30),
lastname VARCHAR(30)
);
Query OK, 0 rows affected (0.00 sec)
```

You can always add the UNIQUE constraint after creating the table with an ALTER statement:

```
> ALTER TABLE Candidates
ADD CONSTRAINT
UNIQUE (lastname);
Query OK, 0 rows affected (0.05 sec)
Records: 0  Duplicates: 0  Warnings: 0
```

Now let's test the Candidates table. Bill Simpson goes in with no problem:

```
> INSERT INTO Candidates VALUES ('Bill', 'Simpson');
Query OK, 1 row affected (0.02 sec)
```

But now when we try to add Jade Simpson, we end up with an error because she has the same last name:

```
> INSERT INTO Candidates VALUES ('Jade', 'Simpson');
ERROR 1062 (23000): Duplicate entry 'Simpson' for key 1
```

SQL TIP

You can drop a unique constraint like the following:

```
ALTER TABLE Candidates
DROP UNIQUE lastname;
```

If that doesn't work in your DBMS, use the following SQL instead:

```
ALTER TABLE Candidates
DROP CONSTRAINT UNIQUE lastname;
```

Using Check Constraints

Check constraints are perhaps the most powerful constraints you can use.

When you create a check constraint, you can check the values about to be inserted into a column to see whether an expression you specify is true; if not, the insertion will cause an error.

You create a check constraint when you create a table with the keyword CHECK and the expression you want to check in parentheses. For example, recall that when we created the Employees table, we set constraints on the id and supervisor columns.

```
CREATE TABLE Employees
(firstname VARCHAR(20),
lastname VARCHAR(20),
department VARCHAR(20),
hiredate DATE,
supervisor INT CHECK (supervisor > 1000 AND supervisor < 2000),
id INT PRIMARY KEY CHECK (id > 1000 AND id < 3000));
```

After installing this constraint, inserting or updating data that violates a check constraint causes an error.

SQL CAUTION

As of this writing, MySQL reads CHECK constraints when you create or alter tables, but doesn't implement them. It gives no errors, but just doesn't make any check constraints active, which is unfortunate if you count on them and expect to see an error if they're not yet supported.

Here's another example. You can add a new column, gender, to the Candidates table we created earlier in this chapter:

```
> ALTER TABLE Candidates
ADD COLUMN gender VARCHAR(1);
Query OK, 1 row affected (0.02 sec)
Records: 1  Duplicates: 0  Warnings: 0
```

And you can add a check constraint after the table is created to check that values that go into the gender field can only be M or F:

```
> ALTER TABLE Candidates
ADD CONSTRAINT
CHECK (gender LIKE '[MF]');
Query OK, 1 row affected (0.02 sec)
Records: 1  Duplicates: 0  Warnings: 0
```

Here's another way to do the same constraint:

```
> ALTER TABLE Candidates
ADD CONSTRAINT
CHECK (gender IN ('M', 'F'));
Query OK, 1 row affected (0.03 sec)
Records: 1  Duplicates: 0  Warnings: 0
```

Now this UPDATE statement causes an error if your DBMS supports check constraints:

```
UPDATE Candidates
SET gender = 'Y' WHERE lastname = 'Simpson';
```

Alternatively, you could have added the check constraint on the gender column when you created the Candidates table in the first place:

```
> CREATE TABLE Candidates
(firstname VARCHAR(30),
lastname VARCHAR(30),
gender VARCHAR(1) CHECK (gender IN ('M', 'F')));
Query OK, 0 rows affected (0.02 sec)
```

SQL TIP

If the CHECK constraint doesn't work in your DBMS, you can use triggers to implement a constraint that works the same way. See the section, "Creating Triggers," later in this chapter.

Using NOT NULL

As you can guess from its name, the NOT NULL constraint makes sure that values inserted into a particular column are not NULL.

For example, here's how you might create the Candidates table used in this chapter, making sure the gender field is not NULL:

```
> CREATE TABLE Candidates
(firstname VARCHAR(30),
lastname VARCHAR(30),
gender VARCHAR(1) NOT NULL);
Query OK, 0 rows affected (0.00 sec)
```

Now when you try to insert data into the Candidates table where the gender field is NULL, you get an error:

```
> INSERT INTO Candidates VALUES
('Bill', 'Simpson', NULL);
ERROR 1048 (23000): Column 'gender' cannot be null
```

Here's how we can specify that the firstname and lastname fields of the Employees table not be NULL when we create the table:

```
CREATE TABLE Employees
(firstname VARCHAR(20) NOT NULL,
lastname VARCHAR(20) NOT NULL,
department VARCHAR(20),
hiredate DATE,
supervisor INT CHECK (supervisor > 1000 AND supervisor < 2000),
id INT PRIMARY KEY CHECK (id > 1000 AND id < 3000));
```

In general, insisting that a field not be NULL means that you have to supply a value for it. So if you have a field that you want to be sure is not left empty, making it NOT NULL is a good choice.

Creating Triggers

SQL triggers are chunks of SQL code that are executed or "triggered" by INSERT, UPDATE, or DELETE actions on a table. Each trigger is connected with a table until you remove it.

So, for example, you can watch data as it is inserted into a table to check whether it's within certain bounds that you set, or alter data as it's inserted or updated, or watch to make sure that inserted data matches key fields in other tables, and so on.

Although trigger creation syntax varies, it's usually close to the following:

```
CREATE TRIGGER trigger_name trigger_time trigger_event
ON table_name FOR EACH ROW trigger_statement
```

Here are the parts of this statement:

- *trigger_name* is the name by which you want to refer to the trigger, for example, when it's time to drop it.

- *trigger_time* is BEFORE or AFTER, and indicates when the trigger fires—before or after the event it triggers on.

- *trigger_event* is INSERT, UPDATE, or DELETE (some DBMSes enable combinations such as UPDATE OR INSERT). This is the action to the table, such as an INSERT operation, that the trigger fires on.

- *table_name* is the name of the table you want to attach the trigger to.

- *trigger_statement* is the set of SQL statements that you want to execute when the trigger fires.

SQL CAUTION

Trigger syntax differs between DBMSes, because it's not laid out in the ANSI standard. We see examples in various DBMSes here, but when creating complex triggers, check your DBMS's documentation.

Let's look at a working example on the Employees table. Say that when you insert a new row, you want to make sure that the employee's last name is capitalized. We do that with a trigger named upper.

We start by setting the end-of-line delimiter to // so we can use semicolons in the trigger definition:

```
> DELIMITER //
```

Then we create a trigger named upper:

```
> DELIMITER //
> CREATE TRIGGER upper
```

We set the trigger to fire before data is inserted into the Employees table:

```
> DELIMITER //
> CREATE TRIGGER upper
BEFORE INSERT ON Employees
```

Now we use FOR EACH ROW:

```
> DELIMITER //
> CREATE TRIGGER upper
BEFORE INSERT ON Employees
FOR EACH ROW
```

Next, we add a BEGIN ... END block for the trigger statement:

```
> DELIMITER //
> CREATE TRIGGER upper
BEFORE INSERT ON Employees
FOR EACH ROW
BEGIN
...
END;
```

In the trigger's code, we can refer to the newly inserted row as NEW (or :NEW or INSERTED). So we can convert the inserted last name to uppercase:

```
> DELIMITER //
> CREATE TRIGGER upper
BEFORE INSERT ON Employees
FOR EACH ROW
BEGIN
SET NEW.lastname = UPPER(NEW.lastname);
END;
```

SQL TIP

If we used a *trigger_time* of AFTER instead of BEFORE, we would have access to the old data that was replaced using the predefined variable OLD instead of NEW.

And we end with the // delimiter:

```
> DELIMITER //
> CREATE TRIGGER upper
BEFORE INSERT ON Employees
FOR EACH ROW
BEGIN
SET NEW.lastname = UPPER(NEW.lastname);
END;
//
Query OK, 0 rows affected (0.02 sec)
```

SQL CAUTION

Some DBMSes won't let you use INSERT or UPDATE inside a trigger if it triggers on INSERT or UPDATE.

That sets up the upper trigger. We can set the end-of-line delimiter back to a semicolon:

```
> DELIMITER ;
```

To test the trigger, let's insert a new employee, Tony Curtis, into the Employees table:

```
> INSERT INTO Employees VALUES
('Tony', 'Curtis', 'Sales', '20120615', 2004, 1909);
Query OK, 1 row affected (0.00 sec)
```

And we can look at the Employees table to see whether Tony Curtis's last name was indeed converted to all capital letters:

```
> SELECT * FROM Employees;
+-----------+----------+------------+------------+------------+------+
| firstname | lastname | department | hiredate   | supervisor | id   |
+-----------+----------+------------+------------+------------+------+
| John      | Wood     | Sales      | 2012-01-15 | 1001       | 1501 |
| Mary      | Green    | Sales      | 2012-01-15 | 1501       | 1601 |
| Daniel    | Grant    | Sales      | 2012-01-15 | 1501       | 1602 |
| Nancy     | Jackson  | Accounting | 2012-02-20 | 1501       | 1701 |
| Tom       | Smith    | Accounting | 2012-03-15 | 1701       | 1801 |
| Jessica   | Smith    | Accounting | 2012-03-15 | 1701       | 1901 |
| Tony      | CURTIS   | Sales      | 2012-06-15 | 2004       | 1909 |
+-----------+----------+------------+------------+------------+------+
7 rows in set (0.00 sec)
```

As you can see, the trigger worked.

Trigger creation syntax differs from DBMS to DBMS. Here's how a trigger might look in SQL Server (note the use of INSERTED instead of NEW):

```
> CREATE TRIGGER upper ON Employees
FOR INSERT, UPDATE
AS
SET INSERTED.lastname = UPPER(INSERTED.lastname);
```

Here's what it might look like in PostgreSQL and Oracle (note the use of :NEW instead of NEW):

```
> CREATE TRIGGER upper BEFORE INSERT ON Employees
FOR EACH ROW
BEGIN
SET :NEW.lastname = UPPER(:NEW.lastname);
END;
```

In MySQL, it might look like the following:

```
> CREATE TRIGGER upper BEFORE INSERT ON Employees
FOR EACH ROW
BEGIN
SET NEW.lastname = UPPER(NEW.lastname);
END;
```

Dropping Triggers

You can delete triggers with the DROP TRIGGER statement:

```
DROP TRIGGER upper;
```

SQL CAUTION

When you drop a trigger, it's gone. If you want to get it back, you have to re-create it.

The Least You Need to Know

- A primary key is a specified field for a row that contains a unique value among all rows that you can use to identify records. DBMSes usually sort on primary key columns by default.
- A foreign key is the value in a field, usually in another table, that corresponds to the current field in the present table.
- Unique constraints constrain values in fields to be unique across the same column in all rows of a table.
- Check constraints let you perform checks to make sure data entered into a particular column matches the restrictions you place on it.
- Triggers let you execute SQL code of your choosing when an INSERT, UPDATE, or DELETE operation occurs for a particular table.

Advanced SQL Topics

In This Chapter

- Checking a condition with IF ... THEN ... ELSE
- Testing with CASE ... END CASE
- Executing SQL statements repeatedly with LOOP
- Working with WHILE
- Working with REPEAT ... UNTIL
- Skipping to the next iteration of a loop with ITERATE

This chapter looks at some advanced topics to give you more SQL power—in particular, flow of control statements for use in stored procedures.

Flow of control statements are an important tool in your SQL toolkit, because they let your SQL scripts branch (take alternate paths), depending on the conditions you specify.

For example, say that you want to check on the sales records of various employees and transfer them to the accounting department instead of sales if their sales are less than a certain level. You can do that with the IF statement, which reads their sales figures from a table or tables, checks whether the total is above a certain cutoff, and if not, transfers them to the accounting department.

Or you might need to trim back your staff by checking everyone's hire date and firing those hired after a certain date.

That's the idea—with flow of control statements, you can make decisions in your SQL code and let the flow of control branch as you like.

SQL CAUTION

In nearly all DBMSes, flow of control statements are to be used only inside stored procedures. For some reason, many DBMSes' documentation neglects to mention that fact, and so individuals are frustrated. So please bear in mind—the flow of control statements in this chapter are meant to be used inside stored procedures.

As always with advanced topics, please be aware that the syntax your DBMS uses for the topics in this chapter might vary.

We begin with the most popular flow of control statement: the IF statement.

Using IF ... THEN

You use IF ... THEN statements to check a condition, and if that condition is true, you execute the SQL code you specify (if the condition is false, the SQL code is not executed).

Here's the IF statement's syntax:

```
IF condition
THEN statement
END IF;
```

If *condition* evaluates to true, *statement* (which might actually involve many SQL statements) is executed. If not, then *statement* is not executed.

Here's an example. Say that you want to check the temperature, as stored in a variable named @temperature. If it's greater than 72 degrees, you want to move it back to 72 degrees. You can use an IF ... THEN statement to handle the logic required here.

You start by creating a procedure named, say, checktemp():

```
> DELIMITER //
> CREATE PROCEDURE checktemp( )
```

Then add the BEGIN and END keywords to surround the body of the procedure:

```
> DELIMITER //
> CREATE PROCEDURE checktemp( )
BEGIN
...
END;
```

We set the temperature to 90 degrees:

```
> DELIMITER //
> CREATE PROCEDURE checktemp( )
BEGIN
SET @temperature = 90;
...
END;
```

Now we can check whether the temperature is over 72 degrees with an IF statement:

```
> DELIMITER //
> CREATE PROCEDURE checktemp( )
BEGIN
SET @temperature = 90;
IF @temperature > 72 THEN
...
END;
```

If the temperature is above 72, we set it to 72 instead:

```
> DELIMITER //
> CREATE PROCEDURE checktemp( )
BEGIN
SET @temperature = 90;
IF @temperature > 72 THEN
SET @temperature = 72;
...
END;
```

And finally, we end the IF statement with END IF and use // to end the stored procedure.

```
> DELIMITER //
> CREATE PROCEDURE checktemp()
BEGIN
SET @temperature = 90;
IF @temperature > 72 THEN
SET @temperature = 72;
END IF;
END;
//
Query OK, 0 rows affected (0.02 sec)
```

Now we set the end-of-line delimiter back to a semicolon:

```
> DELIMITER ;
```

And call the checktemp() function:

```
> CALL checktemp();
Query OK, 0 rows affected (0.00 sec)
```

If the IF statement worked, the temperature will be set to 72 degrees; if not, it will be set to 90. Let's look like this:

```
> SELECT @temperature;
+--------------+
| @temperature |
+--------------+
| 72           |
+--------------+
1 row in set (0.00 sec)
```

Using ELSE

IF statements can also contain ELSE statements, whose code is executed if the IF statement's condition is false.

Here's the syntax of an IF statement that includes an ELSE statement:

```
IF condition
THEN statement_1
ELSE statement_2
END IF;
```

If *condition* is true, *statement_1* is executed; if condition is false, *statement_2* is executed.

For example, say you're buying ice cream for the crowd, and everyone wants chocolate except Dave, who wants strawberry. Let's put
together a procedure named geticecream() that handles this.

We start by creating the procedure, which takes one argument,
person:

```
> DELIMITER //
> CREATE PROCEDURE geticecream(IN person VARCHAR(20))
BEGIN
...
END;
```

First, we check whether the person argument equals 'Dave,' and if so
set the variable @icecream to strawberry:

```
> DELIMITER //
> CREATE PROCEDURE geticecream(IN person VARCHAR(20))
BEGIN
IF person = 'Dave' THEN
SET @icecream = 'strawberry';
...
END IF;
END;
```

If the person argument does not hold Dave, we can set the ice cream
type to chocolate in an ELSE clause:

```
> DELIMITER //
> CREATE PROCEDURE geticecream(IN person VARCHAR(20))
BEGIN
IF person = 'Dave' THEN
SET @icecream = 'strawberry';
ELSE
SET @icecream = 'chocolate';
END IF;
END;
//
Query OK, 0 rows affected (0.00 sec)
```

After setting the end-of-line delimiter back to a semicolon, we can
call the geticecream() function, passing it a value of 'Dave':

```
> CALL geticecream('Dave');
Query OK, 0 rows affected (0.00 sec)
```

Because the person is Dave, we expect the @icecream variable to be set to strawberry, and it is:

```
> SELECT @icecream;
+------------+
| @icecream  |
+------------+
| strawberry |
+------------+
1 row in set (0.00 sec)
```

On the other hand, say that we pass a person that's not Dave through the geticecream() procedure:

```
> CALL geticecream('May');
Query OK, 0 rows affected (0.00 sec)
```

In this case, @icecream is set to chocolate:

```
> SELECT @icecream;
+-----------+
| @icecream |
+-----------+
| chocolate |
+-----------+
1 row in set (0.00 sec)
```

As you can see, IF … THEN … ELSE statements are a powerful tool for decision making in SQL procedures.

Using CASE … END CASE

The CASE statement lets you test whether a variable is equal to any of several test values and execute code corresponding to the first test that's true:

```
CASE variable
    WHEN value_1 THEN statement_1
    [WHEN value_2 THEN statement_2]
    ...
    [ELSE statement_else]
END CASE
```

If no case's condition is true, the code in the ELSE statement is executed.

Here's an example. Say that you have a procedure, getday(), which accepts the day of the week as an argument, and sets the value in the variable @day with a comment on the day (for example, Thursday's comment is "Nearly there"). Writing this procedure is simple with a CASE statement to handle all the possible days.

We start by creating the procedure:

```
> DELIMITER //
> CREATE PROCEDURE getday(IN day VARCHAR(20))
BEGIN
...
END;
```

Then we add the CASE statement using the passed argument, day (see Chapter 12):

```
> DELIMITER //
> CREATE PROCEDURE getday(IN day VARCHAR(20))
BEGIN
CASE day
...
END CASE;
END;
```

Now we're able to add the WHEN statements to handle the various days:

```
> DELIMITER //
> CREATE PROCEDURE getday(IN day VARCHAR(20))
BEGIN
CASE day
WHEN "Sunday" THEN SET @day = "Day Off";
WHEN "Monday" THEN SET @day = "Darn";
WHEN "Tuesday" THEN SET @day = "Oh well";
WHEN "Wednesday" THEN SET @day = "Working, working, working";
WHEN "Thursday" THEN SET @day = "Nearly there";
WHEN "Friday" THEN SET @day = "TGIF!";
WHEN "Saturday" THEN SET @day = "Day Off";
...
END CASE;
END;
```

And we add an **ELSE** statement to take care of any illegal arguments:

```
> DELIMITER //
> CREATE PROCEDURE getday(IN day VARCHAR(20))
BEGIN
CASE day
WHEN "Sunday" THEN SET @day = "Day Off";
WHEN "Monday" THEN SET @day = "Darn";
WHEN "Tuesday" THEN SET @day = "Oh well";
WHEN "Wednesday" THEN SET @day = "Working, working, working";
WHEN "Thursday" THEN SET @day = "Nearly there";
WHEN "Friday" THEN SET @day = "TGIF!";
WHEN "Saturday" THEN SET @day = "Day Off";
ELSE SET @day = "Not a valid argument";
END CASE;
END;
```

And we end the whole procedure with the **//** end-of-line delimiter:

```
> DELIMITER //
> CREATE PROCEDURE getday(IN day VARCHAR(20))
BEGIN
CASE day
WHEN "Sunday" THEN SET @day = "Day Off";
WHEN "Monday" THEN SET @day = "Darn";
WHEN "Tuesday" THEN SET @day = "Oh well";
WHEN "Wednesday" THEN SET @day = "Working, working, working";
WHEN "Thursday" THEN SET @day = "Nearly there";
WHEN "Friday" THEN SET @day = "TGIF!";
WHEN "Saturday" THEN SET @day = "Day Off";
ELSE SET @day = "Not a valid argument";
END CASE;
END;
//
Query OK, 0 rows affected (0.00 sec)
```

After setting the end-of-line delimiter back to a semicolon, we call the getday() procedure with Monday:

```
> CALL getday('Monday');
Query OK, 0 rows affected (0.00 sec)
```

And we can check the @day variable to make sure it was set correctly by the CASE statement:

```
> SELECT @day;
+------+
| @day |
+------+
| Darn |
+------+
1 row in set (0.00 sec)
```

Success. Let's try Wednesday:

```
> CALL getday('Wednesday');
Query OK, 0 rows affected (0.00 sec)
```

And we check @day again:

```
> SELECT @day;
+--------------------------+
| @day                     |
+--------------------------+
| Working, working, working |
+--------------------------+
1 row in set (0.00 sec)
```

So the CASE statement does its job.

Using LOOP and LEAVE

The SQL LOOP statement lets you execute SQL statements repeatedly:

```
Label: LOOP
Loop statements
END LOOP;
```

Here, *Loop statements* is executed forever, over and over. Because you probably want to finish the loop at some point, you can use a LEAVE statement to jump out of the loop:

```
Label: LOOP
Loop statements
[LEAVE Label;]
END LOOP;
```

Let's see this in practice with a procedure called looptest(). In this procedure, we loop 10 times, adding 1 to a variable named @a each time.

First, we create the procedure:

```
> DELIMITER //
> CREATE PROCEDURE looptest()
BEGIN
...
END;
```

Next, we initialize @a to 0 and then start the loop:

```
> DELIMITER //
> CREATE PROCEDURE looptest()
BEGIN
SET @a = 0;
Looper: LOOP
...
END LOOP;
END;
```

Then we increment @a by 1 each time through the loop:

```
> DELIMITER //
> CREATE PROCEDURE looptest()
BEGIN
SET @a = 0;
Looper: LOOP
SET @a = @a + 1;
...
END LOOP;
END;
```

As written, this loop would go on forever, so let's terminate it with a LEAVE statement. We check whether @a has exceeded 9, and if so, leave the loop:

```
> DELIMITER //
> CREATE PROCEDURE looptest()
BEGIN
SET @a = 0;
Looper: LOOP
SET @a = @a + 1;
IF @a > 9 THEN
LEAVE Looper;
END IF;
END LOOP;
END;
```

And we can end the procedure with a // end-of-line delimiter:

```
> DELIMITER //
> CREATE PROCEDURE looptest()
BEGIN
SET @a = 0;
Looper: LOOP
SET @a = @a + 1;
IF @a > 9 THEN
LEAVE Looper;
```

```
END IF;
END LOOP;
END;
//
Query OK, 0 rows affected (0.06 sec)
```

Now we can call the looptest() procedure:

```
> CALL looptest();
Query OK, 0 rows affected (0.00 sec)
```

And check the value left in the @a variable:

```
> SELECT @a;
+------+
| @a   |
+------+
| 10   |
+------+
1 row in set (0.00 sec)
```

As you can see, the looptest() procedure left a value of 10 in the @a variable, just as we expected.

Using WHILE

The WHILE loop keeps executing while a condition you specify remains true. Here's the syntax:

```
Label: WHILE condition DO
Loop statements;
END WHILE;
```

Let's see this at work in a procedure named dowhile(). In this procedure, we increment a variable from 0 to 20.

We start by creating the procedure:

```
> DELIMITER //
> CREATE PROCEDURE dowhile()
BEGIN
...
END;
```

Next, we set a variable named @a to 0:

```
> DELIMITER //
> CREATE PROCEDURE dowhile( )
BEGIN
SET @a = 0;
...
END;
```

Now we set up the WHILE loop. We want to increment @a to 20, so the termination condition if the loop is @a < 20:

```
> DELIMITER //
> CREATE PROCEDURE dowhile( )
BEGIN
SET @a = 0;
WHILE @a < 20 Do
...
END WHILE;
END;
```

And inside the loop, we can increment @a each time:

```
> DELIMITER //
> CREATE PROCEDURE dowhile( )
BEGIN
SET @a = 0;
WHILE @a < 20 Do
SET @a = @a + 1;
END WHILE;
END;
```

We end the procedure with a // end-of-line delimiter:

```
> DELIMITER //
> CREATE PROCEDURE dowhile( )
BEGIN
SET @a = 0;
WHILE @a < 20 Do
SET @a = @a + 1;
END WHILE;
END;
//
Query OK, 0 rows affected (0.00 sec)//
```

Now we can call the dowhile() procedure:

```
> CALL dowhile();
Query OK, 0 rows affected (0.00 sec)
```

And finally, we check the value left in @a to confirm that it's really 20:

```
> SELECT @a;
+------+
| @a   |
+------+
| 20   |
+------+
1 row in set (0.00 sec)
```

Sure enough, the WHILE loop did its work.

Using REPEAT ... UNTIL

Another loop is the REPEAT ... UNTIL loop, which repeats until a condition that you specify is satisfied:

```
Label: REPEAT
Loop statements
UNTIL condition
END REPEAT;
```

Let's put this to work in a procedure named dorepeat():

```
> DELIMITER //
> CREATE PROCEDURE dorepeat()
BEGIN
...
END
```

We can start off with @a set to 0:

```
> DELIMITER //
> CREATE PROCEDURE dorepeat()
BEGIN
SET @a = 0;
...
END
```

Then we can set up the REPEAT loop, which runs until @a exceeds 29:

```
> DELIMITER //
> CREATE PROCEDURE dorepeat( )
BEGIN
SET @a = 0;
REPEAT
...
UNTIL @a > 29 END REPEAT;
END
```

Inside the loop, we increment @a each time through:

```
> DELIMITER //
> CREATE PROCEDURE dorepeat( )
BEGIN
SET @a = 0;
REPEAT
SET @a = @a + 1;
UNTIL @a > 29 END REPEAT;
END
```

We end the procedure with a // end-of-line delimiter:

```
> DELIMITER //
> CREATE PROCEDURE dorepeat( )
BEGIN
SET @a = 0;
REPEAT
SET @a = @a + 1;
UNTIL @a > 29 END REPEAT;
END
//
Query OK, 0 rows affected (0.00 sec)
```

Now we run dorepeat():

```
> CALL dorepeat( );
Query OK, 0 rows affected (0.00 sec)
```

And check the value left in @a:

```
> SELECT @a;
+------+
| @a   |
+------+
| 30   |
+------+
1 row in set (0.00 sec)
```

As you can see, @a was incremented to a value of 30 by the REPEAT loop.

Using ITERATE

You use the ITERATE statement inside loops, and it means "continue with the next time through the loop."

In other words, if you have a loop of four statements, all four statements are executed, each time through the loop, one after the other:

```
Label1: LOOP
Statement 1
Statement 2
Statement 3
Statement 4
END LOOP;
```

On the other hand, if you put an ITERATE statement after the first two statements, then only the first two statements are executed before the loop starts over.

```
Label1: LOOP
Statement 1
Statement 2
ITERATE Label1;
Statement 3
Statement 4
END LOOP;
```

So now you short-circuited the loop to become a loop of only two statements.

SQL CAUTION

You can only use ITERATE inside loop statements like LOOP, REPEAT, and WHILE.

Let's look at an example in a procedure called doiterate():

```
> DELIMITER //
>CREATE PROCEDURE doiterate()
BEGIN
...
END
```

Inside the procedure, we set up a loop:

```
> DELIMITER //
>CREATE PROCEDURE doiterate( )
BEGIN
label1: LOOP
...
END LOOP;
END
```

And inside the loop, we keep incrementing a variable named @a:

```
> DELIMITER //
>CREATE PROCEDURE doiterate( )
BEGIN
SET @a = 0;
label1: LOOP
SET @a = @a + 1;
...
END LOOP;
END
```

If the value in @a is less than 40, we jump to the next time through the loop, using ITERATE:

```
> DELIMITER //
>CREATE PROCEDURE doiterate( )
BEGIN
SET @a = 0;
label1: LOOP
SET @a = @a + 1;
IF @a < 40
THEN ITERATE label1;
END IF;
...
END LOOP;
END
```

If @a is 40 or above, we leave the loop with LEAVE:

```
> DELIMITER //
>CREATE PROCEDURE doiterate( )
BEGIN
SET @a = 0;
label1: LOOP
SET @a = @a + 1;
IF @a < 40
THEN ITERATE label1;
END IF;
LEAVE label1;
END LOOP;
END
```

The final step is to end the procedure with the // end-of-line delimiter:

```
> DELIMITER //
>CREATE PROCEDURE doiterate()
BEGIN
SET @a = 0;
label1: LOOP
SET @a = @a + 1;
IF @a < 40
THEN ITERATE label1;
END IF;
LEAVE label1;
END LOOP;
END
//
Query OK, 0 rows affected (0.17 sec)
```

Now we call the doiterate() procedure:

```
> CALL doiterate();
Query OK, 0 rows affected (0.00 sec)
```

And we check @a to confirm that it does hold 40:

```
> SELECT @a;
+------+
| @a   |
+------+
| 40   |
+------+
1 row in set (0.00 sec)
```

So the ITERATE statement did what it was supposed to do.

The Least You Need to Know

- The IF ... THEN ... ELSE statement lets you make decisions and execute code depending on whether or not a condition is true.
- The CASE ... END CASE statement lets you test multiple conditions and execute SQL depending on which condition is true.
- The LOOP ... LEAVE statement lets you execute SQL statements repeatedly until you leave the loop with the LEAVE statement.

- The WHILE loop lets you execute SQL statements repeatedly while a certain condition you specify remains true.
- The REPEAT … UNTIL loop lets you execute SQL statements repeatedly until a condition you specify becomes true.
- The ITERATE statement lets you skip to the next iteration of the loop in loop statements.

Creating and Administrating User Accounts in SQL

In This Chapter

- Creating user accounts with or without passwords
- Creating remote users
- Assigning users privileges

This chapter is about creating new user accounts in SQL and granting those users various database privileges. If you're the administrator of your database, you need this skill to add new users to the database.

When you've added new users, you can also grant them access privileges to your database, allowing some actions but not others. Let's take a look at how this works.

Creating New User Accounts

Say you're the administrator of your DBMS, and you're the only one who can log in to it. After a while, you decide it's lonely at the top, and you want to add other users.

But just how do you do that? Are there special files you have to edit? Special programs to run? In most DBMSes, you can create new user accounts in SQL, and we'll take a look at the process here.

Users are stored in an internal SQL table in most DBMSes, so if you can find that table, you can edit it directly to add new users with INSERT or UPDATE statements. But finding the name of the table to work with isn't easy. For example, it's mysql.user in MySQL, and manipulating it yourself is error-prone, so it's better to add new users the way we do in this chapter.

It's common to specify users as *'user_name'@'host_name.'* This tells your DBMS that the user's name is *user_name,* and the host they'll be logging in from. For example, 'richard'@'localhost' specifies a user name richard, who will be logging in the localhost.

You usually don't need to specify the host name for a user if you don't want to—you can use a % wildcard instead. So 'richard'@'%' means that your DBMS will not check Richard's host name when he logs in.

To actually create a new user, you use the CREATE USER statement, as shown in the following:

```
CREATE USER user_specification
    [, user_specification] ...
user_specification:
    user [IDENTIFIED BY [PASSWORD] 'password']
```

Creating User Accounts with No Password

Let's create an account for the user name Richard, who will log from the localhost. To give Richard an account with no password, use CREATE USER:

```
CREATE USER
```

To specify Richard's account, add this:

```
CREATE USER 'richard'@'localhost';
```

Okay, let's do it. Log on to your DBMS as an administrator, or root. Note that you have to have the top-most privileges in your DBMS to be able to create new user accounts:

```
>
```

Switch to the database you want to add the new user to:

```
>USE corporation;
```

Alright, now create Richard's account, with no password:

```
> CREATE USER 'richard'@'localhost';
```

It looks like it worked. But did it? You can check by logging in as Richard, or by checking the internal table that keeps track of users.

For example, in MySQL, that table is called mysql.user, and you can take a look at it directly. Note that it's a big table with many columns, and so it will wrap here:

```
> SELECT * FROM mysql.user;
+------------+----------+-----------------------------------------------+-
+--------------+-------------+--------------+--------------+-----------
--+---------------+-------------+-----------+------------+-----------
---------+------------+--------------+-------------+----------------
-------------+---------------+--------------+--------------------+--
----+----------------+-------------+---------------------+---------
---+----------+------------+-------------+--------------+-----------
------+-----------------+--------------------+
| Host       | User     | Password                                      |
| Insert_priv | Update_priv | Delete_priv | Create_priv | Drop_priv
v | Shutdown_priv | Process_priv | File_priv | Grant_priv | Referenc
dex_priv | Alter_priv | Show_db_priv | Super_priv | Create_tmp_table
_tables_priv | Execute_priv | Repl_slave_priv | Repl_client_priv | C
riv | Show_view_priv | Create_routine_priv | Alter_routine_priv | Cr
iv | ssl_type | ssl_cipher | x509_issuer | x509_subject | max_questi
dates | max_connections | max_user_connections |
+------------+----------+-----------------------------------------------+-
+--------------+-------------+--------------+--------------+-----------
--+---------------+-------------+-----------+------------+-----------
---------+------------+--------------+-------------+----------------
-------------+---------------+--------------+--------------------+--
----+----------------+-------------+---------------------+---------
---+----------+------------+-------------+--------------+-----------
------+-----------------+--------------------+
| localhost | root     | *B1C8657FC5DC25635892B01F82A9082F581DFDC5 |
| Y           | Y           | Y            | Y            | Y
  | Y             | Y            | Y         | Y          | Y
         | Y          | Y            | Y           | Y
             | Y             | Y            | Y                  | Y
    | Y              | Y           | Y                   | Y
    |          |            |             |              | 0
      | 0               | 0                    |
| localhost | richard  |                                               |
| N           | N           | N            | N            | N
  | N             | N            | N         | N          | N
         | N          | N            | N           | N
             | N             | N            | N                  | N
    | N              | N           | N                   | N
    |          |            |             |              | 0
      | 0               | 0                    |
```

continues

continued

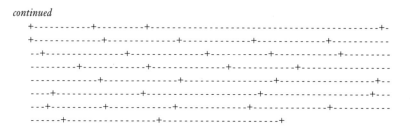

If you study this data, you can see a root account (with an encrypted password of B1C8657FC5DC25635892B01F82A9082F581DFDC5) and a richard account, with no password. This is just what you wanted.

So that creates the richard account, which allows Richard to log in from the localhost with no password.

You can also create the account so that Richard can log in from any host, like this:

```
> CREATE USER 'richard'@'%';
```

This means Richard can log in from any host. Of course, creating new user accounts with no password is inherently dangerous because it's so insecure. Let's take a look at creating new user accounts with passwords.

Creating User Accounts with Passwords

Let's create an account for a person named Jessica, using a password of opensesame. You start with CREATE USER:

```
CREATE USER
```

Specify Jessica's user name:

```
CREATE USER 'jessica'@'localhost'
```

Finally, give Jessica a password with an IDENTIFIED BY clause like this:

```
CREATE USER 'jessica'@'localhost' IDENTIFIED BY 'opensesame';
```

Did it work? In MySQL, for example, you can take a look at the user table:

```
> SELECT * FROM mysql.user;
+-----------+---------+---------------------------------------------
+-------------+-------------+---------------+-------------+---------
--+---------------+--------------+-----------+-------------+------
---------+-----------+---------------+--------------+---------------
-------------+--------------+--------------+--------------------+
----+---------------+-----------------------+---------------------+
---+----------+-------------+---------------+-------------+---------
------+-----------------+----------------------+
| Host      | User    | Password
| Insert_priv | Update_priv | Delete_priv | Create_priv | Drop_pr
v | Shutdown_priv | Process_priv | File_priv | Grant_priv | Refer
dex_priv | Alter_priv | Show_db_priv | Super_priv | Create_tmp_ta
_tables_priv | Execute_priv | Repl_slave_priv | Repl_client_priv
riv | Show_view_priv | Create_routine_priv | Alter_routine_priv |
iv | ssl_type | ssl_cipher | x509_issuer | x509_subject | max_que
dates | max_connections | max_user_connections |
+-----------+---------+---------------------------------------------
+-------------+-------------+---------------+-------------+---------
--+---------------+--------------+-----------+-------------+------
---------+-----------+---------------+--------------+---------------
-------------+--------------+--------------+--------------------+
----+---------------+-----------------------+---------------------+
---+----------+-------------+---------------+-------------+---------
------+-----------------+----------------------+
| localhost | root    | *B1C8657FC5DC25635892B01F82A9082F581DFDC5
| Y         | Y       | Y           | Y           | Y           | Y
  | Y           | Y         | Y           | Y           | Y
    | Y         | Y         | Y           | Y           | Y
      | Y         | Y         | Y           | Y
    | Y         | Y         | Y           |
    |           |           |             |             | 0
      | 0         | 0         |             |
| localhost | richard |
| N         | N       | N           | N           | N
  | N           | N         | N           | N           | N
      | N         | N         | N           | N
        | N         | N         | N           |
    | N         | N         | N           |
    |           |           |             |             | 0
      | 0         | 0         |             |
| localhost | jessica | *CD084AF663D43EC51ADA2C369B9478DFDE41533F
| N         | N       | N           | N           | N
  | N           | N         | N           | N           | N
      | N         | N         | N           | N
        | N         | N         | N           |
    | N         | N         | N           |
    |           |           |             |             | 0
      | 0         | 0         |             |
+-----------+---------+---------------------------------------------
+-------------+-------------+---------------+-------------+---------
--+---------------+--------------+-----------+-------------+------
---------+-----------+---------------+--------------+---------------
-------------+--------------+--------------+--------------------+
----+---------------+-----------------------+---------------------+
---+----------+-------------+---------------+-------------+---------
------+-----------------+----------------------+
```

Jessica has been added, along with her password, which is encrypted as CD084AF663D43EC51ADA2C369B9478DFDE41533F.

> **SQL CAUTION**
>
> If you're after ultra-security, here's something you should know. Some DBMSes record all SQL statements in a history table, which means the password you enter in plain text here will be recorded in that table. To get around that, use the PASSWORD() function to convert the password to a code like CD084AF663D43EC51ADA2C369B9478DFDE41533F and use that code, to the IDENTIFIED BY clause.

And if you don't want to limit Jessica to having to log in from a particular host, you can specify that any host is okay for her to log in on:

```
CREATE USER 'jessica'@'%' IDENTIFIED BY 'opensesame';
```

You've seen how to create new user accounts, both with and without passwords. But you may not want to grant all new users the same privileges. For example, you may not want to give some users INSERT privileges on tables, restricting what they can do with database tables.

Let's take a look at how granting privileges works.

Granting Privileges

Say you're in charge of the master database and have been asked to let the boss's nephew see it. You have no great respect for the boss's nephew, and you worry that he can do a lot of harm.

Wouldn't it be nice if you could restrict the boss's nephew to using SELECT statements so he could read the database, but not change it? He wouldn't be able to use INSERT, DELETE, UPDATE, CREATE, or other possibly dangerous statements.

With privileges, you can restrict the pesky nephew's access to only using SELECT statements on tables. That's the kind of restriction that granting privileges is all about.

After you create a new user with the CREATE USER command, you'll usually follow that up with a GRANT statement, indicating what privileges you want to grant the new user.

Besides just SELECT, you can also let the new user use UPDATE statements, INSERT statements, CREATE statements, and so on.

The way you typically use GRANT is as follows (*priv_type* can be found in Table 16.1):

```
GRANT priv_type [(column_list)]
[, priv_type [(column_list)]] ...
ON [object_type] priv_level
TO user_specification [, user_specification] ...
[REQUIRE {NONE | ssl_option [[AND] ssl_option] ...}]
[WITH with_option ...]

object_type:
    TABLE
  | FUNCTION
  | PROCEDURE

priv_level:
    *
  | *.*
  | db_name.*
  | db_name.tbl_name
  | tbl_name
  | db_name.routine_name

user_specification:
    user [IDENTIFIED BY [PASSWORD] 'password']

ssl_option:
    SSL
  | X509
  | CIPHER 'cipher'
  | ISSUER 'issuer'
  | SUBJECT 'subject'

with_option:
    GRANT OPTION
  | MAX_QUERIES_PER_HOUR count
  | MAX_UPDATES_PER_HOUR count
  | MAX_CONNECTIONS_PER_HOUR count
  | MAX_USER_CONNECTIONS count
```

As you can see, the GRANT statement is a whopper, and is best understood with multiple examples.

Which privileges can you grant? The individual privileges are items like SELECT, UPDATE, and so on, and a typical list of the privileges a DBMS allows (privileges usually vary by DBMS) appears in Table 16.1.

Table 16.1 Privileges You Can Grant

Privilege	Meaning
ALL [PRIVILEGES]	Grants all privileges at specified access level except GRANT OPTION.
ALTER	Allows use of ALTER TABLE.
ALTER ROUTINE	Allows stored routines to be altered or dropped.
CREATE	Allows database and table creation.
CREATE ROUTINE	Allows stored routine creation.
CREATE TEMPORARY TABLES	Allows use of CREATE TEMPORARY TABLE.
CREATE USER	Allows use of CREATE USER, DROP USER, RENAME USER, and REVOKE ALL PRIVILEGES.
CREATE VIEW	Allows views to be created or altered.
DELETE	Allows use of DELETE.
DROP	Allows databases, tables, and views to be dropped.
EVENT	Allows use of events for the Event Scheduler.
EXECUTE	Allows the user to execute stored routines.
FILE	Allows the user to cause the server to read or write files.
GRANT OPTION	Allows privileges to be granted to or removed from other accounts.
INDEX	Allows indexes to be created or dropped.
INSERT	Allows use of INSERT.
LOCK TABLES	Allows use of LOCK TABLES on tables for which you have the SELECT privilege.
PROCESS	Allows the user to see all processes with SHOW PROCESSLIST.

Privilege	Meaning
RELOAD	Allows use of FLUSH operations.
REPLICATION CLIENT	Allows the user to ask where master or slave servers are.
REPLICATION SLAVE	Allows replication slaves to read binary log events from the master.
SELECT	Allows use of SELECT.
SHOW DATABASES	Allows SHOW DATABASES to show all databases.
SHOW VIEW	Allows use of SHOW CREATE VIEW.
TRIGGER	Allows trigger operations.
UPDATE	Allows use of UPDATE.
USAGE	Synonym for "no privileges."

Let's take a look at some examples.

Granting All Privileges

We'll start by granting all privileges to a new user, including the option to let the new user grant privileges to others. In this case, we'll create a new user account for Dan on the localhost, and then grant privileges.

SQL CAUTION

Note that you yourself must have privilege X if you want to grant privilege X to other users.

Here's how it works. First, create the user 'dan'@'localhost':

```
> CREATE USER 'dan'@'localhost' IDENTIFIED BY 'letmein';
```

That creates Dan's user account. Now it's time to grant him some privileges. You want to grant Dan all available privileges, so start with the GRANT statement like this:

```
> GRANT ALL PRIVILEGES
```

Next, specify what databases you're granting privileges on. This can be a list of database names, but in this case, we want to grant Dan maximum privileges, so we'll use *.* to indicate that we want to grant Dan all privileges on all databases:

```
> GRANT ALL PRIVILEGES ON *.*
```

Next, specify who you are granting privileges to—that is, 'dan'@'localhost':

```
> GRANT ALL PRIVILEGES ON *.* TO 'dan'@'localhost';
```

Great, now you have created the dan account and given it all privileges. You can take a look at the results in your DBMS's user table. For example, that would look like this in MySQL:

```
> SELECT * FROM mysql.user;
+------------+---------+-----------------------------------------------+-
+-------------+-------------+------------------+------------------+------------
--+------------------+-------------+------------+-------------+---------
-----------+-------------+-------------+------------------+------------------
------------+-------------+-------------+------------------+---------+--
----+------------------+-------------+------------------+---------+---
---+------------+-------------+------------------+-------------+-----------
------+------------------+----------------------+------+
| Host       | User    | Password                                      |
| Insert_priv | Update_priv | Delete_priv | Create_priv | Drop_priv
v | Shutdown_priv | Process_priv | File_priv | Grant_priv | Referenc
dex_priv | Alter_priv | Show_db_priv | Super_priv | Create_tmp_table
_tables_priv | Execute_priv | Repl_slave_priv | Repl_client_priv | C
riv | Show_view_priv | Create_routine_priv | Alter_routine_priv | Cr
iv | ssl_type | ssl_cipher | x509_issuer | x509_subject | max_questi
dates | max_connections | max_user_connections |
+------------+---------+-----------------------------------------------+-
+-------------+-------------+------------------+------------------+------------
--+------------------+-------------+------------+-------------+---------
-----------+-------------+-------------+------------------+------------------
------------+-------------+-------------+------------------+---------+--
----+------------------+-------------+------------------+---------+---
---+------------+-------------+------------------+-------------+-----------
------+------------------+----------------------+------+
| localhost | root    | *B1C8657FC5DC25635892B01F82A9082F581DFDC5 |
| Y           | Y           | Y                | Y                | Y
  | Y             | Y            | Y         | Y          | Y
    | Y         | Y            | Y          | Y
      | Y            | Y               | Y                | Y
    | Y              | Y                   | Y                  | Y
  |            |             |                  |             | 0
    | 0         |             | 0                |             |
```

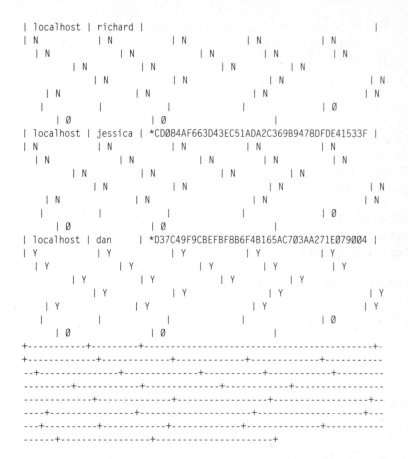

```
| localhost | richard |                                              |
| N               | N               | N             | N            | N
   | N               | N                | N             | N           | N
      | N              | N            | N              | N
         | N            | N            | N              | N.
         | N            | N            | N             | N.
      | N               | N            | N             | N
         |              |             |              | 0
      | 0              | 0            |
| localhost | jessica | *CD084AF663D43EC51ADA2C369B9478DFDE41533F |
| N               | N               | N             | N            | N
   | N               | N                | N             | N           | N
      | N              | N            | N              | N
         | N            | N            | N              | N
         | N            | N            | N             | N.
         |              |             |              | 0
      | 0              | 0            |
| localhost | dan     | *D37C49F9CBEFBF8B6F4B165AC703AA271E079004 |
| Y               | Y               | Y             | Y            | Y
   | Y               | Y                | Y             | Y           | Y
      | Y              | Y            | Y              | Y
         | Y            | Y            | Y              | Y
         | Y            | Y            | Y             | Y.
         |              |             |              | 0
      | 0              | 0            |
+-----------+---------+-------------------------------------------+-
+-------------+-------------+-------------+-------------+-----------
--+---------------+-------------+-------------+-------------+--------
---------+-------------+-------------+-------------+-------------
-------------+---------------+-------------+-------------------+---
----+---------------+-------------+---------------+-------------+---
---+----------+------------+-------------+-------------+-----------
------+-----------------+-------------+--------------------+
```

Note that the fields following the dan account, although hard to read here, have all Ys in them, indicating that that privilege is granted to Dan. By contrast, note that Jessica's account, which we created earlier in the chapter but did not assign any privileges to, has all Ns in the privileges field, indicating that she doesn't have any privileges.

In fact, there's usually an easier way to take a look at user privileges. In MySQL, for example, you can use the SHOW GRANTS statement:

```
> SHOW GRANTS FOR 'dan'@'localhost';
+------------------------------------------------------------------
--------------------------------------------------+
| Grants for dan@localhost
                                             |
+------------------------------------------------------------------
--------------------------------------------------+
```

continues

continued

```
| GRANT ALL PRIVILEGES ON *.* TO 'dan'@'localhost' IDENTIFIED BY PAS
49F9CBEFBF8B6F4B165AC703AA271E079004'                             |
+-----------------------------------------------------------------
-----------------------------------------------------------+
```

That's how to grant all privileges on all databases. Now let's take a look at narrowing the number of databases the user has privileges on.

Specifying Which Database the User Has Privileges On

In the previous example, we granted the user all privileges on all databases. But what if you only want to grant a user privileges on a single database?

Let's create a new user named Jason and give him all privileges on our Corporation database to see how this works.

First, create the Jason user:

```
> CREATE USER 'jason'@'localhost' IDENTIFIED BY 'letmein';
```

Then use GRANT to grant Jason all privileges on the corporation database:

```
> GRANT ALL PRIVILEGES
```

Now specify that you want to grant privileges on the Corporation database like this:

```
> GRANT ALL PRIVILEGES ON Corporation.*
```

The reason you use Corporation.* is to grant access to all tables in the Corporation database. Finally, specify to whom you're granting privileges:

```
> GRANT ALL PRIVILEGES ON Corporation.* TO 'jason'@'localhost'
```

You'll see these changes mirrored in the user table of your DBMS. For example, in MySQL, that looks like:

```
> SELECT * FROM mysql.user;
+------------+---------+------------------------------------------
+-------------+-------------+-------------+-------------+---------
--+---------------+-------------+-----------+-------------+-------
```

```
---------+------------+---------------+------------+---------------
------------+--------------+-------------------+-------------------+
----+---------------+------------+-----------------+-------------------+-
---+----------+-----------+------------+--------------+---------
------+-----------------+----------------------+
| Host      | User   | Password
| Insert_priv | Update_priv | Delete_priv | Create_priv | Drop_pri
v | Shutdown_priv | Process_priv | File_priv | Grant_priv | Refere
dex_priv | Alter_priv | Show_db_priv | Super_priv | Create_tmp_tab
_tables_priv | Execute_priv | Repl_slave_priv | Repl_client_priv |
riv | Show_view_priv | Create_routine_priv | Alter_routine_priv |
iv | ssl_type | ssl_cipher | x509_issuer | x509_subject | max_ques
dates | max_connections | max_user_connections |
+------------+----------+----------------------------------------
+-------------+--------------+--------------+--------------+---------
--+---------------+--------------+------------+------------+-------
---------+------------+---------------+------------+---------------
------------+--------------+-------------------+-------------------+
----+---------------+------------+-----------------+-------------------+-
---+----------+-----------+------------+--------------+---------
------+-----------------+----------------------+
| localhost | root   | *B1C8657FC5DC25635892B01F82A9082F581DFDC5
| Y          | Y           | Y           | Y           | Y
| Y          | Y            | Y           | Y            | Y
| Y          | Y           | Y           | Y
| Y          | Y           | Y           | Y
| Y          | Y           | Y           |
|            |             |             |             | 0
| 0          | 0           |
| localhost | richard |
| N          | N           | N           | N           | N
| N          | N            | N           | N            | N
| N          | N           | N           | N
| N          | N           | N           | N
| N          | N           | N           |
|            |             |             |             | 0
| 0          | 0           |
| localhost | jessica | *CD084AF663D43EC51ADA2C369B9478DFDE41533F
| N          | N           | N           | N           | N
| N          | N            | N           | N            | N
| N          | N           | N           | N
| N          | N           | N           | N
| N          | N           | N           |
|            |             |             |             | 0
| 0          | 0           |
| localhost | dan     | *D37C49F9CBEFBF8B6F4B165AC703AA271E079004
| Y          | Y           | Y           | Y           | Y
| Y          | Y            | Y           | Y            | Y
| Y          | Y           | Y           | Y
| Y          | Y           | Y           | Y
| Y          | Y           | Y           |
|            |             |             |             | 0
| 0          | 0           |
```

continued

```
| localhost | jason   | *D37C49F9CBEFBF8B6F4B165AC703AA271E079004
| N             | N             | N             | N             | N
     | N             | N             | N             | N             | N
          | N             | N             | N             | N
          | N             | N             | N                             |
     | N             | N             | N                             |
     |             |             |             | 0
     | 0                     | 0                     |
+-----------+---------+-------------------------------------------
+-------------+------------+-------------+-------------+---------
--+---------------+-------------+-------------+------------+-------
---------+------------+---------+-------------+------------+-------
-------------+-------------+---------+-------------+----------------+
----+------------+---------+------------------+----------------+-
---+----------+-----------+--------------+------------+---------
------+----------------+-------------+-----------------+
```

You can see that Jason has Ns in the privilege fields because he doesn't have general privileges over all databases. Instead, you can see that Jason has privileges on the Corporation database this way:

```
> SHOW GRANTS FOR 'jason'@'localhost';
+-----------------------------------------------------------------
-----------------------------+
| Grants for jason@localhost
                             |
+-----------------------------------------------------------------
-----------------------------+
| GRANT USAGE ON *.* TO 'jason'@'localhost' IDENTIFIED BY PASSWORD
FBF8B6F4B165AC703AA271E079004' |
| GRANT ALL PRIVILEGES ON 'corporation'.* TO 'jason'@'localhost'
                             |
+-----------------------------------------------------------------
-----------------------------+
```

Very nice. Now let's see if we can't grant privileges on a specific table.

Specifying Which Table the User Has Privileges On

Let's say we want to grant all privileges on the Employees table in the Corporation database, but just that one table, to Jennifer.

First, create the Jennifer user:

```
> CREATE USER 'jennifer'@'localhost' IDENTIFIED BY 'letmein';
```

Then use GRANT to grant Jennifer all privileges on the Corporation database's Employees table:

```
> GRANT ALL PRIVILEGES
```

Specify that you want to grant privileges on the Corporation database's Employees table like this:

```
> GRANT ALL PRIVILEGES ON Corporation.Employees
```

The reason we use Corporation.Employees is to grant access to the Employees table in the Corporation database.

Finally, specify to whom you're granting privileges:

```
> GRANT ALL PRIVILEGES ON Corporation.Employees TO
➥   'jennifer'@'localhost';
```

Great, that gives Jennifer all privileges on the Employees table. You can look in the user table to find Jennifer:

```
> select * from mysql.user;
+-----------+----------+-------------------------------------------+
 -+-------------+-------------+--------------+-------------+----------
---+----------------+--------------+-------------+------------+--------
----------+-------------+-------------+------------+---------------
--------------+-------------+--------------+----------------+-
-----+----------------+-------------------+-------------------+--
----+----------+------------+--------------+-------------+----------
-------+----------------+---------------------+
| Host       | User     | Password                                  |
 | Insert_priv | Update_priv | Delete_priv | Create_priv | Drop_priv
iv | Shutdown_priv | Process_priv | File_priv | Grant_priv | Referen
ndex_priv | Alter_priv | Show_db_priv | Super_priv | Create_tmp_tabl
k_tables_priv | Execute_priv | Repl_slave_priv | Repl_client_priv |
priv | Show_view_priv | Create_routine_priv | Alter_routine_priv | C
riv | ssl_type | ssl_cipher | x509_issuer | x509_subject | max_quest
pdates | max_connections | max_user_connections |
+-----------+----------+-------------------------------------------+
 -+-------------+-------------+--------------+-------------+----------
---+----------------+--------------+-------------+------------+--------
----------+-------------+-------------+------------+---------------
--------------+-------------+--------------+----------------+-
-----+----------------+-------------------+-------------------+--
----+----------+------------+--------------+-------------+----------
-------+----------------+---------------------+
```

continues

continued

```
| localhost | root    | *B1C8657FC5DC25635892B01F82A9082F581DFDC5 |
  | Y           | Y             | Y              | Y             | Y
   | Y           | Y             | Y            | Y             | Y
      | Y           | Y            | Y            | Y
       | Y           | Y           | Y
    | Y           | Y              | Y                      | Y
  |           |            |             | Ø
     | Ø          | Ø                |
| localhost | richard |                                        |
  | N           | N             | N             | N             | N
   | N           | N             | N             | N             | N
      | N           | N           | N            | N
       | N           | N          | N
    | N           | N             | N                      | N
  |           |            |             | Ø
     | Ø          | Ø                |
| localhost | jessica | *CD084AF663D43EC51ADA2C369B9478DFDE41533F |
  | N           | N             | N             | N             | N
   | N           | N             | N             | N             | N
      | N           | N           | N            | N
       | N           | N          | N                        |
    | N           | N             | N                     |—N
  |           |            |             | Ø
     | Ø          | Ø                |
| localhost | dan     | *D37C49F9CBEFBF8B6F4B165AC703AA271E079004 |
  | Y           | Y             | Y              | Y             | Y
   | Y           | Y             | Y            | Y             | Y
      | Y           | Y            | Y            | Y
       | Y           | Y           | Y
    | Y           | Y             | Y                      | Y
  |           |            |             | Ø
     | Ø          | Ø                |
| localhost | jason   | *D37C49F9CBEFBF8B6F4B165AC703AA271E079004 |
  | N           | N             | N             | N             | N
   | N           | N             | N             | N             | N
      | N           | N           | N            | N
       | N           | N          | N                        |
    | N           | N             | N                      | N
  |           |            |             | Ø
     | Ø          | Ø                |
| localhost | jennifer | *D37C49F9CBEFBF8B6F4B165AC703AA271E079004 |
  | N           | N             | N             | N             | N
   | N           | N             | N             | N             | N
      | N           | N           | N            | N
       | N           | N          | N                        |
    | N           | N             | N                      | N
  |           |            |             | Ø
     | Ø          | Ø                |
+------------+----------+---------------------------------------------+
 -+-------------+-------------+-------------+-------------+----------
  ---+-------------+-------------+-------------+-------------+-------
  ----------+-------------+-------------+-------------+-------------+
  -------------+-------------+-------------+-------------+---------+-
  -----+-------------+-------------+-------------+-------------+--
  ----+-------------+-------------+-------------+-------------+---------
  -------+-------------+---------------------+
```

To find Jennifer's specific privileges, we check this way:

```
> SHOW GRANTS FOR 'jennifer'@'localhost';
+---------------------------------------------------------------------------
----------------------------------+
| Grants for jennifer@localhost
                                  |
+---------------------------------------------------------------------------
----------------------------------+
| GRANT USAGE ON *.* TO 'jennifer'@'localhost' IDENTIFIED BY PASSWORD '*D37C49F9
CBEFBF8B6F4B165AC703AA271E079004' |
| GRANT ALL PRIVILEGES ON 'corporation'.'employees' TO 'jennifer'@'localhost'
                                  |
+---------------------------------------------------------------------------
---------------------------------+----------------------------------+
```

As you can see, Jennifer has all privileges on the Employees table.

Granting Specific Privileges

Let's see how to grant specific privileges to a user. For example, say you want to give Mike most of the privileges on the Employees table—except DROP, which means he can't delete the Employees table.

First, create the Mike user:

```
> CREATE USER 'mike'@'localhost' IDENTIFIED BY 'peanut';
```

Then use GRANT to grant Mike specific privileges on the Corporation database's Employees table:

```
> GRANT SELECT,INSERT,UPDATE,DELETE,CREATE
```

In this case, you grant the SELECT, INSERT, UPDATE, DELETE, and CREATE privileges to Mike and omit the DROP privilege.

Next, specify for what database or table Mike is getting his privileges:

```
> GRANT SELECT,INSERT,UPDATE,DELETE,CREATE
ON corporation.Employees
```

And finally, specify that you're granting these privileges to Mike:

```
> GRANT SELECT,INSERT,UPDATE,DELETE,CREATE
ON corporation.Employees
TO 'mike'@'localhost';
```

That's it. We can verify the grants to Mike this way:

```
> SHOW GRANTS FOR 'mike'@'localhost';
+----------------------------------------------------------------
------------------------------+
| Grants for mike@localhost
                                    |
+----------------------------------------------------------------
------------------------------+
| GRANT USAGE ON *.* TO 'mike'@'localhost' IDENTIFIED BY PASSWORD
   ➡ '*FD62797ED464C2843942A9167CC0521779D68862' |
| GRANT SELECT, INSERT, UPDATE, DELETE, CREATE ON 'corporation'.'employees' TO
'mike'@'localhost'              |
+----------------------------------------------------------------
------------------------------+
```

Here's another example. Say you wanted to give Tina just SELECT privileges on the Employees table. That works like this.

First, create a Tina user:

```
> CREATE USER 'tina'@'localhost' IDENTIFIED BY 'beachball';
```

Then use GRANT to grant Tina only SELECT privileges:

```
> GRANT SELECT
```

Next, you have to specify on what database table Tina is getting her privileges:

```
> GRANT SELECT
ON corporation.Employees
```

And finally, specify that you're granting these privileges to Tina:

```
> GRANT SELECT
ON corporation.Employees
TO 'tina'@'localhost';
```

And that's all it takes. Here's the result:

```
> SHOW GRANTS FOR 'tina'@'localhost';
+----------------------------------------------------------------
------------------------------+
| Grants for tina@localhost
                                    |
+----------------------------------------------------------------
------------------------------+
```

```
| GRANT USAGE ON *.* TO 'tina'@'localhost' IDENTIFIED BY PASSWORD
➡  '*032F31C6561FFB44745E58AF4A3E68498B7F8589' |
| GRANT SELECT ON 'corporation'.'employees' TO 'tina'@'localhost'
                             |
+-------------------------------------------------------------------------
```

As you can see, Tina has SELECT privileges on the Employees
table.

Letting Users Grant Privileges

You might want to let other users grant privileges themselves, and
you can do that. We'll create a new account named Ed with all privileges, and let Ed grant privileges to others.

First, create the Ed account:

```
> CREATE USER 'ed'@'localhost' IDENTIFIED BY 'letmein';
```

Now it's time to grant some privileges.

You want to grant Ed all available privileges, so we start with the
GRANT statement like this:

```
> GRANT ALL PRIVILEGES
```

Next, specify what databases we're granting privileges on. Here, that
will be *.*:

```
> GRANT ALL PRIVILEGES ON *.*
```

Specify who we are granting privileges to—that is, 'ed'@'localhost':

```
> GRANT ALL PRIVILEGES ON *.* TO 'ed'@'localhost'
```

Finally, indicate that you want to let Ed grant privileges to others as
well by adding WITH GRANT OPTION:

```
> GRANT ALL PRIVILEGES ON *.* TO 'ed'@'localhost' WITH GRANT OPTION;
```

Great, now we've created the ed account and given it all privileges,
and let it also give privileges to others.

You can check that like this:

```
> SHOW GRANTS FOR 'ed'@'localhost';
+------------------------------------------------------------------------------
-----------------------------------------------------------------+
| Grants for ed@localhost
                                                              |
+------------------------------------------------------------------------------
----------------------------------------------------------+
| GRANT ALL PRIVILEGES ON *.* TO 'ed'@'localhost' IDENTIFIED BY PASSWORD
    ➡  '*D37C49F9CBEFBF8B6F4B165AC703AA271E079004' WITH GRANT OPTION |
+------------------------------------------------------------------------------
-----------------------------------------------------+
```

As you can see, Ed has been granted all privileges, and can grant
privileges to others.

The Least You Need to Know

- You create new user accounts with the CREATE USER
  statement.
- In the CREATE USER account, you specify the new user's
  password.
- You grant privileges to use with the GRANT statement.
- To grant a privilege, you have to have that privilege.
- To allow users to grant privileges to others, you use the WITH
  GRANT OPTION with the GRANT statement.

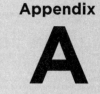
* A wildcard that matches anything appropriate to where it appears in an SQL statement.

column A vertical set of fields in a database table, all with the same data type.

commit Doing this to a transaction writes all its changes to the underlying database.

constraint A limitation on the values a column can hold.

cursor A location in the result set of an SQL query. You can move cursors up and down in result sets, fetching records from various locations at will.

database A container for tables.

expression A term that SQL can evaluate to a value.

field A single cell in a table.

foreign key A value in one table that must appear in a column you specify in another table.

index A presorted version of the data in a column or columns from a table, used to speed filtering and sorting.

join An SQL statement that takes data from two or more tables.

local variable A variable declared and used inside a stored procedure. It is not accessible outside the procedure.

NULL When a cell contains this value, it contains no value at all. Typically, this means the data in the cell hasn't been initialized.

primary key A guaranteed unique identifier for each record.

query   An individual statement that performs an action.

roll back   Undoing a transaction.

row   Holds a record in a table, such as a record for each student in a class. Each row is divided into columns, such as the name column and grade column. Thus, rows are collections of data items (held in columns) to make a record.

savepoint   A marked location in a transaction that an SQL user can roll back to.

SQL   Stands for Structured Query Language, a language that talks to databases and allows users to store, manipulate, and extract data.

stored procedures   Chunks of SQL code that can be run over and over again.

subquery   A nested SQL statement that returns a value or values that are then further checked, usually in a WHERE clause.

table   A grid with rows and columns that holds data.

transaction   A set of sensitive SQL statements that you want to either complete without error or undo entirely.

trigger   Chunks of SQL code that are executed—or "triggered"— by INSERT, UPDATE, or DELETE actions on a table. Each is connected with a table until you remove it—that is, drop it.

VARCHAR   A variable-length character string.

Using Different DBMSes with the Example SQL

This appendix explains how to get an interactive command prompt for various DBMSes so that you can enter the examples in this book.

DB2

Here's how to enter and run SQL statements in DB2:

1. Start the Command Center.

2. Click the **Script** tab.

3. Enter your SQL in the script text box.

4. Click the **Execute** button or select the **Execute** item in the Script menu.

The results are displayed in the lower window. To see the results in grid format, click the **Results** tab.

The Command Center also has an interactive SQL statement facility called SQL Assist. You can find it by clicking the **Interactive** tab.

Macromedia ColdFusion

Here's how to enter and run SQL statements in ColdFusion:

1. Use the ColdFusion Administrator program to create a new ColdFusion page, with a .cfm extension.

2. Create a <CFQUERY>...</CFQUERY> element.

3. Supply a name for the NAME attribute and supply a data source for the DATASOURCE attribute.

4. Enter your SQL between the <CFQUERY> and </CFQUERY> tags.

5. Use a <CFDUMP> or <CFOUTPUT> element to display the results.

6. Save the page in any executable directory beneath the web root directory.

7. Execute the page by opening it in a web browser.

The results of your SQL statement will appear in the web page, as displayed by the <CFDUMP> or <CFOUTPUT> element.

Microsoft Access

Here's how to enter and run SQL statements in Access:

1. Start Microsoft Access.

2. When prompted, open the database you want to work with.

3. In the Database window, select **Queries**.

4. Click the **New** button and select **Design view**.

5. Close the **Show Table** dialog that opens without selecting any table.

6. From the View menu, select **SQL view**. The Query window opens.

7. Enter your SQL into the Query window.

8. Click the **Run** button to switch to the Datasheet view, where the results will appear in a grid.

You can switch back and forth between SQL view and Datasheet view as needed to change your SQL and to see the results of that SQL.

Microsoft SQL Server

Here's how to enter and run SQL statements in Microsoft SQL Server:

1. Start the SQL Query Analyzer application from the SQL Server program group.

2. When prompted, enter your login information. You may need to start SQL Server if appropriate.

3. After the Query window opens, select the database you want to work with from the drop-down DB list box.

4. Enter your SQL into the query text box.

5. Click the **execute Query** button.

The results of your SQL query will appear in the smaller window beneath the Query window.

MySQL

Here's how to enter and run SQL statements in MySQL:

1. Start a Windows command prompt window (a DOS window) from the Accessories program group.

2. Type **mysql** and press **Enter**. Depending on how you configured MySQL, you may have to enter - **u** *username* **-p** on the command line in addition to mysql. Enter your password if prompted by MySQL.

3. Select a database to use by entering **USE** *databasename*.

4. Enter your SQL (end SQL statements with a semicolon) and press **Enter**.

The results of your SQL query will display directly in the command window beneath your SQL.

Oracle

Here's how to enter and run SQL statements in Oracle:

1. Start SQL*Plus Worksheet directly or from within Oracle Enterprise Manager.

2. When prompted, enter your login information.

3. Enter your SQL into the top pane of the SQL*Plus Worksheet window.

4. Click the **Execute** button.

The results display in the bottom window.

PostgreSQL

Here's how to enter and run SQL statements in PostgreSQL:

1. Start a Windows command prompt window (a DOS window) from the Accessories program group.

2. Type **psql** and press **Enter**. To make the psql utility, use a particular database, and then type **psql** *databasename*.

3. Enter your SQL at the => prompt, terminate each SQL statement with a semicolon, and press **Enter**.

The results of your SQL query display directly beneath your SQL.

Sybase

Here's how to enter and run SQL statements in Sybase:

1. Execute the SQL Advantage program that comes with Sybase.

2. When prompted, enter your login information.

3. When the Query window opens, select the database you want to work with from the drop-down list on the toolbar.

4. Enter your SQL into the Query window.

5. Click the **Execute** button, or select **Execute Query** menu item from the Query menu.

The results of the query are displayed in a new window.

Index

G-H

I

Q-R

S

CHECK OUT THESE
BEST-SELLERS

More than 450 titles available at booksellers and online retailers everywhere!

 Grammar and Style — SECOND EDITION
978-1-59257-115-4

 Word Search Puzzles
978-1-59257-900-6

 Glycemic Index Weight Loss — SECOND EDITION
978-1-59257-855-9

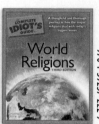 World Religions — THIRD EDITION
978-1-59257-222-9

 U.S. History GRAPHIC ILLUSTRATED
978-1-59257-785-9

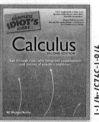 Calculus — SECOND EDITION
978-1-59257-471-1

 Positive Dog Training — SECOND EDITION
978-1-59257-483-4

 Personal Finance in Your 20s & 30s — FOURTH EDITION
978-1-59257-883-2

CD INCLUDED!

 Learning Spanish — FIFTH EDITION
978-1-59257-908-2

 Wine Basics — SECOND EDITION
978-1-59257-786-6

 Microsoft Windows 7
978-1-59257-954-9

CD INCLUDED!

 Music Theory — SECOND EDITION
978-1-59257-437-7

 The Perfect Resume — FIFTH EDITION
978-1-59257-957-0

 Organizing Your Life — FIFTH EDITION
978-1-59257-966-2

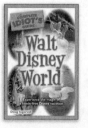 Walt Disney World
978-1-59257-888-7

ALPHA

idiotsguides.com